D0935692

Love, Marriage, and Friendship in the Soviet Union

Ideals and Practices

by Vladimir Shlapentokh

PRAEGER

PRAEGER SPECIAL STUDIES • PRAEGER SCIENTIFIC

New York • Philadelphia • Eastbourne, UK
Toronto • Hong Kong • Tokyo • Sydney

Shlapentokh, Vladimir.
   Love, marriage, and friendship in the Soviet Union.

   Bibliography: p.
   Includes index.
   1. Marriage—Soviet Union. 2. Love. 3. Women—Soviet
Union. 4. Friendship. I. Title.
HQ734.S5765 1984   306.8'1'0947   84-15943
ISBN 0-03-071541-5 (alk. paper)

*To the memory of my parents,
and my friends in Russia
who loved them.*

Published in 1984 by Praeger Publishers
CBS Educational and Professional Publishing
a Division of CBS Inc.
521 Fifth Avenue, New York, NY 10175 USA

© 1984 by Praeger Publishers

All rights reserved

3456789 052 987654321

Printed in the United States of America
on acid-free paper

Acknowledgments —————————————————————————

I would like to thank the Ford Foundation and the National Council for Soviet and East European Studies for financial support of the project, "Social Values in the Soviet Union," which allowed the preparation of this book.

I would also like to express my gratitude to members of the Department of Sociology at Michigan State University who, in various ways, made my first years of residence in the United States comfortable and productive. My special gratitude to my friends— Ellen Mickiewicz, Ralph Smuckler, Bernie and Ada Finifter, Bob Solo, and Stan Kaplowitz—whose intellectual and moral support were so important for me in this period. I would also like to express my love and respect for many Soviet sociologists with whom I have had the honor and pleasure of cooperating and communicating face to face for more than two decades.

I also want to express my deep gratitude to Rachel Burd, my project editor, who displayed an extreme patience in dealing with me and to whom I am thankful for many important suggestions. And my special thanks to Lynda Sharp for her high evaluation of my first comprehensive book on Soviet society published in this country.

My special gratitude should also be expressed to Katherine McCracken and Kim Schopmeyer who courageously confronted my English and tried to make sense of it as far as was possible. I am especially grateful to Kim Schopmeyer for valuable comments that allowed me to improve the text.

Table of Contents ──────────────────────

List of Tables ———————————————

Introduction

The ultimate goal of this book is to show how the private life of the Russians and the other peoples, especially in the realm of love and marriage, is affected by various developments in the economy, politics, and ideology of Soviet society. Frederick Starr (1982), in his exciting book on jazz in the Soviet Union, very convincingly showed that the history of this genre of music "is coded with the defining characteristics of the entire social organism." This is all the more true with regard to relations between men and women. There were two periods in Soviet history when romantic love and long–term marriage, as values, were separated and set against each other. In the first period, it was official ideology that favored the confrontation of these two values; in the second period, public opinion advanced this notion. Between these two periods, there were times when official ideology reunified these values into the idea of one life–long, romantic marriage.

The last period of Soviet history—the period of liberalization after the Stalin era—will receive most of our attention. I will try to show how relatively new images of the relations between men and women have emerged in this period.

The evolution of attitudes toward love and marriage in post–Stalinist Soviet society was determined by some important trends, inherent in transitional periods of this sort. Among these trends are: the diminishing acceptance of official ideology, the strengthening of individualistic orientations, the emergence of more or less free communication between people, progress in the social sciences combined with the publication of more realistic literary works. This last phenomenon is especially significant, for it strongly shapes public opinion and creates the possibility of public self–reflection. Society begins to become aware of itself, of the many ongoing processes, and begins to get a good sense of what, in everyday life, is typical and what is not.

When a revolutionary society moves beyond a period of mass terror, many universal trends begin to manifest themselves much more actively than before (Shlapentokh 1982a). To a considerable degree, this is the result of an intensification of all types of exchange with the world abroad. As an illustration, sexual equality has presumably been firmly established in Soviet life since the Revolution. However, it was only after 1953 (aside from a brief period after the Revolution) that the orientation of women toward independence and equality in the family—by now a worldwide trend—became a significant factor in Soviet life.

Although any social process or event can arouse interest, the evolution of attitudes toward the values of love and marriage is especially interesting to study. In addition, any process or event can be seen as an indicator of other social phenomena. Under the specific Soviet conditions, attitudes toward love and marriage are very sensitive indicators of attitudes toward other values, such as individual freedom and privacy. Thus, data on the attitudes of Soviet people toward the notion of dating services (as to whether such services should exist or not) can perhaps be treated as a unique source of information about people's stance toward other, more fundamental issues in Soviet life. Using such data for this purpose is my second, auxiliary aim here.

The Soviet woman cannot complain, any more than her Western counterpart, of indifference toward her. The bibliography on Soviet women is rather rich and surpasses that on a number of other, no less acute, social problems in the Soviet Union. But what is striking is that while in books devoted to studying Soviet women there are almost always chapters on marriage and sexual relations, the role of love in modern Soviet life is practically ignored. This issue has been touched on, for the most part, only in connection with the discussions in Soviet literature in the 1920s, principally about the writings of Alexandra Kollontai. It is typical that, in the index of the best recent book about Soviet women (Lapidus 1978), there is not listing for "love," though in the same index (comprising about 400 terms and names), one can find such terms as "Obkom Bureau, women in," "polygamy," and "avoidance or transcendance of sex orientations."

It is not easy to explain why love in Soviet life has not attracted the attention of Western researchers who are otherwise so meticulous in their studies of even minor aspects of Soviet reality. Perhaps this can be attributed to the positivistic methodology that prevails in the majority of Western (especially American) investigations of Soviet society. This methodology has compelled researchers to concentrate only on those phenomena in Soviet life that can be documented with "hard" data. Attitudes toward relatively concrete issues is perhaps the one area, beyond actual behavior, that has been explored in studies based on positivistic methodology. Yet "value," from this perspective, appears too vague a concept to be employed in empirical investigations.

Love, even more than other social values, is difficult to study in a rigorous way. This is true even in America and other Western societies. Still, there is another reason that love has attracted so little attention in studies of Soviet women: the lack of interest, among many Sovietologists, in the role of ideology in Soviet life and their underestimation of its influence on every phenomenon in the lives of the Soviet people. Meanwhile, in official ideology, love has been regarded as a significant value ever since the Revolution. It has permeated the mass media, literature, and art, and it confronts the Soviet people continuously in their everyday lives. Love is one of rather few official values that has nearly always enjoyed the sincere support of the people and, as such, has stimulated great emotions and expectations. This has resulted in very important consequences for "real" human behavior, particulary in the sphere of love and marriage.

Perhaps with the development of humanistic sociology and its various offshoots, like existential sociology and the sociology of emotions, new researchers studying Soviet women, the relations between the sexes in Russia, as well as other analogous issues in other societies will give love the attention it deserves.

Along with love and marriage, this book deals as well, if to a lesser extent, with friendship. In some respects, friendship is analyzed here as an institution that contrasts with marriage in a variety of ways. The Soviet state has always been ambivalent toward love and supports marriage and the family with a number of reservations. The attitudes of the state have been less ambivalent and more decidedly hostile toward friendship. However, the hostility toward friendship has always been well hidden. Yet this animosity is revealed by the fact that only a very few studies of friendship have been conducted in Soviet social science, and nearly all of them have been devoted to friendship among children. But friendship plays an extremely important role in the lives of Soviet people, and the exploration of love and marriage, without the investigation of friendship (even if only in a perfunctory way because of lack of data) would be very incomplete.

The major goal of this book is to give readers a reasonably comprehensive picture of human relations in Soviet society. I use the term "comprehensive" not in the sense that I promise to give an exhaustive account of this aspect of Soviet life. I mean, rather, to reconstruct, as far as my knowledge and imagination allow, a multi-dimensional or Gestalt view of human relations.

Such an objective necessitates that, in addition to analyzing the available sociological data, I resort to some impressionistic data, because sociological studies in the Soviet Union far from cover all the important issues of this domain. It might be added, however, that many other spheres of Soviet life are in an even worse position in this respect.

Of course, impressionistic data such as fiction, films, and official mass media (not to mention my personal experiences) do not stand well in competition with well organized and conducted sociological studies. However, if I followed only the severe, if nonetheless fair, prescriptions of positivistic methodology, I would be forced to abandon the pleasure of presenting to my readers my vision of Soviet society in its fullness.

Aware of all the possible biases that can haunt me in my adventure, I can, however, console myself with the recognition that even very "objective" studies are strongly influenced by what Alvin Gouldner (1970) has called the "domain assumptions" of sociologists, i.e., the values, feelings, and life story of the investigator. Attempts to negate all of these would result in only the most sketchy image of life in a socialist society.

1

How to Study Interpersonal Relations ——— in Soviet Society

THEORETICAL PERSPECTIVE: HUMAN RELATIONS IN A SOCIETY WITH A DECAYING IDEOLOGY

The subject of this book is the microworld of the Soviet people: the interpersonal relationships between spouses, lovers, and friends. It is impossible, however, fully to understand many aspects of these relationships, in particular their dynamics and uniqueness compared to those of Western societies, if we do not take into consideration the most important features of the Soviet system, and of its evolution, during the last three decades.

The comparison of the period under Stalin with the post–Stalin era underlies the analysis of love, marriage, and friendship in Soviet society. Of course, in its principal characteristics, Soviet society is the same in both periods. Yet, there are also significant differences between the two periods, and these differences have strongly affected the nature of interpersonal relations in the USSR.

Two key factors account for the radical differences in human relations between the Stalin and the post–Stalin eras. First, there has been a significant reduction in the scale and intensity of political repression since 1953. Second, and relatedly, the prominence of ideology in the lives of the Soviet people has diminished.

Political repression, or more accurately, the fear of repression, constitutes the most critical feature of a society of the Soviet type.* Without repression, the political elite, deprived of "normal"

---

*Ultimately, and most important from a political point of view, it is not repression in itself, but the fear of it that is so significant. For this reason, in different historical contexts, the same amount of repression begets fear of varying intensity. Nonetheless, "objective" indicators of repression, such as the number of arrests or dismissals from jobs for political reasons, are quite reasonable predictors of human fear.

legitimation through free elections, could not prevent the emergence of organizations independent of the state. Without repression, the elite could not impede public and private criticism of the system and its regime, restrict contact with the West, or control the many other activities that are regarded as dangerous to the maintenance of the Soviet system. Yet the scope of political repression is not constant and, in fact, changes under the influence of a variety of circumstances over time. And life in Soviet society is strongly influenced, both directly and indirectly, by the degree of repression existing at any given moment.

The role of political repression is so significant that it is useful to describe various periods of Soviet history according to the intensity of repression. Thus, we can identify periods of severe repression as well as periods of moderate or mild repression. The post–Stalin era, on the whole, can be characterized as moderately repressive compared with the very repressive prior period. But even within the post–Stalin period, there are considerable differences between, for example, the 1960s and 1970s.

The acceptance of ideology represents the second factor whose dynamics have had an important impact on human relations in Soviet society. Unlike political repression, which can change in intensity in any direction (i.e., from a period of mild or moderate repression back toward more intensive repression, or the reverse), the role of official ideology changes largely in one direction—to diminishing acceptance.

While to a considerable degree repression and ideology vary independently of each other, they also tend to reinforce each other. Thus, the relaxation of mass repression tends to result, if with some lag, in the diminished impact of ideology on the population. The degree to which the scale and intensity of repression influence the level of ideological fervor depends to a strong degree on a "third variable": the historical context. The fear engendered by repression is all–encompassing when people strongly believe in the historical legitimacy of a new power, and when they believe that others support the new system. This is characteristic of the first period following a revolution.

But with the passage of time, when the discrepancies between proclaimed goals and reality become more and more obvious, and when people—despite the terror—begin to realize that others, too, are questioning the legitimacy of the system, the foundation for the decline of ideology is laid. The cessation of mass terror then triggers the more rapid decay of ideology, and ultimately this process is irreversible. The political elite may return again to the tools of massive repression, after a period of moderation or even liberalism. However, this time only relatively few people will reconstruct their mentality to start loving "Big Brother" or even to accept his legitimacy. Even new generations, who did not experience the period of disillusionment, are unlikely to be transformed, through fear, into sincere advocates of the system. And, conversely, the radical reduction in political repression after 1953 could not halt, indeed furthered, the erosion of ideology and its acceptance.

But most important for our purposes here, the transition of Soviet society from a period of severe repression toward one of moderate repression has much and variously affected all aspects of Soviet life. And the realm of human interpersonal relations has also been greatly affected by this radical change in so central an aspect of the Soviet system.

The goal of this book is to demonstrate, through concrete analysis, how the political realities in the USSR after 1953 had an impact on the most intimate sides of Soviet life. It will be shown how the Soviet people, with a diminished fear of the authorities and a skeptical view of official ideology, altered the character of their relations with spouses, lovers, and friends.

I also suggest that the role of hedonistic values is increasing in societies across the world. New generations in all countries display heightened aspirations and demonstrate a diminished willingness to curb their egoistic desires and submit them to societal or group goals. In socialist society, particularly in the USSR, this seemingly universal tendency has been greatly enhanced by the specific conditions of society at a time when political repression and ideology have lost their prior significance.

Soviet official ideology has always cultivated, above all, the societal values of patriotism and allegiance to the party and the state. All values related to interpersonal relations, with few exceptions, have been neglected or treated with tolerant hostility. As a result, when Soviet ideology began to lose its influence on the behavior of most of the population, a growing number of Soviet individuals found themselves in a sort of moral vacuum. They found themselves to be deprived, not only of the collectivist official values, but also of other moral values capable of curbing their egoistic drives. Paradoxically, the Soviet people made a leap from a nearly ascetic society to a rather permissive one, and today they look as much, or more, unbridled and indulgent than the citizens of Western societies with their glorification of the individual.

In this connection, it is not surprising that the majority of Soviet people are deprived of serious and genuine links to any social group whose goals could be regarded as their own. They feel no true allegiance to organizations, such as the Party, the young communist organizations, or trade unions. Only a few maintain close ties with a church, and there are no independent professional organizations to which Soviet people can be really devoted. Only in the workplace do we find a sphere of activity with some importance for the Soviet individual. This is not because the office or factory is an organization with which the individual can identify, for any place of work is perceived as simply another arm of the state. Rather it is because among coworkers, with whom so much time is spent, the Soviet individual finds friends who can be relied upon. Actual allegiance to the work organization is minimal: even official Soviet data reveal that the long–term attempts of the authorities to instill in the minds of Soviet people "the feeling of being master of their own enterprise" have failed.

Thus, the Soviet individual confronts the all–powerful state, armed only with nihilism and a readiness to use all kinds of tricks to "beat the system," without the real support of any association or small group, beyond family and friends. In terms of "material behavior," moral nihilism is combated in contemporary Russia only by the values related to the family and friendship (and, of course, by fear of sanctions from the state or public opinion). However, this privatization of the Soviet mentality is not so strong that it prevents a growing number of people from skidding into the abyss of moral permissiveness.

In many cases in history, the decay of a dominant official ideology has been accompanied by the rise of a new ideology that offered alternatives to the moral values of the *ancien régime* (see Duvignaud 1973). This occurred in Russia during the period of the revolution, when the religious morals and the values of "class society" were replaced by the new "proletarian morals," which accorded wanton behavior no tolerance and strictly checked the instincts of revolutionaries.

Today in Russia, however, the eroding official ideology is not confronted with an adequate rival. It is true that nationalism and religion are on the rise in the country. But, while many are willing to declare themselves as religious, only a few are actually influenced by religious proscriptions in their behavior. About nationalism, insofar as it is not organically linked to religion, it can be said that it advances as a "positive" value only absolute allegiance to a given nationality, and does not profess its own specific values regulating human relations. And while the Western system of values, with its cult of "enlightened individualism," has made some progress among educated Soviet people, it has not rooted itself significantly in the mentality of the majority of the people.

On the basis of these considerations, I here advance the hypothesis that as a socialist society leaves the period of mass repression, it moves toward a condition of widespread anomie, as people rapidly lose confidence in the dominant values and norms and, indeed, trespass against them in their everyday behavior. What is occurring in the Soviet Union, as well as in other socialist countries, is similar to the responses to anomie that Robert Merton described as "retreatism" and "rebellion": not only are the accepted means to achieve goals abandoned, but the very goals approved by the dominant value system are also cast aside (Merton 1957, pp. 140, 153–57).

The majority of the Soviet people have discarded such values as the building of communism or the interests of the state as their life goals and are rather absorbed in the maximization of their personal interests in consumerism, power, prestige, sex, and alcohol (despite the hostility of official ideology toward these hedonistic values). The change in the structure of goals among the Soviet population over the last three decades is closely connected with the tremendous rise in aspirations, especially among the younger generations. This growth of aspirations, which represents the most important social phenomenon of Soviet postwar history, is a product of both political factors and of the remarkable growth in education and mass media, especially television (which provides an awareness of high living standards previously unknown).

Although the standard of living in the USSR rose steadily in the 1960s and 1970s, aspirations, themselves a product of this rise, grew even faster. This created a situation, skillfully analyzed in Durkheim's theory of anomie, in which aspirations outpace the possibility of their fulfillment (Durkheim 1933 and 1951; also see Ginzberg 1980).

This gap between aspirations and their satisfaction, along with the erosion of the acceptance of official ideology, has been one of the decisive factors accounting for the emergence of the state of "normlessness" in Soviet society. Like Merton's "innovator" (1957), a growing number of people have lost respect for the officially–approved means of achieving their goals and have resorted to variant semi–legal and illegal means to satisfy their aspirations (or even their basic needs).

At the same time, the anomie observable in socialist society has a number of specific features unknown to societies described by theorists of this phenomenon. Virtually every Soviet individual is regularly engaged in the infraction of dominant moral norms and laws. Indeed, few could survive in socialist society without the regular violation of the rules and principles proclaimed by the state.

This anomic behavior takes one of two distinct forms, depending upon the attitudes toward the dominant norms taken by those who violate them—either hypocrisy or cynicism. A growing number of Soviet people, especially the young, only barely conceal their contemptuous attitudes toward official moral values. On the other hand, a considerable proportion of the population, seeking to avoid viewing themselves as selfish and egoistic, resort to a relatively sophisticated mental construction, wherein they find regular excuses for the violation of norms. This preserves at least a superficial respect for the norms and even allows them to insist on their observance by others. (I will deal with this issue in greater detail in the next sections.)

The most specific feature of anomie in a Soviet–type society, however, is its strong relationship to the state. Most anomic acts committed by individuals in a socialist society are directed against the state. Because of this, many such acts take on a strong political flavor, even though they may be more directly linked to more intimate spheres of life, such as interpersonal relations.

In fact, the state may actually encourage violations of its own norms, while nonetheless concealing such violations from the public. The role of the "second economy," which is based largely on illegal or semi–legal activities, is illustrative here. The "second economy" is quietly tolerated, for it plays a vital role in making available goods and services that the official economy fails to provide. However, the most important contribution of the state to the problem of anomie is the institutionalized lying on the part of the authorities in socialist society. Mass media, educational institutions, political leaders, and managers lie systematically, providing the citizenry with the justification for their own deceptive actions. Since "the lie" is an organic part of many anomic situations and actions, its existence as a "normal" institution in Soviet society greatly exacerbates the demoralization of the population.

Nonetheless, it would be erroneous to underestimate the degree of compliance to the dominant norms by the Soviet people.

There are three reasons that account for most of the cases in which Soviet people meet the demands of the official ideology. First, the Soviet state remains a very strong force, capable of rewarding conformist and punishing nonconformist behavior. The desire to gain the approval of the authorities constitutes an important stimulus for large numbers of people to conform, even if they do not miss the opportunity to cheat on the state when the situation arises.

Second, many people, who themselves do not observe the dominant norms, still demand this from other people, and as a result, create a public atmosphere that chastises the violators of norms and applauds their observers.

Third, some official values, despite the general decay of ideology, continue to be internalized by a considerable number of people. Chief among these values is patriotism. Of course, there is a great difference between verbal, even if quite genuine, support for these values and the behavior that such values prescribe, and not all people who consider themselves to be inspired by patriotism are ready to make even modest sacrifices for the sake of the nation.

Nonetheless, however significant the factors that force the Soviet people to observe the dominant norms are, anomic behavior is still a centrally important phenomenon in Soviet society. I will attempt to substantiate the hypothesis of the growing role of anomie in Soviet life in the analysis of inter-personal relations in Soviet society, focusing particularly on relations between men and women, and between friends. My goal is not only to portray how anomie flourishes in this sphere of Soviet life, but to show also how the Soviet people build up new norms in their interpersonal relations in order to adjust them-selves to their personal values.

VALUES FOR ME AND VALUES FOR OTHERS

The problem of love, marriage, and friendship in the Soviet Union will be approached here from the values perspective (Rokeach 1973). This means that I will put emphasis on these issues as social values, and on the attitudes of the people and the elite toward these values. Additionally, I will attempt to analyze the evolution of these values and the attitudes toward them.

The distinction between two types of social values has a special bearing on this investigation. We can distinguish 1) value–ideals, or "goal" values, and 2) "real" or "practical" values. These types of values are distinguished by the different intensity of involvement of an individual—a bearer of these values—in their realization in behavior. This distinction is almost always observed by actors in real social life. People regard some values, and the cognitive structures related to them, as socially desirable and sincerely support their observance by others, but do not treat them as relevant for themselves. At the same time, other values are actually realized in the behavior of those who support them verbally. The first type can be termed "values for others," and the second type "values for me" (Kluckhohn 1951; Shlapentokh 1980 and 1982a).

In this connection, two kinds of supportive behavior with regard to a given value should be acknowledged. We can distinguish "material behavior," which requires a relatively substantial expenditure of time and material resources and assumes some risk, from "verbal behavior," with its lesser outlay of limited resources. To some degree, it can be contended that "values for me" are related to "material behavior" whereas "values for others" relate to "verbal behavior." The provisional nature of this distinction, however, is evident (Schuman and Johnson 1976).

"Romantic love" and "romantic marriage" are examples of values that alternatively play the role of "values for others" and "values for me" for different categories of the Soviet population. Soviet ideology has lent an historically unique strength to both of these values. But with the weakening of this ideology, many Soviets now regard these same values as good values—for others.

THE CONFLICT OF VALUES

The analysis of love and marriage as values, as with that of any other value, can be fruitful only if the existence of a permanent conflict between nearly all values is taken into full consideration. Individuals quite often try to profess their allegiance to values that may contradict each other. Love and marriage, sex and love, love and children, friendship and marriage, love and social status are examples of potentially conflicting values for which even in the individual conscience priorities must in some way be established.

Conflicts between values are manifested when we move from

thought to behavior. The implementation of any value requires various limited resources—time, money, emotions, and so forth. For instance, people must make decisions about how to allocate time between the profession to which they are devoted, the spouse they deeply respect, the children to whom they wish to be good parents, and perhaps a lover who is secretly adored.

THE HETEROGENEITY OF SOVIET SOCIETY

Considering the attitudes of the Soviet people toward various values—in this case love, marriage, friendship—it is necessary to underscore that it is possible to discuss the "average" Soviet woman and the "average" Soviet man only in a rather limited way, given the diversity of Soviet society. Analysis requires not only the singling out of traditional social and demographic categories, but also using psychological groups who hold the same views on the same values. The Soviet people bolster very different images of the ideal marriage and love, and they have different ideas on the roles of sex and children in their lives.

Let us take, for instance, Soviet women. They are torn between the desire to espouse and implement various values that are in deep contradiction with each other. As a result, Soviet women may be divided into different groups, with differing accents on certain values. Some women give priority to marriage, some to professional activity, some to love, others to sexual pleasure, cultural life, or mutual psychological understanding with men. And women are no less divided on the principal merits of marriage: some look first for stability, some for psychological harmony, some for sexual compatibility, others for material well–being. Such diversity in the value orientation of the Soviet people is a direct result of the "de–ideologizing" of Soviet society and the diminishing role of central values. This sometimes makes it difficult to understand trends in Soviet society because these trends appear to be mutually exclusive.

This diversity creates special problems with the use of various "hard" data, such as the divorce rate or the birth rate, because the same indicator may be relevant to opposing trends. For example, the rise in the divorce rate may reflect not only the growth of anti–marriage attitudes, but also the increasing importance of the family, for many people now, for this reason, are demanding more of their partners. The decline in the birth rate, in its turn, may be regarded as an indicator of the decrease of the value of children in people's lives; but at the same time, it may be regarded as a result of the growing concern of parents about the quality of upbringing of their offspring, making it desirable to reduce the number of children.

Similarly, the growing number of single women serves as an indicator of the frustration of females incapable of finding marriage partners; but it may also be evidence of the refusal of many women to marry men who do not suit their new image of what a husband should be. The growth of education leads to an increase in the role of romantic love in human life, but it also stimulates relativism and contributes to the declining significance of the family.

IMAGES AND VALUES

The value approach to the study of love and marriage presupposes the special interest of the author in the images held by people. The concept of "value" itself assumes that people can evaluate objects in the world only if they possess some images of these objects. Strictly speaking, people evaluate not "real" objects, but their perceptions of these objects, a fact that was underscored by William Thomas and Florian Znaniecki (1918) in their seminal work in which values were first the main subject of empirical investigation. Images are not mirror reflections of the "real" objects they substitute for in the human mind. Besides the "real" objects, many other factors influence human perceptions—particularly dominant values, personal interests, and experiences.

Therefore, the images of love and marriage held by the Soviet people, like images of all other phenomena, are exposed to the impact of diverse variables. These images change because of the evolution of ideology, literature, and the arts. In emphasizing the values perspective, I will use not only "soft" data about people's attitudes toward values, but also "hard" data describing "material behavior" as well. Normally, studying attitudes is regarded as a means of better understanding and predicting behavior (see, for instance, Schuman and Johnson 1976). Here I will do the opposite. I will regard behavior as an activity, the study of which can help us to comprehend people's attitudes toward social values—here marriage and love. As someone once said, the word is sometimes more important than the deed, and the lowering of the status of behavior as a source of information on mental activity can have its rewards.

TABLE 1-1: Combinations of Attitudes toward Love, Sex, and Marriage

| | Love is Important | | | Love is Not Important | |
| | Important Component of Love | | | Sexual Contacts Are: | |
	Agape	Eros	Both	Important	Unimportant
Marriage					
Important	1	2	3	4	5
Unimportant	6	7	8	9	10

Source: Compiled by author.

In my attempt to follow the evolution of love and marriage as values in Soviet history, I will use the so–called morphological procedure and single out the most significant of possible combinations of attitudes to these two values. In constructing different types of these combinations, I will use some elementary concepts from the sociological literature, in particular the distinction between two components of love: *agape*, the spiritual component; and *eros*, the sexual component (Rubin 1973). For the purpose of simplification, I will rely on this dichotomy and will omit several factors influencing images of love and marriage (see table 1-1).

Each cell in the chart above is equated to an image of relations between men and women that people regard either as ideal or as practically positive. This table may be said to contain all historically significant images of the relations between the sexes that have played a role in Soviet history.

THE SOVIET RESPONDENT ON LOVE AND MARRIAGE

The data on which this study will largely be based were collected by Soviet sociologists during the last two decades. In evaluating the quality of these data we should separately consider the Soviet respondent and the Soviet sociologist.

Let us begin with the first. There are a number of issues that, when included in questionnaires, would not elicit sincere responses from Soviet people. Marriage and love, however, are not among these. Soviet respondents do not fear any unpleasant consequences direct or indirect, whatever their attitudes toward love and marriage, or even their behavior in this field. (Perhaps this assertion cannot be extended to issues related to homosexuality and other sexual deviations regarded in the Soviet Union as criminal activity.)

Of course, various factors do affect the responses of Soviet citizens and can produce a gap between these answers and their "real" views, feelings, and behavior in the sphere of interpersonal relations. Three kinds of factors are particularly important. First of all, the great influence of social prestige should be stressed. This is relevant to both values of marriage and love. The point is that these values, which are actively supported by official ideology, are to some degree internalized by most Soviets (the degree of this internalization will be discussed later on). As a result, the values enjoy considerable prestige in the Soviet mentality, and this significantly affects the reaction of Soviet respondents to questions probing their attitudes toward marriage and love and their behavior in that sphere.

The mechanism of rationalization also taints data elicited from Soviet respondents when they speak on these issues, especially when their responses have to do with the past. Respondents, for instance, often perceive their emotions before their wedding in light of the current state of their marriage.

Another psychological mechanism—the so-called coping mechanism—should be mentioned here, too. To enable individuals to adapt as much as possible to a situation they cannot or do not wish to change, this mechanism produces feelings that may substitute for genuine love in human consciousness. The vagueness of the notions of "love" and "happiness" helps the coping mechanism to operate. For this reason, the Soviet respondent is extremely sensitive to different formulations of the same question on love and marriage. Often, even the slightest rewording of the question can radically change the results of a survey. Respondents react especially strongly to the subject of a question: are they being asked about the role of certain values in their own lives, in the lives of people in their milieu, or in the lives of everyone in the country?

Respondents are also strongly influenced by the degree of concreteness of a question: does a sociologist want to know their views in general, their ideal image of the given value, or their practical view on this subject? The best Soviet sociologists are well aware of all the pitfalls to be encountered by those who conduct surveys.*

---

*One of the best books on marriage is by Vladimir Boiko, a Leningrad sociologist. This book contains a brilliant section devoted to the empirical validity of people's answers to some questions in his survey (Boiko 1980, pp. 152–215)

Exposed to the influence of all these and a number of other factors, Soviet respondents do not differ in this regard from respondents in the West. For this reason, it may be contended that the quality of Soviet and Western data on this subject is quite comparable, though differences in value systems should certainly be taken into consideration. The prestige of love, for example, in the USSR and, say, in the United States or Japan, is not the same.

THE SOVIET SOCIOLOGIST OF LOVE AND MARRIAGE

It is remarkable that, even with the general deterioration of Soviet sociology in the 1970s, publications on marriage and related subjects (the number of children in a family, divorce, and some others) have not diminished (as is the case, for instance, with works on the mass media or on youth) but perhaps have even improved since the 1960s. Publications in the early 1980s, which will be used profusely in this book, are so good that they can even compete with those from the branch of Soviet sociology that was best in the 1970s—rural sociology.

Soviet sociologists specializing in marriage and the family are much more complicated figures than Soviet respondents. They are doubtless in a much easier position than many of their Soviet colleagues who tackle issues much more rigidly controlled by the Soviet elite than marriage and love. However, the pressure of political and ideological constraints should not be underestimated, even in this branch of Soviet sociology.

Like any other Soviet sociologists, those who study the problems of the relations between the sexes have to respect, or at least not directly counter, certain official values related to the domain of investigation or values of general importance. Thus, it is unacceptable for sociologists who plan to publish their findings to attack love and marriage bluntly. Among the official values to which Soviet researchers must subscribe are the homogeneity of Soviet society and, implicit in this, the social and ethnic heterogeneity of Soviet marriage.

Along with official values, sociologists must additionally consider the current aims of domestic and foreign policy. Thus, worries of the elite about the decline of the birth rate and about juvenile delinquency must be considered a direct signal to sociologists to treat such issues as of major importance in their work. At the same time, the policy of detente has not eliminated the necessity of emphasizing the radical difference in the relation between the sexes in capitalist and communist societies. However, détente has allowed cooperation between Soviet and Western sociologists, including international conferences in the Soviet Union (Kharchev 1977), as well as reflections about general trends in the sphere of marriage and the family (Kharchev and Matskovskii 1978).

The role of official values in the sociology of marriage and the family—which is considerable, if not as pervasive in other fields—emerges in a clear division between ideological, managerial, and "professional" specialists. As is true in other areas of sociology, the first two groups are predominantly oriented to meeting the demands of the Soviet elite. Abounding in the publications of ideological sociologists are considerations of the heterogeneity of the Soviet family, its principal distinction from the bourgeois family, and statements about the devotion of Soviet men and women to love as the basis of marriage (see, for example, Slesarev 1978, p. 196).

Managerial sociologists, with practical orientations, do not confront any official values, but they try to adapt themselves to new realities and to the managerial interests of the elite. These sociologists, unlike the first kind, regard their main task not so much as the defense of official Soviet values vis-à-vis marriage and family, but the elaboration of the real policy of the State in this field, which is closely intertwined with demographic issues. These sociologists, and not those who are anxious to manifest their ideological impeccability, now play the leading role in this branch of Soviet sociology (Kharchev 1979, 1982; Iankova 1978, 1979; Iurkevitch 1970).

"Professional" sociologists in this area avoid official values and ideological issues as much as possible. They approach marriage and related demographic problems with a broad perspective (including Western experience) and insist on analysis that is multifaceted, objective, and undistorted by ideological constraints. This accent on a scientific approach versus an ideological one is an even more salient peculiarity of these sociologists (for example, see Kon 1967; Golod 1977, 1982; Vishnevskii 1982; Urlanis 1977, 1978; Matskovskii 1981; Arutiunian 1980; Perevedentsev 1982a; Volkov 1977, 1979, 1981).

Soviet works on marriage and the family are influenced by more than simply the political and cultural context in which empirical data have been collected and analyzed. Again, as in many other domains of sociology, investigations in this area are affected by the personal traits of the sociologists. The personal view of sociologists of marriage and love, affecting all stages of empirical investigation, have been shaped under the influence of such factors as the sex of the sociologist, age, marital experience, ethnic origin, place of residence, social milieu, and so on. Since empirical data produced by Soviet sociologists, like that produced by sociologists of any other country, can hardly be interpreted as "absolutely objective," the generalizations they make, purportedly on the basis of these data, may often be more reliably regarded as reflecting the sociologist's own stance toward love and marriage rather than that of their respondents. Espousing different concepts of love and marriage in Soviet life and affording these concepts an influence on their data, Soviet authors on this subject become eloquent, empirically well-outfitted exponents of views shared by millions of Soviet people. It is certainly a pity that we cannot simultaneously receive data on the numbers of adherents of each concept.

I am far from imagining that my own empirical studies done in the USSR are exempt from the influence of all these extra-scientific factors. A few words about my investigations devoted to the marriage problem are in order. I conducted two studies connected with a public debate on dating services sponsored by the Soviet newspaper *Literaturnaia gazeta* (Literary Gazette).

The first of these studies, in the late 1960s, was based on a content analysis of 500 letters sent by participants in this discussion to the newspaper. Since this set of letters constitutes a self–selected sample, a question about representativeness is appropriate. To solve this problem, I have used ideas developed elsewhere (Shlapentokh 1976; see also Shlapentokh and Chernets 1977). In a case like this, we are dealing with the so–called inverse problem in statistics, where the task is not to select a representative sample, but, given an existing sample, to reconstruct a universe that the given sample approximately represents. In this case, as sociodemographic data reveal, we have at our disposal a sample that chiefly represents single women between 20 and 50 years of age with a college education.

The other study, done in 1977, had two parts. One was based on letters sent to the newspaper after the discussion was resumed after a six-year hiatus. A sample of 500 letters, which this time represented about 10,000 letters received by the newspaper after it published two marital advertisements, were analyzed in the same way as had been done in 1969–70. The other part of the study surveyed all readers of the newspaper. Since about 80 percent of all readers of *Literaturnaia gazeta* are people with higher education, the sample could be taken to be somewhat representative of the Soviet intelligentsia as a whole.*

However I might wish to embellish the quality of my own data, I have to concede that, like data produced by other Soviet sociologists, they share a number of weak points. For one, those who investigate marriage and the family have conducted almost no nationwide research.[†] They do not even have data representing single republics, administrative regions (oblast), or large cities. Leningrad has played a particularly prominent role in these investigations, like the role of Novosibirsk in studies of migration and of prestige of professions. The best works about Soviet marriage are based on Leningrad data (Boiko 1980; Vasil'eva 1981; Baranov 1981; Golod 1982). But not one of these works can pretend to use data representing all Leningraders, or even some categories of them. The same is true of other areas researched in Soviet studies of marriage and the family—Moscow (Iankova 1979; Kisilieva and Rodzinskaia 1982; Sysenko 1981), Bielorussia (Iurkevitch 1970), Estonia (Tiit 1982), Kiev (Chuiko 1975), and others.

With the present state of representativeness of Soviet data on marriage and the family, I have only one option—to use local data and, comparing them, try to detect some regularities. Soviet sociologists, who recently started to generalize accumulated data and to have recourse to secondary analysis, are using this approach (Kharchev and Matskovskii 1978). It should be noted that the comparison of regional data is hampered by low comparability of information, a flaw deeply inherent in Soviet empirical studies, strange as it may seem for a presumably highly centralized society. This circumstance has been increasingly recognized by Soviet sociologists, including those studying marriage and the family.[‡]

---

*The survey was based on a nationwide area multistage random sample. About methodological aspects of this sample, see Shlapentokh 1976; Petrenko and Iaroshenko 1979; Muchnik et al. 1980; Muchnik et al. 1978.

[†] As exceptions, some surveys executed by the Central Statistical Board can be mentioned, along with my own 1977 study. These surveys did not propose mainly to study problems of marriage and the family, but did touch on some issues related to them (Darskii 1972, 1978; Belova and Darskii 1972; Belova 1975).

‡Having collected data about divorces produced by many Soviet researchers, Kharchev and Matskovskii, the authors of the first Soviet book based on secondary analysis of data on marriage and the family, came to a sad conclusion about the comparability of these data. They remarked that each investigator had used his own classification of motives for divorce as well as his own procedures for gathering information (1978, pp. 142–43).

In the evaluation of Soviet data on marriage and love, we will pay special attention to the phenomenological quality of these data. We have already listed some factors affecting perceptions of love and marriage. In this area, until very recently, Soviet researchers, as well as the majority of their counterparts in the West, ignored this vital methodological problem. Now the situation has begun to change. Kharchev's last book contains a number of reasonable considerations on the subject (1979, pp. 31–32, 191).

However, using Soviet as well as American data, secondary analysts have been too often ruled only by their methodological intuition in their attempt to estimate the influence of various factors on opinions on marriage and love expressed by respondents.

FRIENDSHIP AS AN OBJECT OF STUDY IN THE USSR

Friendship has been the object of study in Soviet social science only rarely. Kon's book, *Friendship*, published in 1980, was the first significant treatment of this subject. (This book was based upon Kon's article, published in 1973 in the magazine *Novyi Mir*, and his booklet published in 1973.) Even as one of the most knowledgeable Soviet sociologists, who fastidiously monitors the sociological literature, Kon could use in his book no more than half a dozen articles on friendship, of which all but one were devoted to relations between children. He was forced to devote only a tiny fraction of his book to friendship among Soviet adults. He undoubtedly also felt himself politically much safer in discussing friendship among people under age 18, or friendship among German romantics in the first half of the 19th century. The single empirical study, which he cites profusely, was carried out by Losenkov and himself and focuses on high school students.*

It is notable that Galina Andreieva, one of the most politically sensitive of Soviet social scientists, in her book, *Social Psychology*

---

*The bibliographic reference book on social psychology, which covers the period from 1970 to 1978, does not contain a single article or book (besides those by Igor Kon) that has "friendship" in the title (Fedorina 1983). The L'vov philosopher Veniamin Zatsepin devoted a small section to friendship in his book, *Happiness as an Issue in Social Psychology*, which came out in 1981. This section simply repeats some theses from Kon's book, including his limited empirical data.

(1980), the first serious publication of this sort in the Soviet Union, did not find room for even a brief discussion of friendship. This is true despite the fact that she allotted a considerable portion of the book to descriptions of various concepts related to interpersonal relations.

Soviet social scientists manage to study some issues related to friendship only in the context of investigations of other topics, such as value orientations or the use of leisure time. Soviet social scientists avoid friendship as an object of study largely because, in exploring friendship between adults, they must inevitably touch on such a cardinal issue as the conflict between friendship and the Soviet political and economic order. It is characteristic that, in the Soviet textbook *Marxist Ethics*, the authors did not find a place for even the mention of friendship (Titarenko 1980).

In the West, and particularly in the United States, friendship is not among the most popular subjects of scholarly interest. However, nearly every textbook on social psychology contains at least one section on this issue, and there are a number of significant publications on friendship (see, for example, the recent works of Reisman 1981; Farrell and Rosenberg 1981). At the same time, when comparing the volume of publications on friendship in the two countries, it is necessary to remember that the place of friendship in the system of personal values is much higher among Soviets than Americans and that interest in the problems of friendship in the Soviet Union is extremely high.

2

Love and Marriage in Soviet Ideology and Policy Before and After 1953

LOVE AND REVOLUTION

Love has played a specific role in Marxist ideology. This can be accounted for by Marxists' bluntly negative attitude toward marriage and the family, as with any other institutions of bourgeois society. As far back as the *Communist Manifesto* (1848), Marx and Engels proclaimed the necessity of the destruction of this institution.

The Marxists singled out love as a phenomenon absolutely incompatible with bourgeois marriage, seen to be based on mean, mercantilistic calculations and on the enslavement of women. In such marriage, free and equal relations between a man and a woman, which can be founded only on love, were viewed as impossible. Divorce was therefore praised as a necessary guarantee of such relations and the equality of women.

Russian Bolsheviks, headed by Lenin, accepted this postulate without reservation. Moreover, a considerable part of the Russian liberal prerevolutionary intelligentsia shared this attitude to the question of marriage and divorce. Romantic love and passion had been highly respected in classical Russian literature (Turgenev, Dostoevsky, Chekhov). And the absence of the right to divorce was condemned by this intelligentsia—as will be recalled from Tolstoy's *Resurrection*.

Another approach, hostile to official values of love and marriage in prerevolutionary Russia, was engendered by the so-called nihilistic movement in the 1860s. Representatives of this movement, women and men, with their accent on the absolute equality of the sexes and on professional careers for woman, rejected the decisive role of sexual relations in marriage, either praising marriage based on love—*agape*—or else justifying unrestrained sex. At the beginning of the twentieth century, especially after the defeat of the revolution in 1905, among the Russian intelligentsia, relations based exclusively on sexual contacts or as ends in themselves, were widely praised. This, too, was reflected in a number of literary works of that time.*

In the first years after the Revolution, Lenin and his staff preserved the attitudes on marriage and the family that they had professed before the Revolution. This was unlike the radical changes in Lenin's attitudes about many other key issues—the agrarian question, the national movement, the army, and others, which changed immediately after the Revolution. At this stage, Soviet official ideology largely emphasized negative values, in order to destroy millions of enemies of the new regime. The destruction of the family was an important step in broadening the social basis of the new order because it allowed the recruitment of youth and, to some degree, women in the fight against heads of families belonging to classes and strata hostile to the Revolution. The antireligious and antichurch tenor of the diatribes against marriage and the family should not be overlooked either.

The attitude of the Soviet leadership was formulated by Lenin in the Revolutionary period: "The Communist ethic opposes vulgar and dirty marriage without love and praises proletarian civic marriage with love."† (Vospominaniia oV.I. Lenin, v. 2, 1957, p. 484).

Lenin and his colleagues regarded the introduction of the freedom to divorce as a central precondition for the implementation of the new concept of marriage—which can, without exaggeration, be called a form of romantic marriage.

Lenin's view of marriage underlay the first Soviet marital code (1918). The most significant features of this code were the declaration of the freedom to divorce and the nonrecognition of marriages registered by the church. Despite these novelties, the

---

*A detailed description of attitudes toward marriage and sexual life before the Second World War can be found in the excellent book of Richard Stites, *The Women's Liberation Movement in Russia* (1978).

†Lenin's stance toward marriage was very much like Engels's: "If only marriage based on love is moral, it lasts only as long as love continues. But the duration of the feeling of individual sexual love of different individuals is very different, and once this feeling has withered, or is replaced by new, passionate love, divorce comes to be good for both partners as well as for society." (Marx and Engels, *Sobraniie Sochinenii*, Vol. 21, p. 85).

new law supported marriage and the family as social institutions.

Lenin's attitudes toward marriage in the postrevolutionary period once again mirrored his sagacity as a politician, which distinguished him sharply from many revolutionaries who tried to ground real life on negative values only. Lenin's defense of marriage, even if in its romantic version, was only one example of how his policy was directed not only at the destruction of the old order, but also the consolidation of a new one.

In contrast to the next period under Stalin, in the first decade of Soviet history, the elite had no absolute control over the people. Moreover, even the rank and file in the Party were not rigidly manipulated, as they were to be. Lenin's concept of marriage did not prevail in the Party, especially among young members. The concept satisfied neither women nor men. Having affirmed the State's support of legal marriage, the new notion encountered the animosity of those women activists who continued to consider marriage a bourgeois institution by definition, inconsistent with the true equality of women and men. These women were inspired by one of many attractive romantic ideas cultivated by Marxism—the idea that the new society would take up all tasks previously performed by the family, including fostering children. The preservation of the family by the new marital law was a disappointment to the true believer of this Marxist vision. As long as the family persisted, it was argued, women would have to fill their old roles, even if with some modern modifications. Thus, they could not achieve true equality with men and wholly devote themselves to the public cause, the building of a new society. The most ardent advocate of these attitudes was Aleksandra Kollontai.

Even more active opposition to Lenin's concept of marriage came from the great number of young male Communists, and a considerable number of young women, who saw in absolute sexual freedom an important achievement of the Revolution. Being direct successors of Russian nihilism and the prerevolutionary decadence, these exponents of the so-called "glass-of-water" theory, to which a love act was equated, regarded the official support of marriage as an obstacle to the sexual hedonism presumably sanctioned by Marxist ideology (Stites 1978, pp. 358–76).

In the debate over marriage, attitudes toward romantic love were extremely varied. The official position, as had been indicated, was very supportive of it. The great focus on divorce as one of the major achievements of the Russian Revolution—Lenin underscored this many times—was an indirect manifestation of the role that official Soviet ideology attributed to love. The official image of love identified it with passion, which alone morally justified marriage. In such a context, divorce might be regarded as the price for the preservation of marriage as a social institution. Declaring love-passion, in accordance with the attitudes of Marx, and especially Engels, as the only morally permissible basis of a couple's cohabitation, the Soviet leadership immediately began to blur the line between the registered and the unregistered common life of a man and a woman.

The first step in this direction was already made in the first marital code in 1918. But the next, and most radical, step which equated two kinds of marriage, registered and unregistered, was made in the second marital code in 1926. This code also simplified further the procedures for divorce. Of course, there were also pragmatic motives for the official recognition of unregistered cohabitation. The rising unemployment at the time of the NEP (New Economic Policy) put unwed mothers and illegitimate children in very difficult positions. With the recognition of common law marriage, the new code compelled fathers of children of such unions to support them materially.

With the installation of this rule, Soviet official ideology departed openly, to the dismay of many true believers, from the idea that the state would take care of children and other domestic responsibilities in order to free women more completely. But, however pragmatic the impetus for the new marital code had been, its emergence would have been impossible without the official ideological stance toward marriage as founded on romantic love. If only economic considerations lay at the bottom of this code, it would be difficult to see why it made divorce even easier than in the code of 1918.*

The stance of Party feminists toward love was very complicated: putting woman's social role foremost, they could not praise love, the passion-love that absorbs human life and subjugates everything to itself. Therefore, they had only two options—either shift the emphasis in love from sexual passion, from *eros*, to *agape*, to mutual spiritual attraction of both individuals involved in social activity for a common cause; or deny love generally and replace it with unrestrained sexual contacts freed of deep emotional involvement.

---

*There are different points of view on the role of ideology, or theory, in real life in the Soviet Union. Carr, for instance, denies the importance of it, at least with respect to sexual morality in postrevolutionary Russian (1958:31). Others, including myself, hold the contrary view (Stites 1978:75).

Aleksandra Kollontai was a brilliant and outspoken representative of the first view. It was she who advanced the concept of "winged eros." In her famous "winged eros" articles, Kollontai described love: "Love is composite, a complex combination of friendship, passion, maternal tenderness, affection, sympathy of spirit, concern, habit, and many other nuances of feelings and experience" (see Stites, 1978, p. 352). Thus, Kollontai was the first Soviet theorist of spiritual love, of Soviet *agape*—the submission of sexual pleasure to higher values.* Four decades later, her view, though without acknowledgment, would be incorporated into a new notion of rational marriage advanced by Soviet sociologists as an upshot of the crisis in sexual relations. A number of feminists also joined the partisans of sexual libertinism in their attack on love, arguing that not only were marriage and the family altogether the product of the old society, love was as well.

Thus, with the consolidation of the state and with the strengthening of control over the masses as a first task while Lenin was yet alive, the Soviet leadership launched a campaign in favor of marriage. Yet, they lacked enough power to present their views as the only ones congruent with the major postulates of Marxist ideology. They even had to cede to the pressure of public opinion within the Party and, in 1926, make marriage an institution even looser than as defined in the code of 1918.

However, from the middle of the 1920s the Soviet leadership started to pursue ideological activity against the antimarriage attitudes among Party members. An offensive was launched against both trends—the one that proclaimed love without marriage and the other that rejected love as well as marriage.† The logic of these polemics led Soviet officials, such as Lunacharskii, Iaroslavskii and Riasanov, not only to the defense of marriage, but to charges against sex and consequently against the key role of romantic love in life in general. As is usual in debates between people who refer for support to the same source of ideological authority, official figures started promiscuously to brand pro-

---

*By the irony of history, thanks to some other statements of hers, mainly against marriage as such, Kollontai became in some Soviet sociological and historical works a symbol of the sexual libertinism of the twenties.

†In the ideological offensive against the devotees of permissive sex and the cult of love, Lenin was included through the posthumous publications of his letters to Inesse Armand and the content of his conversations with Clara Tsetkin (see Vospominaniia oV.I. Lenin, v. 1 and 2, 1957).

ponents of "winged" or "unwinged" love as people affected by bourgeois views and perversions.

The fight against sex reached its apex in the works of Aron Zalkind. Using Freud's ideas about the sublimation of energy, he insisted that love and sex are by definition hostile to the new society because they divert energy from socially useful activity. Although pure ascetic attitudes toward love and sex were later repudiated by official ideology (Volfson 1929), such attitudes were in some way absorbed into it and contributed to the formation of a new ideal of marriage for Stalin's era of Soviet history.

Also of great weight is another peculiarity of the "sexual Thermidor," to use the term employed by Richard Stites (1978). This has to do with the relation between the state and marriage. Among other accusations against capitalist society, Marx and Engels stressed its pernicious influence on relations between men and women. Since a majority of positive statements about the future society were simply the ideas of bourgeois life turned upside down, Marxists initially insisted that in their society, as Engels put it, relations between two individuals would be their own business only.*

In their persistent efforts to establish order, as they perceived it, Soviet leaders rejected the assumption that the state should not interfere, and by the end of the twenties, the right of society, the right of the state to supervise family life in one way or another, was asserted more and more.

IMAGES OF MARRIAGE AND LOVE IN STALIN'S TIME

Stalin completed the formation of a new official image of marriage in Soviet ideology. Certainly he eliminated any public resistance to his image of marriage and compelled everyone who touched on the problem of the relations between the sexes, in a novel or in a philosophical work, to conform to this image strictly.†

---

*Even at times when another approach became dominant, Nikolai Bukharin seemed to persist in his opinion that Party interference in family affairs was "petty bourgeois."

†Richard Stites astutely compares two books of the Soviet scholar Volfson. In his first book, which came out in 1929, Volfson treated the family as doomed to extinction in the new society. Some years later, the same man exalted monogamous marriage and exhorted readers to have recourse to divorce and abortion only in extreme cases (Stites 1978, p. 388).

Stalin was perhaps even more aware than Lenin of how important a stable family is for a totalitarian state. In such a state, members of a family should be more loyal to the state than to each other.* Stalin tried to preserve this heritage of the civil war as much as possible. On a grand scale, at all critical stages of his rule—during the collectivization and the purges of the mid thirties—the political police used people as informers and even as witnesses for the prosecution against their relatives, parents, and even children (see Orlov 1953; Solzhenitsyn 1975).

But beyond this, Stalin, like other potentates, believed the stable family was an additional bond that weakened people's inclination to opposition activity, made them seek material well-being, and so made them much more dependent on the state. Moreover, thanks to the overwhelming fear of "Big Brother," the family took up a mutual responsibility for all its members and kept them from all kinds of antistate activity.

In this context, the family's responsibility for bringing up the new generation was particularly crucial for Stalin. Since the state, for many reasons, turned out to be incapable of controlling the socialization process completely and children had to spend considerable time outside the state system of education, a stable family became an important participant in this process. Of course, it was very clearly established that the family was to play the auxilliary role and unhesitantly follow the prescriptions of official institutions. Stalin regarded the family's contribution as valuable in indoctrinating the youth, and he turned out to be absolutely right.†

---

*It would be extremely unfair to Stalin to suppose that it was only he who wanted to submit the family to the interests of a totalitarian state. Hitler and Mao did the same. Of course, each exploited the traditions of his country. Thus, the Chinese leader tried to capitalize on the traditional experience of the Chinese family and Confucianism, and suggested that family loyalty should be extended to "the larger family of the revolution"—namely, the state. Like Stalin and Hitler, Mao used the young as agents inside the family: their functions were to inculcate the new ideology in the elders of the family, as well as to inform on those who did not comply with it.

†Adult members of the great majority of Soviet families in Stalin's time almost never indulged in frank discussions about their impressions of their current life. Out of fear for their children, they communicated with them in the same terms the children learned in official places. Parents who shared their critical attitudes with their children (if they had any) were very rare and such discussions are described in the literature as extraordinary events (see Grigorenko 1982).

Pronatalistic considerations were, of course, of no minor importance for Stalin when he shaped his policy. Various economic and, especially, military demands explain Stalin's strong anti-Malthusian stance and his energetic pronatalist policy. Here the family was an irreplaceable institution.

It would hardly be possible to guess the priorities Stalin attributed to the various functions of the family. Unmanageable as it is even in issues of current social life, the question of priority of motives and relative importance of causes is all the more beyond our cognitive possibilities when the question concerns the past. In any case, it is clear that it was the highest interest of the state, not of the individual, that moved the creator of the Soviet empire to include the problems of the family, and even love, in the realm of his preoccupations.

In developing a new official image of marriage, Stalin had to submit to some constraints. One of the most important was ideological continuity. He was too close to the Revolution, and appreciated Marxist phraseology too much, to forego it in the solution of any ideological problem, even if this solution was essentially in stark contradiction to the spirit of Marxism and the Revolution. Even his successors, three decades after his death, have not dared publicly to revise one postulate of Marx and Engels without speaking of Lenin.*

For this reason, Stalin had to adjust his image to the Marxists' concept of romantic marriage as marriage based on genuine love, and in contrast to the mercantilism of bourgeois wedlock. But such a concept, at least as it was perceived in the 1920's, did not meet his requirements. The point is that in the alliance—of marriage and love—it was the latter that had to play the leading role and to determine the duration of marriage. It was just this circumstance that compelled Party officials, as early as the middle 1920's, to move away from Lenin's image of marriage, with its accent on love and divorce. In their polemics against those who praised freedom of love (either in true devotion to great affection,

---

*Among these three figures, Engels turned out to be the most vulnerable. Stalin indulged in some remarks critical of Engels on his view of the role of procreation in human history as something equivalent to the role of economy. These precedents established, some Soviet scholars have dared, not without some fear and with growing self-respect, to cast cautious doubt on some of Engels's thoughts.

like Kollontai, or simply as a justification to sexual libertinism), Party puritans were bent on disqualifying love generally as a dominant or even as a positive factor in the lives of the builders of the new society. Stalin did not consent to such deviation from a significant postulate of Marxism-Leninism. So, with the hot debate of the 1920's behind him, he reinstated Lenin's image of romantic marriage, but with a difference not easily perceived at first glance.

Stalin had no intention, for the reason explained above, of declaring war against love. All he did was introduce into the ideal image of marriage, and even of love, a modification that brought about a new official image. Stalin changed the priority of elements in Lenin's image to emphasize stability—at the expense of love-passion. In some sense, this modification even strengthened the value of romance because from now on it had to be eternal, at least lifelong. As a result, a new image of ideal marriage was created—an image of marriage based on lifelong, unfailing love.

Stalin did his best to realize this new image of long-term marriage. Curiously, he injected his image into the Soviet legal system. In this process, which lasted about twenty years, there were two high points. One was in 1936, the year a marital reform was adopted, revoking the freedom of abortion and making divorce more difficult than before. An intensive ideological campaign preceded, as is usual in the Soviet Union, the adoption of the new law. The further strengthening of the Soviet family, denunciations of divorce, free love, and sexual frivolity were the main themes.

To understand the real meaning of this campaign in Soviet life, we must remember that it was waged at the time of rising terror. Thus, any official exhortations, even if they concerned intimate matters, bore the ominous marks of direct threats to those who would not observe the recommendations.

The next high point in Stalin's drive for the implementation of the official image of marriage took place during extraordinary times—World War II. At that time, in 1944, the new law not only further complicated the divorce process, but also revoked those articles of the marital code of 1926 that equated registered and unregistered marriage. Along with these legal measures, Stalin established Party control over the marital and extramarital behavior of Soviet people, members of the Party above all. This Party intrusion into the relations between men and women became a typical feature of Soviet life, which in a milder form remained true in Soviet life until lately.*

Indeed, an editorial in *Pravda* recently used words that could have been read in the same newspaper sixty years ago: "Mercantilist marriage—this concept belongs to the old society. Socialist morals reject everything that smacks of bigotry or insults the purity of the alliance of two people: match-making, church weddings, bride-prices. There is only one approach—love. Love, integral and creative" (*Pravda*, September 27, 1983).

As in the past, the family is still regarded as one of the most important social institutions. The last Soviet Constitution contains a special article on the family that begins with the words: "The family is under the protection of the state." (*Konstitutsiia (Osnovnoi Zakon) Souza Sovietskikh Sotsialisticheskikh Respublik*, Moscow, 1977). And, in a recent decision of the Central Committee and the government, devoted to the family, it is stated that "the family is one of the highest moral values of socialist society" (*Pravda*, March 13, 1981).

Facing the Party and a mass audience, the Soviet elite presumably hold, as before, to the old image of marriage. But apart from this audience, it allows itself and its experts—in particular sociologists—to entertain other views.

I will discuss the latter views of Soviet sociologists on love and marriage at a later point, but now I will turn to an even more eloquent indicator of the divergence between official ideology as it is displayed in the mass media, official literature and art, and the views of officials. I mean the legal and semi-legal practices controlled by the elite. Although insisting on the old image of marriage, since 1953 the Soviet elite has, however, liberalized the marital laws, reinstated the right to abortion, and made divorce easier once more. As a part of the general weakening of control over the nonpolitical sides of private life, the interference of Party organizations into the relations between the sexes has become much less frequent than before.†

---

*Since love was presumed to be the unique basis for marriage, formal decisions of Party committees about marital and extramarital relations almost literally required that an unfaithful husband not only restore his marriage and marital life, but also *love* the wife he had betrayed. The regulation of intimate relations by the Party has been an object of derision in the country for a long time. However, many Soviet women continue to consider party committees as final instances in which to force unfaithful husbands to stay with them, protect daughters from philanderers, and punish profligates of both sexes.

†Again, we should be cautious about exaggerations on both sides—

Having made durability one of the major merits of marriage, Stalin inevitably came into conflict with love as passion, love based on sexual affections. But he rejected the views of those Party puritans who treated love, and especially preoccupation with love, as a manifestation of bourgeois decadence. Otherwise, his concept of marriage would have lost any traits of particularity and would have been indistinguishable from the old image sanctioned by the church. Stalin's desire to restore the institutions, major and minor, of prerevolutionary Russia—a desire that was manifested by the end of his rule in sometimes ridiculous forms*—did not extend to the institution of marriage. Marriage was to be pre-dominantly Soviet, as conceived by the founders of scientific Communism, with as little deviation as possible.

The solution to the problem was found in a decisive shift in the notion of love from *eros* to *agape*, from sexual to spiritual affection. Of course, this deemphasis of the sexual component in love was against direct quotations from Engels and, in essence, against Lenin too. As was remarked earlier, the importance Engels and Lenin—implicitly if not explicitly—attributed to divorce re-flected their views that the Communist ethic recognized only marriage based on true love-passion. Neither referred to other things beyond love that could justify two people maintaining a common life, if love left them.

Since the stability of marriage was a prime concern for Stalin, his iron logic led him to the conclusion that passionate, sex-pervaded love and officially supported love had to be separated. In accordance with this line, sex gradually came to be removed from public life. Very soon, by the beginning of the thirties, Soviet society became in its appearance one of the most puritanical in the world.

Literature, art, and the mass media were transformed into fields in which even mention of the sexual side of life was

underestimation and overestimation of the magnitude of changes in this, as well as other areas of Soviet life. For all this erosion of the pressure on private life, the statute that does not allow a couple who cannot prove they are married to rent a hotel room has not been abolished nor has the prohibition against receiving any other persons in a hotel room, including other guests of the hotel, after 11 p.m. This use of hotel personnel for puritanical purposes has been derided by some brave writers and screenactors (for instance, in a film famous in the sixties, "Our Contemporary")—without noticeable effect.

*Behaving very like Napoleon, he resorted for instance, to old military ranks as well as titles for members of the government (the revolutionary title "commissar" was superseded by "minister"). He reintroduced the uniform in a number of civil departments, and so on.

prohibited. Naked bodies, for instance, completely disappeared from paintings, as did any scenes in movies, plays, or novels that could be even indirectly interpreted as relating to sexual intimacy. Sexual education in schools was out of the question. Moreover, after the war, Stalin reinstated the prerevolutionary system of separate education for girls and boys.

Furthermore, scientific investigation into sexual life was suppressed. If in the twenties a number of interesting explorations of the sexual behavior of the Soviets were carried out, no more were until the sixties.

Freud was declared one of the fiercest foes of Marxism, Communism, and the Soviet way of life. Freudianism, along with pornography, was equated with the most dangerous political activity. The country was plunged so deeply into puritanism that even now it is far from having passed beyond pathological animosity to sex, despite evident progress since the fifties. With all this persecution of *eros*, even if he was "winged," Soviet ideology intensively praised romantic love, epitomized in the spiritual devotion of two people to each other and to the "common" cause.

Soviet reality, as it was shaped by the middle of the 1930s in regard to the role of love, was quite different from the societies described by the three geniuses of anti-utopia—Evgenii Zamiatin, Aldous Huxley, and George Orwell. In one respect, they were all right in their visions of a totalitarian society, its negative attitude toward love-passion as a direct danger to the total enslavement of an individual, and its sheer utilitarianism toward sexual contacts. But, at the same time, they could not envision a totalitarian society in which romantic love, though deprived of sexual pleasure, was not only not persecuted by the state, but even glorified and sanctioned.

IDEOLOGICAL EVOLUTION SINCE 1953

After Stalin, Soviet ideology underwent considerable changes. First of all, it changed from a one-story edifice into a multi-storied one. In Stalin's time, there were no distinctions between the views expressed in the mass media and in professional magazines, between propaganda geared to the masses and information aimed at a select audience—for instance, people in science and culture. This move from universalism to a kind of particularism in ideology (though its scope should not be exaggerated) made Soviet ideology more flexible and somewhat slowed its decay and loss of influence.

Thus, it is possible to present the Soviet ideological system as comprising the following levels: First, the elite; second, experts in various fields of Soviet life; third, Party members; and fourth, the masses. Each level of this sytem is served by particular sources of information and specific media. However, it should be noted that individuals at the highest level have access to all sources of information, whereas those at the lower levels do not. Even experts, for instance, cannot use special sources of information reserved for the elite.

As for marriage and love, their role in the ideology geared to the Party and the masses has not changed significantly since the thirties. The mass media and officially approved novels and movies have continued to boost the Stalinist version of romantic marriage. In this depiction, true Soviet marriage emerges on the basis of spontaneous love, in which the sexual factor plays a secondary role. The marriage should be lifelong, and divorce is considered antisocial. The ideological section of the last Soviet marital code (1968) is not significantly different from the corresponding documents from the Stalin epoch. Its main goals are, it states, the further strengthening of the Soviet family on the basis of the principles of the Communist ethic, the building up of family relations on the basis of the voluntary union of a man and a woman, their feelings of mutual love, of friendship, and of mutual respect, freed from mercantilistic considerations.

The existence of a certain "double-think" in the elite has encouraged not only sociologists, but writers and sometimes even journalists, to try to present the relation between the sexes in a more or less realistic way. It is remarkable that each new literary work with a bold presentation of human relations in this sphere, erotic scenes included, has been perceived by the public as directed against the dominant ideology, even if the authors had no intentions of being involved in any confrontation on political issues.*

---

*Such was the fate of the artistically mediocre film, "Autumn," which emerged in the mid-1970s. This film aroused a stormy reaction, both in the public and among officials, because it was the first film in the USSR to portray positively a pair of lovers each of whom was married to another. Moreover, the lovers were so consumed with love that they had no time to inform us about their professions or about their interests beyond the rapport between themselves.

Moreover, the process of liberalization has gone so far that even in the official textbook, *Marxist Ethics*, the authors come out against those bigots who insist on the removal of "statues of nudes in the parks and are even against acrobatics and ballet." Additionally, they assert that "human psychology is very complicated, and anything that is forbidden may arouse people's heightened, even abnormal, interest, especially among the young." Therefore, the authors boldly defend "the contemplation of Giorgione's 'Sleeping Venus' and even a Renoir 'Nude' (Titarenko 1980, p. 286).*

THE SOVIET FAMILY AS AN AGENT OF THE STATE

Though the ideological and operational position of the Soviet political elite toward the family is much more lenient than was true under Stalin, it continues to consider the family an important agent of its policy. The state expects the family to perform a number of functions.

However, it would be erroneous to presume that all activities expected from the family by the state are always at odds with the interests of ordinary Soviet people. The interests of the state and the population do coincide to some degree in the concern for the procreation of new generations. And the Soviet people also support any action of the government directed toward the alleviation of the plight of the working mother and the improvement of facilities serving women and children such as, for instance, the Decree of the CPSU Central Committee and the USSR Council of Ministers, "On Measures to Increase State Assistance to Families with Children," January 22, 1981, which significantly increases

---

*In the same *Pravda* editorial devoted to the problems of the young family, cited above, the reader finds, along with bombastic sentences and clichés, humanistic reflections on the worries of young couples. The newspaper appeals to young people to be delicate with each other, to try to understand their partner's intentions, and even suggests to young husbands that they "get up at dawn, run to a water-meadow, in order to pick a small flower there for their one and only." Far from defending an ascetic approach to life, the newspaper acknowledges that "the world of the young family is big and multi-colored, and therefore the aspirations of the family grow steadily." The editorial also appeals to various organizations to "do their best for the satisfaction of the desires of young married people." (*Pravda*, September 25, 1983).

the level of material assistance for families with children (see Lapidus 1982, pp. 303–4). In addition, the Soviet population has no objections to the governmental attempts to increase the birth rate in the country, although on the individual level, they completely ignore the political and economic considerations behind the natalistic policy of the state.

There is also a considerable convergence of views between the state and the population with regard to the education of children. Neither want children to be engaged in antisocial or criminal activity, and to some degree support each other in the attempt to halt the growth of juvenile delinquency. But in practice, of course, many Soviet people do not do very much to prevent their children from lapsing into bad habits. The increasing problem of juvenile alcoholism demonstrates how little many Soviet parents are concerned about the social behavior of their offspring.

The Soviet elite continues formally to place an ideological function on the family, demanding that parents do their best to inculcate the current political directives of the leadership. The judicial document, The Statute of Marriage and the Family of the Russian Republic (Moscow 1975) explicitly demands from parents the "education of children by the family in organic combination with social education in the spirit of devotion to the motherland, to communist attitudes toward work, and in the preparation of children for active participation in the construction of communist society." Even officials recognize, however, that the family cannot now play any serious ideological role and that, in fact, it serves more the opposite goal. (I will address this subject in more detail later.)

Yet, the Soviet family, as in the past, continues to be used by the state for its police functions. The family remains responsible for the political behavior of its members, especially children. Parents are in serious trouble if their children, as seniors in high school—or worse, in college—commit actions regarded as politically unloyal or criminal.

The role of the family as hostage to the Soviet authorities is especially clear in the official policy of allowing travel to the West, in most cases, only by those who have family, particularly children. The obvious consequences for family members, in the event of defection, drastically have to curb the likelihood of people not returning home from a mission to the West. Prohibiting trips abroad by entire families also significantly diminishes the probability of defection.

THE FAMILY AS A NEW HOPE IN THE SOVIET ECONOMY

Among many things that displeased the Soviet rulers about family life for many years after the Revolution was its productive activity as an economic unit. Given the notion that each adult, female as well as male, had to participate in social production and be a member of a production collective, the Soviet authorities considered economic activity inside the family as a direct threat to their social and economic system. Time spent in a family business was regarded as time stolen from the state and, hence, was socially unwarranted.

There were also political considerations involved in the opposition to family economic activity. In the view of the state, the existence of independent sources of income makes people more independent of the authorities and may encourage them to engage in activities hostile to the regime.

After the brusque curtailment of the NEP (New Economic Policy), which had allowed small business, family economic activity after the late 1920s continued only in the countryside. Stalin reluctantly permitted the peasants to have their own plots of land, without which they would simply have been unable to survive.

However, while private plots were officially permitted, Soviet ideology intermittently attacked them and derogated the peasants for their interest in them. Moreover, the authorities made it materially very difficult to carry out private agricultural activity, because this deprived the collective and state farmers of the means indispensable to their activities (such as tractor services, fertilizers, or pasture for cattle). The terrible life of the Soviet peasant has been described vividly in a number of novels published after 1953, such as those of Boris Mozhaiev, Vasilii Belov, and Fedor Abramov. After Stalin, the status of private plots improved and the state was much more tolerant than ever before, although continuing their ideological (and sometimes material) attacks on the activities of peasants outside state and collective farms.

If such moderately hostile attitudes toward private plots had existed in the 1930s and 1940s, Soviet peasants would have been the happiest people in the world. However, by the time official policy moved from open animosity to mild disapproval, Soviet peasants themselves had radically changed their attitudes toward family business in the rural economy. With a considerable increase in their incomes flowing from state and collective farms—

the direct result of new, post-Stalin agricultural policy—many peasants lost interest, to a considerable degree, in private plots. This is especially true among the younger generations. Young people in the countryside (quite often having secondary education), unlike their parents, do not want to spend time after work in social production doing additional work in the household. (The time spent on private plots, by those working on collective and state farms, is about 15 hours a week, or one-third of the time spent in social production. This reduces by one-half the leisure time of villagers, compared to city dwellers.) It is typical that, of all the advantages of urban life, rural residents envy most the limited number of hours that industrial workers spend on their jobs. Among rural residents oriented toward urban life, 27 percent named this as the most important characteristic of city life, while leisure was next (21 percent), followed by the better supply of goods (13 percent) (Ryvkina 1976, p. 120).

With their new aspirations, young people not only refuse to deal with private plots, but simply flee the countryside, despite the considerable rise in living standards there (see Zaslavskaia and Kalmyk 1975; Ryvkina 1979; and Shlapentokh 1982b).

Ironically, at the time when the Soviet leadership could celebrate its victory over the peasants' attachment to their own household and nonsocial economic activity, the Soviet rulers radically altered their policy toward private plots. Realizing the earlier fiasco when such activities were more restricted, and in order to make progress in Soviet agriculture and in alleviating the growing food problem, the leadership drastically changed its attitudes in the mid-1970s toward private plots, declaring their full support of peasant activities on them. A special decision was adopted (though not published, for ideological reasons) that not only removed many legal obstacles to peasant efforts on their plots, but also ordered the official ideologues to shift from condemnation to praise of the plots as an important food source. The government even sought to materially aid the peasants with their family agricultural businesses.

This radical shift in official policy toward private plots was reflected in the new Soviet Constitution, adopted in 1977. An article in this constitution confirmed the right of people to have their private plots and declared that "the state and collective farms have to assist citizens in keeping their private plots" (Konstitutsiia (Osnovnoi Zakon) Souza Sovietskikh Sotsialisticheskikh Respublik, Moscow 1977, p. 10). In his report to the 26th Party Congress (February 1981), Brezhnev spoke of the support of private family plots as a fundamental element of Soviet agrarian policy, as if this policy had always been supported by the state (Brezhnev 1981, p. 64).*

It is remarkable that, at this time, the family has begun to be regarded as having an important place in economic activity. In numerous articles, the Soviet press has appealed to peasants, particularly the young, to understand how good it is to have a cow, some pigs, or chickens in their household, and not to be dependent on the vicissitudes of the state supply of food.

The resurgence of the role of the family as an economic unit, however, is not limited to the private plot. More and more frequently, it is suggested that the family plays an almost decisive role, even in social production. In advancing various ideas on how to resuscitate Soviet agriculture, many experts have placed emphasis on the creation of small productive units. These could be responsible for production with minimal governmental interference in their affairs, and granted autonomy for the distribution of income among its members. The best known of the experiments in this area is that conducted by the Kaskhstan agronomist, Khudenko. Indeed, in developing the notion of small production units, more and more the family is suggested as a natural economic organization, which can be burdened with the responsibility of social production, as well as for its own plot.

This idea, which would have been regarded as absolutely heretical a few decades ago, today has become a nearly normal element of economic thinking. For example, *Literaturnaia gazeta* recently published an article with a title that would have been unthinkable ten years ago: "Family Farms." This article enthusiastically described the achievements of a state farm in Estonia, where cattle had been distributed among families who were responsible for the production of meat and milk. Answering the question of why the state farm did this, its director, Il'mar Laurits, bluntly explained: "What is our goal? We want the milkmaids and herdsmen to treat state farm cattle as their own." And then he rather sadly added that "business on family farms so far is going better" (*Literaturnaia gazeta*, November 23, 1983). Having as-

---

*Now the Soviet press again attacks the peasants. However, this time it is not because they have too many pigs or cows in their households which distract them from their work in collective farming, but because many do not want to have cattle at all. "It is not justifiable," states an article in *Ekonomischeskaia gazeta* (Economic Gazette), an organ of the Central Committee, "that many families living in the countryside do not have cattle at all." (April, No. 17, 1983).

serted itself in agriculture, the idea of the new economic role of the family has made its way in other spheres of the economy, particularly in the sphere of services.

It is difficult to predict the reaction of the Soviet population to these advances by the authorities, even if the government were to demonstrate the seriousness of its intentions radically to increase the role of the family in the Soviet economy. The general demoralization of the population, and the reluctance to work hard, as well as a deep disbelief in the consistency of governmental encouragement of private initiative (if even on a limited scale), are significant impediments to eventual developments in this domain. However, a part of the population will definitely respond positively to this new course, if it really takes place, and many social and even political consequences will emerge from the growing economic role of the Soviet family.

SUMMARY

Since the Revolution, the official conceptions of marriage and the family have undergone significant change. In the first period of the Soviet state, ideology was directed at the destruction of legal marriage and the family as the stronghold of the old regime. The pitting of women against men, children against parents, was an important part of the Bolshevik strategy in the acquisition of control over the population and the consolidation of the state.

When this goal had been achieved, the Soviet state radically changed its attitudes toward the family and decided to consider it an important unit, responsible for the reproduction of the population and the political loyalty of its members. To achieve this aim, Soviet ideology drastically modified its attitudes toward love and sex. Since only a stable family could fulfill the tasks assigned to it, sex was driven from the public scene and declared as rather hostile to the building of a new society. The new concept of marriage was created. As with the pre-Revolutionary concept, it regarded divorce as an abnormal phenomenon, but this time it suggested that romantic, even if desexualized love, was the basis for a happy and socially useful alliance of men and women.

After Stalin, the transition of Soviet society from the stage of mass repression and strong ideology to the state of limited repression and weak ideology, affected in many ways the official stance toward marriage, family, and love. Trying to adjust to a new political reality, the Soviet elite relaxed marital laws, permitted abortions, and allowed a humanization of the official image of marriage. At the same time, the political elite continued to consider the family an important arm of the state and moved to a radical revision of the role of family as an économic unit, especially in the countryside.

3

Love and Sex in Present-Day Soviet Life ——

IDEOLOGY AND PERSONAL VALUES

The previous part of this book has been devoted largely to a consideration of love and marriage as official Soviet values. Now we proceed to an examination of the attitudes of Soviet people toward these values.

It is beyond doubt that any official ideology, even if it is imposed on people by coercion, exerts a powerful influence on the thoughts of those who find themselves in a discipline controlled by this ideology. Nonetheless, the existence of a discrepancy between official and personal values (or general attitudes) should not be overlooked, however small it may be. Such a discrepancy can be discerned even at times when terror, coupled with ideology, was reaching its heights.

However strongly ideology can rely on force for imposing its postulates, it always strives to find some support in values that can be treated as inherent in human nature and widespread among different societies (so-called universal values), or that are deeply rooted in the culture of the country where the given ideology came to power. As I showed before, the main thrust of official ideology in the first stage of Soviet history was directed against marriage as a social institution of the old society. In seeking support for this negative evaluation Soviet ideologues could rely on such values as romantic love, the rights of young people to decide their own fate, sexual permissiveness, and the equality of men and women. When the Soviet leadership changed its policy and decided to promote the family to the top of the list of official values, they could this time call for support from the cultural traditions of Russia, particularly Christian religious

39

values. This is also true with regard to those images of romantic marriage that Stalin included in Soviet ideology. Classical Russian literature was very helpful to Stalin here. Since literature is a major subject in Soviet schools and draws the lion's share of a pupil's time, its influence is not to be ignored. Millions of Soviet girls and boys have been brought up with ideal images of great, lifelong love and undying faithfulness. Both Tatiana from Pushkin's *Evgeny Onegin* and Natasha Rostova from Tolstoy's *War and Peace* helped to create models of feelings and behavior of Soviet youth, models that accorded with Stalin's image of the real relations between men and women. It must be underscored that just because of this support by traditional Russian literature and by universal values, the offical images of marriage and love were, to a fair degree, sincerely supported by the bulk of the Soviet people during Stalin's time. It would hardly be wrong to say that these official values were among those that were internalized to a considerable extent by the Soviets.

Soviet experience has convincingly showed how deeply ideology, officially supported and imposed on a people's values, can affect not only their views, but the most intimate aspects of their everyday life. As La Rochefoucauld put it, "There are many people who would never have been in love if they had never heard love spoken of."

Soviet ideology, energetically exploiting classical literature, creating countless novels, plays, movies, and paintings celebrating eternal love as one of the most vital events in life, could not help but bring about a desperate search for romantic love among the young, especially women.*

Of course, the influence of the official values of marriage and love has not been the same for all categories of Soviet men and women. The degree of internalization has ranged from nearly complete adoption of these values to complete rejection, and has always been strongly conditioned by sex, age, level of education, and cultural background. Between the two poles, there are those

---

*Another example of the direct influence of ideology on life is the value of creative and heroic labor. This value has been propagandized since the beginning of industrialization. It, along with some other factors, has led to the shaping of an aversion among young people to the ordinary occupations—particularly menial ones, in industry, agriculture, and commerce. The scope of this phenomenon was discovered only in the mid-1960s by Vladimir Shubkin, who carried out the first sociological investigations of boys' and girls' attitudes to various occupations (Shubkin 1970).

with semi-internalized values. In this connection, the distinction between ideal and practical values (or images) is very important. A considerable portion of the Soviet people has had two images of marriage and love: one for others and another for themselves.

THE HIGH PRESTIGE OF LOVE IN SOVIET SOCIETY TODAY

Speaking very generally, love as a value is highly respected in modern Soviet society. Official ideology and public opinion are seemingly unanimous in regarding love as a precondition for a happy and decent life. In this respect, Soviet society still is, as it was in a previous period, very different from a number of others where love between a man and a woman is treated either inimically or as a matter of no social concern.

Soviet mass media, official literature and art, and the system of education have continued to praise love and to see it as the sole moral basis of marriage, or even as a justification for premarital, and even extramarital, sexual relations.

It is even possible to contend that with liberalization, the rank of love in the hierarchical system of official values has risen somewhat. Since individuals have ceased to be considered only instrumentally, they have acquired, in the ideology, some rights to protect their feelings and personal interest. So, if in Stalin's day marriage as a value was always set higher than love (if the two should be in so undesirable a conflict), now even official ideologues in their capacity as journalists, writers, or professors can assert that sometimes people's feelings or deeds may be condoned, if under special conditions they have sacrificed marriage for the sake of love.

It is hardly possible to find any group in the country who does not share the official view of love. Of course, groups do differ in the role played by love in their systems of values. For instance, women attribute much more importance to love than do men. Available sociological data confirm this expectation (Iurkevitch 1970, p. 27; Golod 1975, p. 132).

There is also evidence that the importance of love increases with the level of education.* The fact that more educated people

---

*So, for instance, in the survey conducted by Sysenko in Moscow (1978), white-collar workers cited the "loss of love" as a reason for divorce more than ten times as often as less educated workers (Sysenko 1982, p. 102).

ascribe a higher status to love than do the less educated is also a useful indicator of the role of ideology in the lives of ordinary people. It shows that love as a particular value has, to some extent, been planted in human consciousness by the mass media, literature, and education. The more people are exposed to these influences, the more distinct and active the role played by love in their way of thinking.

American data also show that the higher the level of education, the more importance is attributed to love. In Rokeach's survey, people with an elementary school education gave love an average score of 13.90, whereas those with college degrees gave it 10.13, on a scale where the highest score was 1 and the lowest 18 (Rokeach 1973, p. 382).

Data showing a high correlation between education and the importance of love are not surprising if we remember that romantic love in general is a product of relatively recent developments, emerging as an important social issue only in the Renaissance. Among those people whose cultures are more firmly wedded to traditional patterns, especially in rural areas, we would anticipate lesser importance attributed to love.

LOVE FOR ME AND FOR OTHERS

I have spoken about the allegiance of Soviet society to love as an abstract value. This is not to deny the great social significance of the most abstract values like God, evil, communism, and so on. However, our understanding of the role of love will be much more penetrating if we consider the role of this value at different concrete levels as well.

The paradigm "for me and for others" seems to be useful in this analysis. This time, however, it will be employed somewhat differently. In its previous application, this approach was used to explain the differences between each individual's attitudes and behavior. In that situation, it was assumed that individuals themselves share the same values that are upheld for "others" to comply with, but find that, at the more concrete level of daily life, certain imperatives impede their being complied with by the individual.

In this case, applying the paradigm to attitudes toward love, we refer to the "values for others" as those that the individual perceives to be important in the lives of others, rather than what they believe *should* be important for others. Whether or not this perception is accurate, it plays a very important role in the shaping of one's own values. Thus, here we focus on the role of love in the lives of the Soviet people, taking into account the images of the importance of this value for other people.

Let us single out four categories of people according to their evaluations of the relevance of love in their own lives and to the lives of others. I will refer to the following table:

TABLE 3.1: Combinations of Attitudes about the Importance of Love

	Love is Important to Others	
Love is Important to Me	Yes	No
Yes	1	2
No	3	4

Source: Compiled by author.

The first group consists of those who believe that love is a universal phenomenon. These people support a romantic, optimistic vision of the role of love in human life. Such a vision was actively disseminated by Marxists and was an essential feature of Soviet ideology until the 1960s. Some elements of this vision, if in diluted form, can still be found in the contemporary ideology. Some Soviet authors still suggest—now more implicitly than explicitly—that every individual possesses some extraordinary gifts and can pursue creative activity in some fields and is endowed with natural inclinations to honesty, friendship, heroism, and so on (see, for instance, Changly 1973). Thus, for this group, love is viewed as a universal phenomenon or at least one that is highly valued by everyone.

The second group is made up of those who believe that love is not a widespread phenomenon and that the majority of people do not experience such a feeling nor consider it particularly important. They view themselves, and perhaps their closest social group, as exceptions, the few capable of real love. This elitist view of love is to be found, as a rule, among the intelligentsia, especially among the most refined part of it.

Members of the third group can be called personal pessimists with respect to love. They are aware of the significance of love for others but view this as an experience they are not likely to encounter. Quite the opposite of the second group, they identify themselves as the deprived, rather than privileged, minority and resign themselves to a life in which love is unimportant. Those who constitute the fourth group may be called either cynics (if they think that love is of no importance in life) or deep pessimists (if they adhere to the opposite judgment).

It is very tempting to try to approximate the size of each of these groups. Soviet sociology has accumulated data that can perhaps make possible such an incursion into this delicate realm of human views and feelings. But before we examine the Soviet data, we should introduce into our analysis a new dimension—the life cycle of Soviet people. In this cycle, the following stages are of special importance: a period before "engagement" (that is, before a decision about whom to marry); a period between getting engaged and getting married; a period of marriage, a period of divorce, and after. Attitudes toward love, as can be expected, strongly depend on the stage of life cycle being experienced. The Soviet data will indicate that as people pass through this series of stages ending in divorce, they tend to move from the optimistic, romantic view of the first group to the relatively dejected pessimism of the third or perhaps fourth group.

The data allow us to get some rough images of the proportion of people who view love as an important value for others, i.e., those making up groups one and three. In a series of studies conducted in the last fifteen years, as many as 80 to 90 percent of Soviet respondents ranked love quite high on a list of important values (Lisovskii 1969; Fainburg 1977; Kharchev and Matskovskii 1978; Kharchev 1979; Iurkevitch 1970).

Two surveys conducted in Leningrad in the 1970s illustrate the pattern. Using Rokeach's scale of eighteen "terminal values," Iadov's sample of engineers ranked love fifth, ahead of other values like material well-being, social recognition, independence, and freedom (1978, p. 90). A survey of young Leningraders found love ranked fourth among a list of thirteen similar values, following friends, health, and interesting work. Indeed, in most cases, love was ranked above family life (Aseiev et al., 1981).

Thus, it appears likely that no more than 10 to 20 percent, at least in these samples, view love as unimportant to their fellow citizens. It is probable that the elitist viewpoint, represented by group two, is not widespread and that the majority of this 10 to 20 percent would be characterized by the personal or universal pessimism of group four.

But how is this romanticism connected with real life, with "material behavior"? Can we contend that in this sphere of life, as in any other, we must deal with two realities—one related to the ideal and normative world in which others should live, and another related to the personal, practical tangible world? Is what we have shown here not this fascinating bifurcation of the Soviet mind, and perhaps of the human mentality generally, where people must accommodate their individuality to group pressure?

In attempting to answer this question, let us move through a typical Soviet life cycle.

ATTITUDES TOWARD LOVE AT DIFFERENT STAGES OF LIFE

We have seen that Soviet people do place great importance on the role of love at an abstract level, that is, when it pertains to other people in general. Yet, when we turn to attitudes toward love in the concrete realm of individual experience, viewpoints appear to change rather drastically. The differences are especially pronounced among those who have passed through the four stages of the marital life cycle.

As an initial indicator of the significance of love in the early stages of the marriage cycle, we employ here the ranking of factors that newly married individuals cite as their motivations for getting married. In a survey of newlyweds conducted by Estonian sociologists in 1972, love was ranked fifth among eighteen motivations to marry. Mutual respect, fidelity, trust, and tenderness were cited as being more significant in the desire to marry (Tiit 1978, p. 143). Chechot (1976) obtained similar results. This suggests that, while the Soviet people attribute great significance to love at an abstract level, the pragmatic concerns facing people in their daily lives seem to compel them to accept less than they consider ideal.

Among people who have experienced actual married life, we seem to find even greater resignation to the idea that love should be of lesser significance in personal life. Most Soviet surveys suggest that less than half of all married respondents maintain a firm belief in the importance of love. In one Leningrad study of married people, mutual love was regarded as fundamentally important for a happy marriage by only 16 percent of all male respondents and 25 percent of female ones (Kharchev 1979, p.

200). In another Leningrad study, the respective figures were 26 percent and 28 percent (Golod 1977, p. 50).[*]

Divorce and the breakup of family life leads to a further increase in pessimism about love. In a number of surveys, Soviet sociologists have classified marriages as either "happy" or "unhappy" (on the basis of the respondents' self-evaluation of marriage). The proportion of people who deny the relevance of love to their marriage from its beginning is much higher in "unhappy" marriages than in "happy" marriages and is as high as 18 percent among men and 28 percent among women (Iurkevitch 1970, p. 27).

Data on divorce are especially significant. As is very often the case, extreme situations help elucidate the "material," behavioral manifestations of a social value. Soviet investigations of divorce have implied that love has not been central to the conflicts that have lead to divorce—at least not as these conflicts were perceived by its participants. In some studies, no more than 10 percent of divorced people referred to a "withering of love" as a motive for the dissolution of marriage (Kolokol'nikov 1976; Pelevin 1972). Moreover, in a number of investigations such a motive was not singled out at all (Chuiko 1975; Soloviev 1977).

Available data suggest that, of Soviet respondents who affirm a belief in love at an abstract level, a considerable proportion think that this value has no relevance to their own life. The data here do not allow us to make more exact computations. But, taking into account that the ratio of divorces to marriages is about 1:3, and that therefore a very great part of the Soviet population must have gone through divorce procedures, that the number of "unhappy" marriages is quite large (Fainburg 1977, p. 72), and that about one-third of single women never get married, it may be asserted that much less than half of the adult Soviet population regard love as a value that has something to do with their own life.

---

[*]The very imperfect character of survey data, as a source of information about human attitudes and feelings in general, and of Soviet surveys devoted specifically to marriage and love, does not allow us to make more subtle distinctions between, for instance, attitudes toward love as a basis for marriage and as a basis for free sexual relations. Nor can we clearly distinguish between people's perceptions based on their own experiences in this domain and perceptions related to the role of love in the lives of others. In interpreting data produced by Soviet sociologists, I have been mostly inclined to treat them as based predominantly on the experience of respondents and related to their own lives.

LOVE, IDEOLOGY, AND SOVIET FEMINISTS

By the mid-1960s, Soviet public opinion, and to some degree the elite, realized that love is a myth for many people—a myth that at best has been playing the role of an unattainable ideal. Public awareness of this should be ascribed not only to sociology, but perhaps more to liberal writers, dramatists, and directors who managed to produce novels, stage plays, and movies containing sober analyses of the relations between the sexes.

With this change of view about the role of love in social life, it became necessary to reassess the place of this value in Soviet history. In response, an extremely interesting, covert discussion of the problem started among Soviet intellectuals, especially among sociologists.*

First of all, it must be remarked that only because love was enshrined and worshipped by official ideology had it become an object of hostility for a considerable part of the intelligentsia and the youth. To some degree, the growth of this skepticism toward love has been supported by some Soviet feminists who, for all their differences from their Western counterparts, also claim more independence for women and consider men, and not only patri-archal society, as their principal foe. Enjoying the active support of only a fairly small proportion of their gender, they see—though in a much milder way than feminists in the United States or their predecessors in post-Revolutionary Russia—in women's devotion to romantic love a serious obstacle to their self-actualization.†

Without rejecting the emotional sphere of life, Soviet fem-

---

*In the course of stabilization in all spheres of Soviet life, a very peculiar style has been established in Soviet social science. It has almost completely excluded overt polemics between scholars. Since the mid-fifties, sociologists, as well as historians, philosophers, and economists, have stopped criticizing each other publicly. Negative reviews of scientific publications have virtually disappeared from magazines and newspapers. It has become practically impossible to discover a more or less serious debate during a symposium. For this reason, it is almost unknown to nonspecialists that between Soviet sociologists and demographers there is a very great divergence of views on the subject under discussion. Among related problems, such an issue as the phenomenon of the childless family is an exception. It is unusually hotly discussed in a variety of publications.

†Gail Lapidus proposes to distinguish three patterns of sex role norms in modern society, the Soviet Union included: 1) a sharp differentiation of male and female roles; 2) the partial assimilation of females into male roles; and 3) the transcendence of gender as the basis for the allocation of social roles (1978, p. 340). Lapidus presents Soviet feminist publicists like Larisa Kuznetsova as proponents of the third approach. It is difficult to agree with this. Of course, Soviet feminist authors favor a more active role for women in some fields of social life, but they are

inists are, however, against treating love as a major value in a woman's life. It is characteristic that Larisa Kuznetsova, one of the most outspoken of the licit representatives of Soviet feminism* in her book, *Women on the Job and at Home* (1980), surveyed all of the modern woman's major problems (major in Kuznetsova's opinion) but did not pay much attention to love. Reminded of a thought of a famous Russian radical writer of the nineteenth century, Alexander Herzen, that for a long time women were "driven in love," Kuznetsova touched on this issue only in connection with the social status of modern women (1980, p. 168).

In the post-Stalinist epoch, recognition of biological and psychological differences between the sexes, like the downgrading of love, has also been directed against official ideology, which has emphasized the determinant role of social milieu.† The apparent

---

very insistent in underscoring biological and psychological differences between men and women. For this reason, when demanding equality with men in housework, they develop the idea of the necessity of redistributing roles between the two sexes, requiring the more intensive participation of women in some spheres and their withdrawal from some others detrimental to their health. With all their misgivings about women's absorption by emotions directed toward men, the most ardent Soviet feminists have never come close to the small group of American feminists and their denunciation of sentiments that can impair women's professional and social status.

*Soviet underground feminist activity is reflected in the magazine *Maria*. About this activity see also *Ms.* 1980 (November) p. 49–56, 80–83 and 102–8. See also *Upp* 1983.

†In this connection, it is necessary to recall that, over the entire period of the 1960s, during the period of liberalization, some Soviet scholars criticized the official concept of humanity that completely ignored the role of biological factors in human behavior and reduced everything to the influence of social milieu. Even the Party philosopher, Georgii Smirnov, Deputy Head of the Propaganda Department of the Central Committee, in order not to appear as a conservative, wrote that "human needs and traits of biological origin should not be ignored. Unfortunately, carried away by social characteristics, some authors forget that this circumstance involves wrong evaluations of human behavior" (Smirnov 1971, p. 48). Some risk-takers (such as the law professor Noi from Saratov or biologist Golubovskii from Novosibirsk) insisted that genetic factors account, to a considerable degree, for criminal behavior. With the rise of political reaction in the 1970s, advancing such concepts as functions of biological factors has become more dangerous. Soviet publications once again began to denounce and derogate these ideas as manifestations of bourgeois ideology (see Dubinin 1983; Dubinin *et al.* 1982).

The author here in no way wishes to take a stand on this issue. He intends only to underscore how, in different historical contexts, the same problem takes on different political colors. Because of this, the transcendence of sex in human society, which is very "progressive" in the American scene, is regarded in the Soviet Union as a derivative of outmoded and obsolete ideology.

similarity between the views of some Soviet authors, such as Kon and Perevedentsev, and some postulates of American functionalist sociology has impelled Lapidus to treat these views as outmoded and conservative since, in her opinion, the transcendence of sex is crucial to modern feminism (1978, p. 325). This is, however, not right and not fair. After a long period when the state very energetically implemented the theory of the transcendence of gender and contended that women can perform any male job, the Soviet intelligentsia has advanced a new ideal of sex differentiation based on real historical experience, which favors a gender division in some spheres of social life.

RESEXUALIZATION OF SOVIET SOCIETY

A short time after the discussion among intellectuals started, it became clear that the relation between love and sexual pleasure was at its center. In fact, such a discussion would have been impossible if Stalin had not died and the country not embarked, after his death, on the path of liberalization. As noted above, Stalin's romantic image of marriage presupposed the exclusion of sex from love. The desexualization of relations between the sexes was one of the significant processes of that time. Now, with the rehabilitation of some human feelings, sex has been gradually, in small doses, reintroduced into Soviet public life, first of all in science—sociology, medicine—then in literature and art. The sexual component began to penetrate novels, plays, and movies.

The leading figure of the resexualization of Soviet sociology has been Igor Kon, one of the most respected figures in the field. In his book, which became famous in the 1960s, *The Sociology of Personality* (even the title sounded then like a challenge to the dominant ideology), he advanced a concept of love not trivial for Soviet readers, in which "the sexual component" had a serious role to play (1967, p. 155). Kon's subsequent publications have developed the subject much further (for instance, 1970, 1978, 1981). In this respect, his article in *Sotsiologicheskiie Issledovaniia*, the Soviet sociological journal (1982), stands out as extremely brave and challenging.

The main message of the article is that sexual activity plays an extremely important role in people's lives and it should be treated as such. Kon was not afraid to say that "modern man carries out in marriage a more intensive and erotically more diversified sexual life than his ancestors because this life does not know now the former seasonal fluctuations (religious abstentions and feasts related to the agrarian labor cycle)." Operating with terminology alien to nonmedical publications, and forced (probably by an editor) to refer to the latest Party decisions, Kon mentioned such an issue as women's orgasms only a few lines from a reference to the 26th Party Congress, in which Brezhnev said two sentences about the acuity of demographic problems in the country (Kon 1982, p. 118).*

Under Kon's influence, one of his graduate students, Sergei Golod, started one of the first surveys since the 1920s which included, to the great surprise of Soviet respondents, some questions about sexual life.† It should not be supposed from this that since then the sexual issue has enjoyed the same rank in Soviet sociology as topics like labor turnover or the choice of occupation after school. Indeed, the question remains in many ways taboo and is treated rather like sensitive political issues. However, at the theoretical level at least, sociologists since Kon's breakthrough can insert a "sexual component" in the examination of problems of marriage and love.

The reappearance of the sexual component has forced Soviet sociologists, as well as representatives of the mass media, literature and art, to express their attitudes to three types of relations between men and women, depending on the presence of love and sexual pleasure in them. To examine these types of relations between love and sexual pleasure, let me again refer to a table:

TABLE 3.2:   Combinations of Attitudes about the Importance of Sexual Pleasure and Love

	Love is Important	
Sexual Pleasure is Important	Yes	No
Yes	1	2
No	3	4

Source: Compiled by the author.

*Despite Igor Kon's heroic efforts to introduce sexual behavior as a "normal" topic in Soviet sociology, he has not been very successful, and his publications on intimate aspects of Soviet life are still exotic in the eyes of Soviet readers. Mikhail Matskovskii made a content analysis of Soviet publications on the family and related issues. He discovered that "sexual relations between spouses" were treated only in four publications over the last thirteen years: In 1968–76 there were three publications of this sort, in 1976–81 only one. At the same time, the topic of the educational function of the family was analyzed in 108 publications, the economic function of the family in thirteen, leisure in the family in thirty-two, and the reproductive function of the family in 146 (Matskovskii 1982, p. 75).

†The first survey of this sort was carried out in Leningrad in 1962.

The first type represents romantic love, just as it was conceived by Engels and Lenin. The second type means sexual relations free of deep emotional feelings. The third type corresponds to the images of love as described by Soviet ideology in Stalin's time. The fourth type denies the significant role of love and sex relations between women and men.

Three categories of sociologists—ideological, managerial, and professional—hold different views on the role of sex in love. Conservative, ideologically oriented sociologists, as well as philosophers, journalists, and writers of the same orientation, adhere to Stalin's image of love and ignore the sexual element of love. Tamara Chumakova can be regarded as a typical representative of this type of Soviet sociologist. In her book (1974) she strongly attacks those authors (Riurikov, Svetlanov) who emphasize the sexual drive as the substance of love. Chumakova is very insistent that the content of love relations is determined by social surroundings. She writes that "love, as a spiritual, moral, and social feeling, does not deny either a class or an individual approach to it" (Chumakova 1974, p. 21). Naturally, she criticizes those who try to treat love as a universal value or universal type of human relation, and defends, as can be seen from the quotation, the class approach to human relations, outmoded in the Soviet Union even in official documents.*

D. Chechot, a law expert who writes on marriage problems, also contends that "the family in a socialist society is based on love both in principle and in most aspects of family life" (Chechot 1976, p. 61).

Another example of the attempts to present the mentality of Soviet people as if still believing in love as a basis of desexualized marriage was the study by B. Ivanov. Having questioned 65 workers, he obviously conflated various alternatives proposed to respondents in the question about the most important traits of their marriage in order to be able to affirm that in marriage, 80 percent of them "appreciate love, moral satisfaction, opportunities for creative activity, and children" (1972, pp. 46–47).

---

*Without delivering figures, Chumakova asserts that the majority of her respondents in answering the question, "What features are the most characteristic of the Soviet family'", chose the following alternative: "Unity of ideals, opinions, feelings of responsibility for society, and common family interests." This assertion looks very suspicious even if we take into consideration the readiness of people to check off any alternatives in closed questions, as well as the apparent conformism of Soviet respondents. No other publications of Soviet sociologists can confirm Chumakova's assertion.

It is curious that when political conservatism in the Soviet Union gained its momentum after the invasion of Czechoslovakia sex was also victimized again. In the early 1970s, one of the best Soviet magazines, *The Journalist*, was accused, and the editor-in-chief Georgii Iakovlev dismissed, under the pretext that a woman in one artistically done picture could be perceived as though naked: her body was shadowed in such a way that it could be imagined to be unclad. By the end of the 1970's and the early 1980s, the accusation of pornography still carries a political flavor and is used to crush political opponents. This happened to a collection of literary works, *Metropol*, which a group of Soviet writers sought to publish in Moscow without censorship.

Professional sociologists—as well as managerial sociologists—are unanimous in recognizing the importance of the sexual element in relations between the sexes and they all consider sexual affection an integral part of love. This thesis may seem trivial, even amusing, but its appearance in Soviet publications in the 1960s was almost a revolution.*

Still, these two groups of sociologists have drawn somewhat different implications from the public rehabilitation of the sexual drive in Soviet life. Professional sociologists have concentrated their attention on the first type of relationship—love based on sex. In their counteroffensive against the bigotry implanted by Stalin, they have energetically emphasized that love without sexual passion is not real love, and therefore that couples from whose life this passion has disappeared should separate. The champion of this view has been Iuri Riurikov, the author of a very popular book among the intelligentsia, *Three Inclinations* (1967) and numerous articles.

Of no lesser importance for professional sociologists has been the second type of relationship between men and women—sex without love. Here the challenge to official ideology has been much stronger than that in praising sexually permeated love. In the end, even official literature and art have not denied that sex exists in human relations. But official ideology has only recognized sex within marriage and has opposed legalization of extramarital sex.

---

*In the early 1960s, one English journalist wrote in an article about sexual problems in the USSR: "This year a book came out in the Soviet Union that began with a sentence that could not have been published a few years ago: 'There is a great difference between a man and a woman.'"

Yet, liberal intellectuals have now begun to justify sexual relations before and outside of marriage. To fully appreciate the meaning of these very often hidden and oblique efforts to infuse sexual problems into Soviet public life, a number of aspects of the Soviet system of values must be taken into consideration.

First of all, in the Soviet political and social context, the advocacy of sexual pleasure has been regarded as one of the episodes in the struggle against totalitarianism and for individuality, much like what occurred in the Renaissance when humanists like Boccaccio saw in sexual permissiveness a radical step toward the happy life of free people. For this reason, the social meaning of the controversy surrounding sex in the USSR and other socialist countries has little in common with its meaning in the West, despite Marcuse's claim that "sexual liberation" is, in essence, antiauthoritarian in the East and West alike.

The struggle against bigotry and for the recognition of sex as an important part of human life has been carried out not only by sociologists, but by nearly the entire intellectual community. Soviet writers have been, of course, among the most active advocates of the realistic approach to this issue. Since 1953, they have consistently increased the role of sex in their novels and poems. They began with the rejection of the idea that sexual relations outside marriage, especially if they are inspired by love, are always immoral. Then they dared to describe sex, even in very reserved ways, worlds away from *Lady Chatterly's Lover*, or, all the more, *The Tropic of Cancer*. However, when in the early 1960s Yevtushenko started a poem with the words, "The bed was unmade," indicating that something had just happened, it was a real sensation in the country. The popularity of Yevtushenko at the time was fantastic: one half of all readers of *Literaturnaia gazeta* named him as their favorite poet in an open question included in our survey in 1968.* In fact, the general resurrection

---

*The prudery of Soviet ideology also makes it impossible to use words in literary works that could be interpreted as vulgar. Insignificant as it may seem in comparison with its other merits, *One Day in the Life of Ivan Denisovich*, the first of Solzenitsyn's publications in the USSR in 1962, acquainted Soviet readers also with the use, even if in a somewhat disguised way, of the word that is an extremely popular component of Russian, "mat", the cursing of the very high rank.

Another breakthrough in the same domain was made recently by Valentin Kataiev (1982) who got permission to use the Russian equivalent of "asshole." (Igor Birman drew my attention to this exotic fact.)

of lyric poetry in the country after 1953 (at the Second All-Union Congress of Soviet Writers it was still rather risky to defend this poetry—see Swayze 1962, pp. 119–20) was directly related to the re-emergence of sex in literature.

The penetration of sex into psychology and medicine was no less thorny than in literature and the arts. Even up to the 1970s, Freud was still treated by Soviet officials only in very negative terms and was a symbol of an unhealthy exaggeration of the role of sexual pleasure in human life. In their attempt to eradicate sexual life from the public scene and to present it as something very nearly like bawdiness or licentiousness, ideologues continued to reduce the entire Freudian heritage to his concept of the libido and did not recognize his other ideas. Of course, the Freudian approach to psychological conflict—especially the idea of the id, ego, and superego, as universal and timeless—only increased the forced anger of Soviet purists enmeshed in historical determinism.

Soviet ideology's hostile stance toward Freud and psychoanalysis only roused interest in them among the intelligentsia. Since Freud's books had not been reprinted since the 1920s, and since even library copies of old editions were not accessible (they are usually kept in special departments of libraries), the price of these books, or their photocopies, reached fantastic levels on the black market. Soviet readers pounced on all books and articles containing any piece of information on Freud, even if the publication was directed at denigrating Freud as much as possible. Only in the late 1960s did liberal Soviet philosophers manage to insert an article on Freud in *The Philosophical Encyclopedia*, which gingerly recognized some "positive" elements of Freud's works.*

In the 1960s, the relaxation of official attitudes toward sexual problems allowed some enthusiasts, headed by Vasil'chenko, to create the first medical unit in Moscow to study human sexual behavior. They managed to publish a few books on this subject, such as *General Sexual Pathology* (1977), which, despite their scientific jargon, became best sellers and were avidly read by everybody who could get their hands on them.

---

*The fact that V. Sysenko recently cited Freud in an article of his without making any critical comment can, in the Soviet context, be regarded as a rather brave act (Sysenko 1979, p. 101).

By the 1970s, medical units of the same character emerged in some other cites—Vilnus, Riga, and especially Leningrad where the physician Sviadoshch acquired public recognition for the management of his laboratories.

As soon as the authorities stopped stigmatizing interest in sexual problems, it became possible to organize lectures on this topic and even to publish popular books on marital life that touched on its sexual aspects.* Lectures on the subject, not at all frequent, usually drew a full house. One of the most popular lecturers in the 1970s was Lubov Gudovich who, as the head of the department on sexual problems in the Kislovodsk medical center, became the most popular figure in town—one of the main resorts of the country (see Stern 1979, pp. 154–55).

Yet, the process of legalizing the sexual issue in Soviet public life has been so slow that only in the late 1960s did it become possible to introduce experiments in sex education in Estonia. In Moscow, however, it became possible only in the early 1980s.

The change in public attitudes toward sex, combined with the rise of education (a critical factor in every sphere of Soviet life) and the greater access to Western styles of life, has contributed to the marked rise of sex as a hedonistic value in the general system of personal values in the USSR. People have become much more demanding of each other concerning sex, both inside and outside of marriage. Sexual disharmony in marriage, which simply did not exist as a public issue in the 1950s or even the early 1960s, is now a subject of serious discussion and even public concern. The Soviet psychologist Rozhanovskaia states that "the sexual aspect of marital life has been increasing," and she cites the East German expert Chalgasch, who contends that sexual conflicts account for the majority of divorces in the DDR (Rozhanovskaia 1981, p. 115).

One of the major factors that has contributed to the sexualization of the Soviet mentality today, according to Igor Kon, is "the drastic increase in female sexual activity." Kon derogates Victorian morality and medical theories that contend that "a decent woman in general does not enjoy sex." He asserts, referring

---

*It is peculiar that the majority of the books on marital life and sex that have come out in the last two decades have been written by authors from East Europe—for example, the East German Neubert's *New Book on Married Life* (1965) has been extremely popular; as has *Love. Motherhood. the Future* (1982) by Frantishek Chorvat, a Slovak.

for lack of Soviet data to Czechoslovakian sources, that the proportion of women from the younger generation who experience orgasm reached 79 percent, against 31 percent among women of the older generation. He further suggests that this sexual awakening of women is a source of conflict between men and women, presumably because now men cannot satisfy the increasing sexual appetites of Soviet women (Kon 1982, p. 118).

ATTACK ON LOVE

Like such values as power and wealth, sexual pleasure as a cathectic value has never been recognized by Soviet ideology, though the elite, almost since the beginning of Soviet history, has sought to possess these as far as could be. It is well known in the Soviet Union that officials engage in numerous sexual affairs with those who depend on them. Beria' s case—about 300 mistresses were attributed to him in the official indictment, per Yskander's story in *Metropol* (1982)—aroused amazement not on moral grounds, but at the vigor of the old chief of the KGB.

Here, as in other cases, the elite have strictly followed the principle: what's good for us is not good for others. For this reason, the legalization of the sexual side of life, and the refusal to treat sexual relations not sanctioned by marriage as moral, have been perceived by Soviet liberals as salient enough aims in their fight against the regime.*

The restoration of sex on the public scene has had another ideological aspect as well. Looking again to our paradigm, we may see that a permissive sex life has been ascribed by ideology only to "others"; this time "we" and "us" have been used to mean all Soviet people, whereas "others" are people in the West. So if ideological sociologists continue to stress, as they did in Stalin's time, the presumed cardinal difference between sexual morals in the West and in Socialist society, professional sociologists take every opportunity to indicate that, with all their differences, the two types of society have a number of features in common.

---

*Orwell was astonishingly aware of this "revolutionary" meaning of the contravention of sexual taboos in a totalitarian society. In the end of a chapter of *1984*, having learned that Julia had had affairs even with members of the inner party (which was a testimony of their corruption and left some hope for their defeat), Smith felt that in making love to Julie he committed not only a sexual, but a political act as well.

By contrast to purely ideological sociologists who continue stubbornly to support major dogmas, sociologists with pragmatic orientations have joined their liberal colleagues in attempts to restore the role of sex in love, if not as directly or actively. However, they have drawn different implications from the restitution of sexual love in Soviet society.

Professional sociologists, as has been said, have found in the sexual basis of love a vigorous argument for freedom in this domain of life. But pragmatic sociologists have come to the conclusion that they must assume the offensive against love. Their logic is clear: if marriage is to be stable, and if love depends on unstable sexual affections, the interests of society require that links between marriage and love, still some years ago seemingly unshaken, should be intentionally weakened. It was Anatolii Kharchev, the leading official theorist in the study of marriage and the family, who launched this, in some ways unprecedented, official attack on love.

Well versed in the tricks used in the Soviet Union to present a change in policy or ideology as completely consonant with old dogma, Kharchev proclaims, at the outset, his absolute respect for love. He attributes to love a key role in the relations between men and women in the future communist society, where the ideals of the founders of Marxism-Leninism are to be completely implemented in this field as elsewhere. By that time, Kharchev wrote, "love will be a major, perhaps the sole, justification of sexual intimacy . . . and will be factually identical to marriage" (Kharchev 1979, p. 354).

As to the role of love in the present socialist society, Kharchev is very pessimistic. He charges at love from different sides. His main aim is to prove that the role of love has been exaggerated and for this he blames literature and art, which have created an unrealistic, sentimental, rosy image of love (Kharchev 1979, p. 187).*

Kharchev writes that "studies show that sexual intimacy based only on love quite often ends, not with marriage, but with disappointment; but at the same time, marriages based on love break up not more rarely, but even more often than marital

---

*Kharchev also criticized his fellow sociologists for overestimating the place of love in Soviet life. He reproaches them for ignorance of factors that move people to attribute to love a much greater role than it really plays in their life (p. 191).

alliances based on more prosaic considerations." In this case, equating love with sexual pleasure, Kharchev, as the ultimate argument in support of his stance, cites Dr. Swiadoshch's data, which show that only 10.5 percent of married men believed that their wives always get pleasure from sexual intimacy (Kharchev 1978, p. 214).

Kharchev further strives to deprive love of its romantic halo. He portrays love as a very vague notion and contends that it is very often erroneously identified with sex; and sexual affection, he continues, is a very precarious feeling that at best can last only a short while (Kharchev 1979, p. 181). He then goes on to deprecate love not only as an unstable value, but also as a value in permanent conflict with other, often more important, values such as honesty, decency, duty, conscience, responsibility (*Ibid.*).

Having denigrated love as a value in various ways, Kharchev can proclaim his main thesis: love and marriage should be divorced. This divorce is so important for him that he is even ready to utter a proposition sacrilegious from the ideological point of view: "there is love without marriage and marriage without love" (*Ibid.*, p. 65).

Thus, Kharchev provides a moral justification for marriage without love. In this way, he embraces a very conservative view of marriage. Moreover, he insists that love is rather dangerous to a good marriage, seeing in love a generator of expectations doomed to be frustrated.

Kharchev suggests to "others," to ordinary Soviet people, that there are many other feelings and values besides love that can make marriage a tolerable and even a pleasurable undertaking. Mutual sympathy and kinship relations are cited as the antithesis of passionate love (*Ibid.*, p. 90).

Kharchev and some other sociologists have developed an idea that not only during the Revolution, but still in Stalin's time, would have been regarded as completely "bourgeois" and deeply alien to the spirit of Marxist-Leninist ideology. This is the notion that there is an inverse correlation between the intensity of love in the courtship period and the happiness of marriage. In other words, the more the fiancés and newlyweds are infatuated with each other, the greater the likelihood that their marriage will come to grief. This concept is advanced even more conspicuously by Sergei Golod, who lends it an even more challenging character.

Golod coins something of an aphorism: "Love is a significant impetus to marriage, but not a serious guarantee of the stability of modern family relations" (1977, p. 50). This Soviet sociologist refers to data of his own as well as those produced by his colleagues to bolster the thesis that love is often a sinister harbinger for wedlock. Among people driven to marriage by love, 19 percent gave negative evaluations of the current state of their conjugal relations, whereas only 13 percent of those who contracted marriage under the influence of "rational considerations" evaluated their marriage as unhappy. Estonian data that Golod refers to also reveal, in his opinion, that the significance of love is diminishing in favor of mutual respect and fidelity (1977, pp. 50–51).

While concurring with Kharchev's and Golod's views, the Estonian sociologist Enni Tiit seeks to soften their categorical severing of all connections between stable marriage and love. She attempts this by watering down the notion of love and opposing it to infatuation. Without denying the importance of the sexual component of love, she links intense sexual feeling only with infatuation. At the same time, she underscores the decisive importance of such components as friendship, mutual respect, and so forth (Tiit 1982, p. 31).

Kharchev's views on this subject, as well as other aspects of marriage, are backed by another leading figure in the sociology of marriage and the family, Zoia Iankova. She states that 30 percent of Muscovites explained their divorce after more than five years of marriage by their strong orientation to romantic love and their neglect of "the prose of life," the more practical imperatives of living. Several other reasons put forth by respondents were also pertinent: an erosion of emotions (12 percent) and difficulties in communications (15 percent) (Iankova 1978).

Soviet creators of classifications of the family's functions, with the exception of Fainburg, also discount love as relevant to current family life. At best, some of them do cite one function that is somewhat associated with love. This is true of Iankova, who speaks of a "sexual-emotional-hedonistic function" (1978, pp. 105–6). Golod follows the same pattern and renders his homage to love by singling out a "hedonistic" function (1977), as does Iurkevich, who speaks of a "sexual function" (1970, p. 70), as do many other sociologists.*

---

*It is curious that in naming the major factors determining the compatibility of spouses, Iurkevich begins with the "ideological unity" of the partners, then continues with "common life goals," "common needs, interests, tastes, customs," "cultural compatibility," and "compatibility of characters." Coming to the end of his list, he cites "physiological adequacy," "love or other mutual inclination," and

The position of the prominent Soviet sociologist Zakhar Fainburg deserves special attention. He can be regarded as a representative of a very small group of Soviet sociologists who may be called romantic neo-Leninists. Outwardly this group shares with the ideological sociologists an allegiance to the old dogmas. But, in fact, they shore up only those dogmas that were dominant immediately after the Revolution, rejecting Stalin's influence, and seek to adjust Lenin's heritage to the modern world. In line with the general vision of this group, Fainburg defends romantic love as a chief value in human relations. He takes a direct stand against the "pessimistic prognosis for the role of love in the future" (Fainburg 1977, p. 38; 1981, p. 145). He is perhaps the only Soviet sociologist who not only did not omit the mention of love in his description of the functions of the family, but even insists that the family's first function is in the preservation of love (Fainburg 1978, p. 12). Making no distinction between love as a value "for me" and a value "for others," he contends that the majority of the Soviet people see in love the key component of marriage. According to his data, even those who judge their marriages unhappy continue to believe in love as a major pillar of it. He claims that only 12 percent of those with an unhappy marriage displayed negative attitudes to love, as against 4 percent among the happily married (Fainburg 1977, p. 136). Fainburg's positive views on the role of romantic love have been criticized by Kharchev who, as was indicated above, thinks that the restoration of prerevolutionary views on love is more suitable to the interests of Soviet society and its elite (Kharchev 1979, p. 180).

Another serious social scientist who, if only in a very abstract form, defends love as the basis of marital relations is Anatolii Vishnevskii. Like Fainburg, Vishnevskii does not want to deny that love is the foundation of stable marriage. Though uttering lofty words about love, instead of the traditional perception of love, he presents love as above all a form of self-actualization, through the "recognition of the personality and the unique individuality of the lover." Yet, having said all these laudatory words about love,

---

"family duties." Sergei Rappoport cannot be rebuked for complete nonchalance about love. He introduces a special compensatory function that has to encompass all aspects of intimate family life. "Sex" finds itself on the list of intimate problems—after housework, hygiene, illness, and conflicts (Rappoport 1977, p. 62). Attacks against the romantic-love complex can also be found in this country. Some U.S. authors (for instance, see Walster and Walster 1978) also contend that because people idealize romance, its loss becomes a source of discontent.

Vishnievskii suggests that the real foundation of a happy family is children (Vishnievskii 1982, pp. 190–97).

In another approach, the social psychologist Gozman attempted to reconcile opposite views on the role of romantic love in marriage by proposing the existence of two types of love: the "pessimistic" and the "optimistic." The first type, which he links to Casler (1974), assumes that the individual has a love-hate relation with the object of his passion. Thus, on the one hand the lover strongly loves those who are capable of satisfying his/her needs, but on the other hand hates this same person who possesses the power to deprive him/her at any moment the satisfaction of needs. For those who experience this type of love, the solidity of their marriage is inversely related to the strength of their passion.

The optimistic form of love is based, in Gozman's opinion, on the concept of needs as advanced by Abraham Maslow (1972). In these cases, love behaves in the opposite way, removing anxiety and creating the atmosphere for psychological comfort. Here the strength of love makes the marriage more stable and secure. Though Gozman seeks to preserve a balanced approach to both visions of love, it is evident that, in his interpretation, "true love" is closer to his "pessimistic" model. Calm and comfortable love, which he describes as an ally of marriage, is depicted as dispassionate and as having little in common with the romantic image of love (see Andreieva and Dontsov 1981, pp. 221–24).

LOVE, SEX, AND PHENOMENOLOGY

It is interesting that discussions on love and sex have forced Soviet sociologists to touch on phenomenological problems. Thus, in analyzing the role of sex in the relations between men and women, sociologists have begun to pay attention to such problems as the human perceptions of one's own feelings. Again, four types of situations can be singled out:

TABLE 3.3: Objective and Subjective Feelings about Love

Subject Considers Own Feelings	"Objectively" Given Feelings	
	Can be Considered as Love	Cannot be Considered as Love
as love	1	2
not as love	3	4

Source: Compiled by the author.

Type two has attracted the special attention of Soviet sociologists in their attacks against love. Professional (Kon, Golod) and managerial (Kharchev, Iurkevich) sociologists have stated that a great number of people, especially women, wrongly perceive their own, as well as their partner's feelings, as love. Their feelings may actually be a sexual aberration, a temporary bodily excitement that has very little in common with love, which is supposed to be the unity of spiritual and sexual affections (Kharchev 1979, p. 188; Kon 1967, p. 155). The ill-judged evaluation of real feelings leads to unfounded expectations and then inevitably to frustration. The concern of Soviet sociologists about the frustration engendered by illusions in personal relations is consistent with their similar worry about illusions leading to frustration in other areas of Soviet life, particulary in the sphere of professional activity (young people, for example, expecting to leave school and get creative work—along with love, much praised by ideology—often fall far short of it) Shlapentokh 1970; Shubkin 1970).

While sociologists focus on type two, Soviet writers and filmmakers prefer to concentrate on another contradictory type—type three. The point here is that despite the growing interest in the sexual aspects of life, Soviet literature and art remain protectors and custodians of love. Developing the humanistic traditions of Russian classical culture, a number of Soviet authors have sought to defend love as a value against sexual pleasure as a goal in itself. Hence, at the center of a novel, play, or movie, we often find a protagonist, young or old, who, having overlooked love, does not understand the real meaning of his intimate relations. One such film, very popular in the 1960s, was titled, *And What If It's Real Love?*

THE SOVIET ELITE, LOVE, AND SEX

The pragmatic-conservative stance toward love has been shared and expressed by many people holding different official positions in the Soviet Union. This stance is closer to the views of the Soviet elite, with their internal, well-concealed contempt of their own ideology and slogans. If they cannot afford to unveil their genuine views on such values as the leading role of the working class, internationalism, or democracy, they can do so to some extent with respect to such values as love. Being by definition cynics (it is impossible to preserve power for long and espouse any ideology but cynicism), they have realized early in their political careers that love, if it exists at all, is something for mavericks, those "others" who cannot pursue truly important goals, individual or social. Not only love, but any other strong affection is probably alien to the type of individuals who belong to the elite in a socialist state, down to the very lowest echelons. The Soviet elite should be credited with a remarkable ability to keep to, in secrecy, their own way of thinking and their private subjective lives. So, any glimpse into this sphere acquires a special significance.*

Given this, the following episode from Soviet history is especially remarkable. Stalin's opposition to most emotion has been well established (Alliluieva 1967; Khrushchev 1970; Djilas

---

*An interesting glimpse into the sexual lives of Soviet *apparatchiks* is provided through a sensational publication in *Kontinent* (1983). The magazine became privy to a top-secret document: the confession of a leading figure in the Uzbek SSR, Iadgar Nasritdinova, one of few Soviet women who have held high positions in the USSR. (She was President of the Uzbek Republic and chair of a chamber in the Soviet Parliament.)

Enmeshed in a nationalist action in the mid-1970s, Nasritdinova sought to avoid harsh punishment by confessing her guilt before Moscow. She provided a detailed description of the lives of Uzbek leaders. A cunning woman, she linked the intensification of anti-Russian sentiment in Uzbekistan to the immoral behavior of local bureaucrats appointed by Moscow, some of whom were ethnic Russians.

The centerpiece of the confession was the portrayal of the lives of her colleagues. For example, the Second Secretary of the Uzbek Central Commitee, Mel'nikov, sent his wife to a psychiatric hospital to enable him to have a love affair with the First Secretary of the Young Communist League, Brodova. A bordello for high officials was created in Tashkent, under the guise of a sanitorium. Martynov, a Central Committee Secretary, who left his family in Moscow, was one of the most frequent visitors. Other prominent guests included Mukhitdinov, First Secretary of the Uzbekistan Party (and later Secretary of the Central Committee in Moscow and Politburo member). Mukhitdinov was also a frequent patron of another exclusive bordello in Sotchi, a principal resort on the Black Sea.

Many other leading figures were involved in various kinds of questionable sexual activities, including many acts prohibited by the Penal Code. (One, a Central Committee Secretary, seduced his daughter-in-law, who later committed suicide. Another, a chair of the Republican Trade Union, attempted to rape his own daughter, inflicting serious injury in the process.) Rashidov, the First Secretary of the Central Committee and alternate member of the Moscow Politburo, was also active in such escapades. Rashidov suffered from stomach trouble. A bordello was created as a branch of a stomach sanitorium for him and an attractive young communist, Tamara Kazakova, enlisted women to serve the First Secretary.

Konstantin Simis, in discussing the Nasritdinova incident, attributes her downfall not to her involvement in nationalist activity, but to her own corruption and to internal struggles between two principal clans in the Uzbek leadership (Simis 1982, p. 60; see also Kamenetskii and Aleksandrova 1983).

1970). Of course, it can be argued that Stalin was an abnormal person, but no one has claimed that members of his leadership, like Molotov, Kalinin, Voroshilov, or Andreiev, should also be counted as such. Still, Stalin arrested and sent into exile the wives of all of these men, without apparently diminishing their activity in support of the regime.

While there are at our disposal only a few publications that can claim to be more or less authentic reflections of the mentality of the elite, they all attest to the extreme indifference, and even hostility, of people from the elite toward any human feelings and certainly to romantic love or passion. It is characteristic how Soviet leaders, Kosygin and Suslov, initially reacted to the desire of Svetalana Alliluieva, Stalin's daughter, to marry an Indian simply because she fell in love with him. They could not understand, as Alliluieva recounts, that these feelings could force her to behave in such an "irrational" way, as in their opinion she did (see Alliluieva 1969).

In the past, the leadership concealed their real attitudes toward love ("We know all about love and such humbug—but let others believe in these old songs"). We can find only one instance when Stalin uttered at least a few words in favor of love. This was his commentary on Maxim Gorki's tale, *Girl and Death*, on behalf of the Soviet elite. And it is noticeable that Piotr Fedosiev, one of the leaders of Soviet ideology,* in describing the role of the Soviet family in the preface to a book, *Change in the Status of Women and the Family* (1977), supported the thesis of Kharchev, leading author of this publication, on the dubious importance of love.

The evolution of the views of the Soviet elite on love can be described according to our paradigm. In the first period, the elite seemed to consider love as a value "for me and for others." In the next period, love was transformed into a value "not for me, but for others." Now, with growing cynicism, the Soviet elite is close to regarding love as a value "neither for me nor for others."

The relationship between pragmatism and ideology in Soviet life is not at all antagonistic, nor does it suppose that pragmatism has a chance of removing ideology from the Soviet scene. The real process is very complex, and ideology continues to preserve its position in Soviet society. This fundamental circumstance reveals

---

*He is a vice-president of the Academy of Science of the USSR, responsible for social science, and a full member of the Central Committee of the Communist Party.

itself even in the treatment of a value as modest in importance as love. For all the tendency to deromanticize love and to remove it from its pedestal because of its disturbing interference with "normal" life, the Soviet elite does this carefully and sustains, as well, ideological sociologists who, as we saw, continue to defend the old image of romantic love as the sole basis of true Soviet marriage.

SUMMARY

The attitudes of the Soviet people toward love are very contradictory, reflecting the complex psychological atmosphere in society. On the one hand, love is one of the most respected values in Soviet society, and in this respect there is no gap between official ideology and popular sentiment. The place of love in the system of Soviet personal values appears significantly higher than in American society.

However, the consensus of the Soviet people on the importance of love in human life holds only if love is regarded at an abstract level. As soon as the Soviet people consider love in personal terms, they are divided into groups with different evaluations of the role of love in their lives. Additionally, the attitudes toward love change with the phases of the life cycle: with experience and age, Soviet people, as people elsewhere, lose their confidence in love. It is natural that it is young people whose expectations about love in their personal lives are the greatest. In the 1960s, a number of Soviet intellectuals (particularly so-called managerial sociologists who try to play the role of experts to the political elite) came to the conclusion that these expectations represent a serious danger to the stability of marriage. Rejecting the old Soviet image of romantic marriage, they advanced the notion that love and marriage should be divorced, and that the overemphasis on love as a precondition for marriage leads to the collapse of conjugal relations, with all the negative implications for society and the state that this implies.

At the same time, liberal intellectuals attempted to reinstate sexual pleasure as a hedonistic value and the right of people to this pleasure, even if it is not combined with love. They also attacked love as it is described in official ideology, literature, and the arts. Thanks to the efforts of liberal writers, poets, and filmmakers, sex was reintroduced into Soviet public life despite the resistance of conservatives.

4

Marriage: Values and Behavior ───────────
after the 1950s

SOVIET DATA ON MARRIAGE

It can be argued that, despite all that has been said about the first decade after the Revolution, marriage as a value, even at the worst of times, has been supported by a considerable portion of the Soviet population who are of Slavic origin, not to mention the non-Slavic peoples of Central Asia, the Caucasus, and so on.

The data on this subject are somewhat limited, however. In one survey of the 1920s, 81 percent of young women and 72 percent of young men declared that they preferred either marriage or a long-term arrangement to brief liaisons (Stites 1978, p. 362). The Stalin era did not leave us any empirical data about attitudes toward marriage and romantic love. The one source of information on this subject presents data gathered during the famous Harvard project, a survey of people who left the Soviet Union under various circumstances during World War II (Inkeles and Bauer 1959).

Some of the questions put to the former Soviet citizens concerned their family lives. Unfortunately, however, the data cannot be broken down to distinguish the 1920s from the 1930s—two very different periods. On the whole, the Harvard project reveals that the family played a significant role in the lives of no fewer than two-thirds of all respondents. Moreover, about half the respondents affirmed that under Soviet conditions their families were becoming even more cohesive (1959, p. 211). Of course, these data can be treated in different, even opposite, ways. For example, this strengthening of the family may be the result not so much of the conservative measures undertaken by the Soviet leadership in favor of the family, but of the increasing role of the family as a refuge from the growing pressure of the state on the individual.

With some modification, I share the latter interpretation. But, however, the data elicited from the Soviet refugees reflect both periods before and after the Revolution. There is no evidence that the respondents made any distinction between them.*

The majority of the Soviet population has maintained a positive attitude toward marriage up to now, and in this area no divergence has emerged between official and personal values. As indicators of the existence and the strength of this attitude, as well as of other dispositions of the individual, the Soviet marriage rate is probably the most useful demographic indicator. The marriage rate not only did not deteriorate in the last two decades, but demonstrated some increase, rising from 8.7 per thousand people in 1965 to 10.9 in 1979 (*Narodnoie Khosiastvo SSSR v 1979*, 1980, p. 35).†

However, it seems that, on the whole, the prestige of marriage in the Soviet Union is higher than in the United States. While in the USSR the marriage rate was growing in the 1970's, in the U.S. the rate fell by one-fifth.

Of course, the marriage rate is a very crude index and is not sensitive to many contradictory trends that counterbalance each other. It is affected by the demographic composition of the population (the proportions of men and women in the marrying age), by the number of divorces and remarriages, and other factors.

---

*This statement can be bolstered by other data from the same project. The respondents were asked about values emphasized in child rearing. Then periods of child rearing were singled out: prerevolutionary (1880–1916), postrevolutionary (1917–1940) and current Soviet (1941). A clear distinction between prerevolutionary and postrevolutionary periods emerged, but the two postrevolutionary periods turn out to be nearly indistinguishable. Thirty-one percent of all non-manual respondents brought up before the Revolution indicated that traditional values were emphasized in their upbringing, whereas only 15 percent reared in the second period, and 12 percent in the third, indicated the same. Emphasis on achievement was pronounced in 34 percent of the first group, and 27 and 23 percent, respectively, for the second and third groups. Other values such as personality development, intellectualism, and individual adjustment, revealed similar patterns. Only the emphasis on political values showed a different trend, growing from 4 to 8 to 12 percent in successive periods (Inkeles and Bauer 1959, p. 221).

†In their positive attitudes toward marriage, the Soviet people hardly differ from people in the West, particularly those in the United States. According to the data of Arland Thornton and Deborah Friedman, three-quarters of a national sample of high school seniors in 1980 said that having a good marriage and family was "extremely important" to them (*ISR Newsletter*, Autumn 1982, p. 8).

For this reason, the growing marriage rate is compatible with tendencies that could be treated as rather inimical to the idea of stable marriage.*

A somewhat curious additional confirmation of positive attitude toward marriage is the following fact: in each census, many more women than men declared themselves married. In 1939, this difference amounted to 178,000; in 1959, 437,000; and in 1980, 1,331,000. It is scarcely possible to put forward an explanation of this phenomenon that could deny that at least Soviet women evaluate marriage positively.

MARRIAGE AMONG SOVIET PERSONAL VALUES

Soviet sociology has accumulated a certain amount of data directly portraying the place of marriage and the family in the value system of the Soviets, and it is notable that there is some consensus among the results obtained by different Soviet sociologists on this subject. Moroever, data from other socialist countries (Poland, Bulgaria) are perfectly consonant with Soviet data.

The major finding of studies of the personal values of people in socialist countries is that the family, directly or indirectly, is give a leading, often the leading position on any list of values ranked by respondents.

It can be said that a "drift to domesticity," if we measure it by the change in the role of family in the system of personal values, has always been one of the most important social and political trends in socialist society (see Inkeles 1980, p. 49).

The family turned out to be the first in importance to respondents in the surveys conducted by Zakhar Fainburg among

---

*The same is true about the average age of grooms and brides which has been decreasing:

	1966	1976
Grooms	29.3 years	25.1 years
Brides	27.2 years	23.4 years

(Urlanis 1977, p. 11; see also Volkov 1981). It is interesting that the average age of American grooms and brides has been increasing since the fifties: for the age of grooms from 22.8 in 1950 to 24.6 in 1980, and the age of brides from 20.3 to 22.1 (U.S. Bureau of the Census, Current Population Report, Series P-20, No. 365, *Marital Status and Living Arrangements*: March 1980, Washington: Government Printing Office 1981: Table A).

workers and engineers in the Ural city of Perm in the 1960s (1969, p. 93), by Iuri Arutiunian among the Moldavians in the early 1970s (1972, p. 18; 1980, p. 151), and by Gevoris Pogosian in Armenia in the late 1970s (1983, p. 164).

Data produced by Vladimir Iadov in his long-term investigations in Leningrad led to the same conclusion. In Iadov's first study, done with Andrei Zdravomyslov in the mid-1960s, he discovered that young workers oriented toward their families exceeded in number any other orientation: 42 percent of the young workers were family-oriented, 23 percent were education-oriented, 8 percent job-oriented, and 12 percent civic work-oriented (Iadov *et al.* 1970, p. 248).

Iadov's next study was devoted to Leningrad engineers.* This time the dominant role of the family as a "terminal" value emerged even more clearly. In the list of 18 terminal values, the family was outranked only by "peace" and "health."† In this survey, as in the surveys of Fainburg and Arutiunian, the family outstrips such values as work, social recognition, active life, and so on (Iadov 1979, p. 56)‡

---

*In this work, Iadov used, as was mentioned before, the methodology proposed by Milton Rokeach (1973).

†Strictly speaking, "peace and a good atmosphere in the country" is incomparable with other values in the list used by the famous Soviet sociologists. The point is that in this list, it is the only value that required from the respondent no individual activity and was at the same time, for obvious reasons, a precondition for human existence generally. So, with zero degree of personal involvement in this value, it is not amazing that having two terrible wars behind them and being kept by propaganda in a permanent state of tension about the danger of another war, the Soviet people sincerely gave first place to "peace, etc." However, in the context of the study in question, the inclusion of such a value creates only informational noise.

‡It is impossible, because of censorship, to find direct data about all 18 terminal values. For the same reason, there are discrepancies between statements and data. So, the contention that the value "peace and a good atmosphere in our society" gained first place is not documented by any figures in combination with data about other values (Iadov, p. 52). The assertion that "family" and "job" shared the third and fourth places is in contradiction with published data (compare pages 52 and 56). Table 12 (pages 56–57) is practically the only place in the book that contains some information about the ranking of values. Even here any data on six (one-third) of the values are absent. The list of absent values is more than remarkable: sagacity, love, peace and good atmosphere, freedom of behavior, equality as equal opportunity for all. Three of the values omitted are under the rigid control of Soviet ideology. Other omitted values probably outran more "important" values. Work is one of these. For all the importance attributed in official ideology to the family, the official status of work is much higher. Because of it, Iadov seems to have been forced not only to exclude data on the ranking of all ultimate values, but

The dominance of the family as a value was revealed even more conspicuously when all respondents were clustered according to their orientation in more or less homogeneous groups. Of eight groups, only the four smallest included those who did not consider family a dominant value. These groups consisted of only 16 percent of all respondents. At the same time, 84 percent of all respondents found themselves in groups characterized by a strong family orientation. Moreover, the authors could affirm that the orientation toward family and job were "balanced" only in one of these groups. Other groups, with 55 percent of all respondents, are described as predominantly oriented toward the family. In evaluating these data, it should be taken into account that a considerable proportion of respondents—one-fifth—were not married, and one-fourth had no children (Iadov 1977, p. 229).*

It is curious that such a "bureaucrat" in Soviet sociology as Anatolii Kharchev, the editor-in-chief of the lone Soviet sociological journal and a man who very cautiously (and in many cases very deftly) wanders through Soviet ideology and politics, did not understand (or refrained from doing so) that data produced by him reveal the denigration of Soviet official values by respondents. About one thousand people in the Vladimir region, asked in 1976–1978 about the influence of various social factors on their mentality, gave conspicuous priority to the family. School, mass media, social organization, the Party, the young communist organization, trade unions, and labor collectives were ranked lower. The same rankings were revealed, as A. Kharchev says with satisfaction, in the 1969 survey of students in higher schools and colleges (Kharchev 1982, p. 17).

Data collected by Sverdlovsk sociologists show that the general mood of the Soviet people depends much more on the

---

also not to have been permitted to show that the family is held higher than work in the value systems of his respondents. Therefore, he had to ascribe to work in an evasive way the third or fourth places. Meanwhile, it is clearly to be seen from the table mentioned that the family received a higher rank in 6 groups out of 8. Moreover, the computation of the average ranking of work (fortunately this is possible because there are data on the size of the groups) reveals that it is lower than the ranking for family—3.58 (this figure is to be detected in another table).

*Here is a typical nuance of the atmosphere Soviet sociologists must work in. In 1977 and 1979, Iadov and his Leningrad colleagues published two books based on the study of engineers. In 1977, they could still insert in a normal way at least some demographic data about their sample. But, in the book that came out two years later, demographic information was limited once more (for instance, data on marital status are placed in a way not admitted in sociological publications, buried somewhere in the middle of the book as auxiliary information—on page 98).

quality of their family life than on other factors, including their work lives. The sociologists categorized groups of people who were satisfied or not satisfied with three elements of their lives: work, family, and leisure. Then it was determined what proportion of the people in each group considered themselves "happy" and "unhappy." The comparison of groups indicated that people who are satisfied with their family lives are more likely to be happy with their lives as a whole. Among those who were satisfied with all three elements of their lives, 46.7 percent considered themselves to be "completely happy," whereas among those who were satisfied only with work and leisure, the proportion indicating complete happiness was only 20.7 percent, a difference of 26 percent, which should be imputed only to the family. The respective difference for work was 22.8 percent, and for leisure, 22.9 percent (Kogan 1981, pp. 172–73).

The significance of marriage is revealed in other indicators, such as the subjective evaluation of one's marital status. A 1970–75 survey of workers in various Soviet cities found that well over twice as many of the divorced as of the married regarded their marital status negatively. Among women, 47 percent of divorced respondents, as against 21 percent of their married counterparts, expressed negative evaluations. Among men, the figures were 35 percent for the divorced, and 16 percent for married respondents (Fainburg 1981, p. 146).

It is clear that marriage is perceived by Soviets as an institution necessary for the satisfaction of a variety of needs. While this is, of course, true of all societies, the specific combination of needs that may be fulfilled in marriage varies. For example, the significance of children to a family in an agricultural setting, where they represent an important source of labor, differs from that of an urban family in which children represent more of an economic drain, more as consumer than producer.

It is difficult, however, to obtain reliable data on the kinds of needs that marriage and family are perceived to fulfill. The available sociological techniques allow neither Soviet nor Western analysis to get quality data, and existing surveys frequently reflect the investigator's perception of social reality. But lacking alternatives, we must rely on the data that are available.

We can distinguish two principal categories of needs that marriage is expected to satisfy. These categories can be applied to the needs that Soviet surveys clearly indicate are important to married life. "Internal" or psychological needs refer to those that relate specifically to the dyadic relationship between spouses, such as the need for a close, intimate relationship with another person to share one's troubles and triumphs. "External" or material and other needs relate to the role of the marriage as a mediator between the individual and the outside world, the state above all in the Soviet context. Here economic needs are important, as is the role of the marriage as an insulator from external pressures, especially those emanating from the state. Some elements of married life, such as children, may alternatively fall into both categories of need fulfillment.

Again, our interpretations of the saliency of these needs in relation to marriage must be drawn from often indirect indicators, such as answers to questions in surveys on the ideal images of partners, or reasons for divorce.* But, on the basis of these data, we can say that the "internal" need for a close relationship with another person, as a protection against the external societal pressures, is paramount for most Soviets in their perceptions of the functions of marriage and family. Among younger age groups, however, the need of children is more likely to be of first rank. "External" economic needs usually play a secondary role, although surveys may underestimate this need because of the impact of dominant values: economic, especially mercantilistic, considerations in the choice of partners are strongly disapproved.

THE FAMILY AGAINST THE SOVIET STATE

It should be noted that the psychological function of the Soviet family is connected with one of many paradoxes inherent in Soviet life. Actively supported by the state and ideology, the Soviet family, since the mid-1950s, has lost much of its instrumental role as an institution effectively used by the state as a means of social control. Since 1953, the Soviet family has gradually emerged as a cohesive unit that confronts the state, rather than serves it. The family is now a refuge for complete ideological relaxation and the expression of genuine views on current events. Here Soviet

---

*The survey conducted by Pankratova (1972) is an exception here. Rural respondents in different regions were asked directly what they appreciate most in family life.

individuals, from members of the Politburo to ordinary workers, acquire what they are deprived of in official life.*

Soviet studies, even those conducted by ideological sociologists like Nikolai Mansurov, indicate that the majority of Soviet people regard the family (along with friends) as the place where they can really elaborate their views on developments in the world. Family and friends are much more important in this role than the educational system, the place of work, or any other area. Asked who influences them the most in the formation of their opinions on vital matters, residents of the Vladimir region, in a 1976–78 study, put family decisively in first place, ahead of school, mass media, and social organizations such as trade unions. The same results were obtained by Semenova (1979), Goriachev et al. (1978), and other researchers.

The family also plays the central role in relations surrounding the "second economy," the enormous unofficial system of distributing goods and services, parallel to the official economy. Members of families trust each other completely about their activities in this realm (e.g., illegal production, bribery, and so forth) and serve as important connections to assist each other in obtaining what they need. Had intrafamily relations remained unchanged from their structure during the Stalin era, the "second economy" could never have approached the scale it has during the last two decades.

The growing antagonism between the state and the family is revealed in another phenomenon, no less important than the

---

*Valentine Rasputin's novel, *Live and Remember* (1980), is a characteristic hallmark of the evolution of Soviet public opinion on the relations between the state and the family. The appearance of such a novel would have been nearly impossible even a few years earlier. The developments in this novel take place during World War II. By the concurrence of various events, Andrei Gus'kov, a young peasant, becomes a deserter and thereby commits one of the most despicable crimes in Russia. He hides close to his native Siberian village, where his wife, Nastena, discovers him. Moved by contradictory feelings—love of her husband and horror toward his cowardly action—she begins to help her husband to survive and to conceal himself from others, including his father. Finding herself pregnant after a secret meeting with Andrei, Nastena explains her condition as the result of a love affair and staunchly endures her shame in the village, but does not betray her husband.

For the first time in Soviet literature, family ties are placed above the state. This case, which reminds one of the plight of Antigone, is diametrically opposed to the glorification of Pavlik Morozov, the thirteen-year-old boy who reported on his father during the collectivization of the 1930s, as well as other cases from this period when family members denounced each other as enemies of the state (I owe this interpretation of Rasputin's novel to Dmitrii Shlapentokh).

"second economy." This is the problem of protection and nepotism among members of the elite. This protection and nepotism flourishes among both national and regional elites.

In this process, the fact that the family is an ideologically supported value is of great importance. It provides the elite with the necessary rationalization for their actions, which result in the interests of families being put above those of the state. As if to confirm Plato's requirement that the philosopher-kings of his ideal republic not have families, Soviet leaders since Stalin have openly promoted their children, wives, and husbands to the highest positions in society (Voslenski 1980). In other socialist countries, such as Bulgaria, Rumania, and North Korea, this phenomenon has taken on grotesque forms, with the wives, sons, and daughters of leaders being appointed to the Politburo. The case of Mao's wife is among the more famous illustrations of this nepotism.

This encroachment of the family structure (along with the system of personal connections) into the structure of the socialist state continues to transform the social relations of these societies. The full implications of this phenomenon will be clear only in the future. Yet, it is now obvious that this rise in the importance of the family in the vested interests of the elite has not only led to a diminished flexibility of the state apparatus, but has also created "models" of social behavior for all strata of the population. This results in the transformation of nepotism from a pathological into a normal social phenomenon.

As would be expected, these patterns of favoritism have begun to insert into socialist societies the elements of a system of inheritance, not only in general social status, but in actual official positions. Since the death of Stalin, we observe the rapidly increasing number of people who inherit the profession and status of their parents in various spheres of social life, particularly politics, art and science. Thus, the family can be regarded as an important mechanism in the process of class formation, and class stabilization, in socialist society.

The confrontation of the institutions of family and state has also led to the emergence of a greater desire for privacy. Until recently, the notion of privacy was, to some degree, alien to Russian life. Although much of this can be traced to long historical traditions, too complex to elucidate here, it can be said that under the Stalin regime, privacy was almost totally eliminated from Soviet life, well beyond traditional patterns. Under Stalin, the family was rather structured against privacy, and in many families people did not feel themselves any safer than in their offices or factories.

With the changing role of the family, and with a glimpse of the possibility of having a place protected from state intervention, the public mind has begun to accustom itself to, and elaborate the principle of, privacy. As one rare indicator of this tendency, we can use some of our data from the survey of readers of *Literaturnaia gazeta* (1977). Leaving aside the general analysis of this survey for the next section, I wish to draw attention here to the following information. Our questionnaire contained a question designed to elicit how inclined unmarried respondents were to recommend the use of a dating service to their relatives and close friends. In considering this data, we should take into account that only one percent of all respondents were opposed to the existence of such services. While one-fourth of the respondents said they would not recommend a dating service to friends or relatives, and about one-half answered that they would do so, the remaining one-fourth rather unexpectedly responded that the matter was a person's private business and that they would not impose their advice on others.

This was a closed question and this alternative was available to respondents. However, given the public support for dating services, we assumed that few respondents would select this alternative. Thus, I must confess, we overlooked the possibility that some respondents would focus on another aspect of the controversy—beyond the utility of dating services—and view it in connection with the right of individuals to make their own decisions on such personal matters. It is notable that this position was most commonly taken by the youngest and most educated readers of *Literaturnaia gazeta*.*

The relative disentanglement of the family and state, and their confrontation as social values, has become very much a part of the public mind. This confrontation extends beyond the areas mentioned above (security, material support, privacy), and occupies a central location in the realm of ideology. The family has become a symbol of the institutions that stand in opposition to

---

*In this respect, the discussion of dating services in the USSR has something in common with the debate in the U.S. on abortion. A considerable proportion of the public in the U.S. insist that abortion is a private matter, and among those who hold this position, the young and college educated also prevail (see the *New York Times*, July 17, 1980).

the state, a development commonly found in nondemocratic societies of all kinds.

The ideological atmosphere has been shaped by the struggles of the state and populace to mold the family to suit their conflicting needs. Paradoxically, it can be noted that the official recognition and support of the family as a social value has made it possible for individuals to turn these values to their own advantage. For example, university students are expected to repay the state for their education by accepting work assignments, often in remote regions of the country. Yet, by appealing to the official support of the family, some graduates can avoid such assignments, arguing that severe familial disruptions would result.

MARRIAGE AS A PRESTIGIOUS VALUE

As was indicated above, the positive attitude among Soviets toward marriage as an important element in life should also account somewhat for the high prestige of this institution. Here we have a kind of feedback loop, where the prestige of marriage is a result of its importance in the lives of individuals, but also further augments its significance for people. In other words, each new generation enters marriage with the preconception that the experience will be positive. This is one example of the "objective" nature of social values: people encounter values as objective forces in life to which they must accommodate themselves, much as they do to the material components of their society.

Certainly, the prestige of marriage and other institutions is shaped by the influence of both official and personal values, which intensively interact with each other. Additionally, the prestige of being married affects men and women in different ways. Women appear to hold marriage in higher regard than men.

To be unmarried, especially never to have been married or to have been left by a husband, is regarded by many women as a humiliating status and as a demonstration of her inferiority. As the heroine of a recent Soviet film, *Family* (1982), responded to her mother (who had rebuked her for being in too much of a hurry to date when her divorce was not yet final), "Don't you understand that to be single is indecent for a woman?"

The great prestige of marriage among women was grasped by Larisa Kuztnetsova, one of the most thoughtful writers on women in the Soviet Union. She writes, "I will not be 'discovering any

America' if I say: yes, a woman fears being alone. Her marital status is vitally important to her. To belong to the institution of marriage is a matter of prestige and ardent and ambitious self-assertion." Of those who did not marry, she writes that they "had no luck," and of a divorcee that "she was left alone" (1981, p. 183).

Only by considering the social prestige of marriage can we understand why the problem of single women in the USSR has taken on such a dramatic tone. Content analysis of letters sent by single women to *Literaturnaia gazeta* in the late 1960s and mid-1970s, reveals that for many single women—even when they are self-supporting, with high status, and with children—their marital status was painful and distressing because they felt inferior. The feelings explain why we labeled one-third of all letters from the late 1960s "letter confessions," for they were so full of lengthy self-reflections, complaints, and descriptions of intimate details of the writers' lives. In contrast, only 5 percent of all letters written by men could be placed in that category.

CONFLICTING ATTITUDES AND BEHAVIOR

In examining the data on people's readiness to marry, we should not overlook two very interesting groups: those who hold negative attitudes toward marriage but have married nonetheless; and those who positively evaluate marriage yet remain unwed.

The first group presumably consists of those who were compelled to marry, forced into public compliance with this value for some reason. These people can be regarded as conformists who do not privately accept the dominant attitudes toward marriage. Soviet data shed some light on this phenomenon, showing something about the proportion of marriages entered into because of the influence of some "circumstances." However, when examining such data at a later point, we must consider that resorting to a reference to "circumstances" (pregnancy, for instance) is not at all a prestigious explanation for why one is married.

The second group whose behavior and attitudes are at odds is much larger and more easily detectable. First of all, of course, this group consists of single people. In 1970, there were 59 million single people, 16 years or older, of whom 20 million were men and 39 million women. Four million men and 28 million women over the age of thirty were single (Sinielnikov 1978, pp. 147–48). In fact, of women over thirty, fully one-third were unmarried (Gerasimova 1976, p. 100).

The contingent of unmarried people comprises those who plan to marry, but are delaying it; those who do not wish to marry; and those who cannot marry because of the lack of a potential spouse. The available data suggest that the third group is significantly larger than the second, especially among women. We have only indirect data on the ratio of single women to single men who are strongly oriented toward marriage. Two advertisements for partners, published in *Literaturnaia gazeta* in 1976, were answered by nearly ten thousand single people (Shlapentokh 1977b). The publication of similar advertisements in local newspapers also received enthusiastic responses. Advertisements that appear in the Latvian evening paper, *Rigas Balls*, draw as many as three hundred responses each.

Unfortunately, Soviet data do not permit even an approximation of the number of people who hold negative attitudes toward marriage. This is partly a result of the vagueness of this idea. People many manifest negative attitudes in subtle ways. They may simply refuse to marry under any circumstances, or they may put forth such demands on potential spouses as practically to exclude the possibility of marrying. Additionally, problems with Soviet data on this issue may also stem from the pressure on respondents to respond in ways consistent with official ideology. One of the few investigations that did detect blatantly negative attitudes toward marriage found that, among rural residents of the regions of Kalinin and Krasnodar, only one to two percent of the respondents could see no value in marriage. This figure reached three percent among women between 23 and 27 years of age, and among men between 28 and 34 (Pankratova 1972, p. 123).

ROMANTIC MARRIAGE AND NEW MODELS OF MARRIAGE IN SOVIET LIFE TODAY

It is clear that the image of marriage imposed by the Stalinist ideology could not withstand all the perturbations of the 1960s and early 1970s. The return of the earlier postrevolutionary notion of the antagonism between marriage and love, the growing skepticism toward love generally, the awareness of the fragility of modern marriage (thanks to statistical and sociological publications), and other factors have led to a discrediting of the official concept of marriage.

Of course, a large part of the population continues to dream about the romantic image of marriage as it was portrayed under Stalin and in sentimental and other forms of literature. After all, what could be better than a marriage undertaken as an alliance of two human beings staying in love until death? Moreover, many Soviet people have come to the end of their lives with such a marriage behind them. It is difficult, however, to estimate the number of such people because surveys only collect data on satisfaction with current marriages: no one has sought to investigate people's conclusions on marriage in the last moments of their lives.

Many things support the thesis that the most highly educated are among the ardent adherents of the romantic ideal of marriage. Yet, as is so often the case, a single phenomenon may give rise to opposite consequences. The growth of education, as will be shown later, is one of the largest factors in the weakening of marriage as a social institution, and in challenging the official image of marriage as based on love. Thus, while the most consistent advocates of romantic marriage are almost exclusively among the intelligentsia, so are the most vocal critics.

After 1953, Soviet ideology could no longer pretend that the romantic ideal of marriage was a dominant norm in Soviet life. The time had passed when the elite could stubbornly adhere to its dogmas and ignore reality or follow Stalin's approach of insisting on the importance of values so openly violated by the elite themselves. After the mid-1950s, the Soviet leadership not only had to accept modifications in the official system of values, including those of love and marriage, but was compelled to tolerate the elaboration of new concepts by the intelligentsia, and even to accommodate the ideology to them. Such a process would have been unthinkable under Stalin.

The evolution of the official concept of marriage has, in many respects, been typical of changes in other areas of ideology. Thus, it has been a movement from a concept strongly permeated by revolutionary, often romantic, ideologies to more pragmatic ones. With the general ideological shift toward more pragmatic visions of the world, the growing significance of utilitarianism and hedonism in the motivations of Soviet people has emerged.

Although developing their new pragmatic image of the normal Soviet marriage, the elite has not simultaneously discarded the old view. Rather, they have encouraged, through mass media, literature, and film, the integration of the new reality with the romantic image of marriage, a common process designed to preserve the continuity of the ideology.

The Soviet intelligentsia (and following them, the entire population), tend to be divided in their images of the "normal" marriage. Some have leaned toward the pragmatic model, while others have advanced their own models of marriage (the "permissive" and "serial" models) or even argued for a model that rejects marriage as a social institution. Underlying these four models are certain notions of the proper relationship between love and marriage. The pragmatic, semiofficial model separates love and marriage, while the unofficial models seek to rescue love and incorporate it into a new type of relationship.

These new images of what the normal marriage is are advanced largely by Soviet sociologists and, to a lesser degree publicists. In describing a certain model of marriage, each sociologist reflects the attitudes and behavior of different social groups. However, when evaluating Soviet publications, it must be taken into account that sociologists have been able directly to collect data only in favor of the pragmatic model. As for the other models of marriage, sociologists can support them only indirectly, with this support being detectable largely in the methodology employed.

Of course, each model of marriage to be discussed in the following chapters is not simply an ideal defended by some people, but a reflection of aspects of real life and real relations between men and women in some parts of society. It can be said that each model represents one pattern of human behavior among many in the relations between the sexes.

Moreover, for many people, each model of marriage represents a certain stage in their life cycles. Starting with romantic marriage, people may move quite often to pragmatic marriage in the next stage of their lives. Other people, beginning with pragmatic marriage exchange it for a permissive, or serial one, and so on. Therefore, many Soviet people have experienced different types of marital behavior. This circumstance also indicates that age is a powerful variable influencing human attitudes toward a specific form of marriage.

SUMMARY

As an abstract value, marriage enjoys the support of the majority of the population, though there are trends in popular opinion clearly hostile to marriage. Marriage is an especially important and prestigious value for women.

The high status of marriage accounts, to a considerable degree, for the transformation of the family into an institution directed against the state. Various sociological studies agree that the family is the leading value among those social values that Soviet scholars dare to include in their surveys. This fact reflects the drift to domesticity in Soviet life that is a direct product of the erosion of Soviet ideology.

Although the majority of the Soviet people have a positive attitude toward marriage at the abstract level, there is a great difference among Soviet people on the character of marriage at the concrete, practical level. A number of people still adhere to the romantic model of marriage; however, the rest of the population regard marriage, as a practical issue, very differently. Each desirable image of marriage has to reconcile in one way or another such conflicting values as love, sex, the stability of children, and the working lives of both men and women.

5

The Pragmatic Marriage ─────────────

MARITAL PRACTICE AND THE IMAGES OF MARRIAGE

When discussing the various patterns in Soviet marital life, it is necessary to distinguish between practice and the images of them in public opinion. Even if the channels of communication are not impeded by pressure from above, it takes time for the various media to disseminate information on new social phenomena. Thus, public awareness of changes lags behind their emergence and development.

There is little doubt that nearly everyone in Soviet society has at least some knowledge of the different patterns of marriage to be discussed. Yet, only in the last two decades has public opinion been effective in shaping the patterns of marital behavior and putting the issues up for wide discussion. The result is that the images and analyses of marriage patterns in popular, literary, and scientific media are a complex interaction of public opinion and the orientations of the investigators. These images then return to condition social practices as people come to be influenced by the authority of what is viewed as public opinion, especially if it is adopted by one's immediate social group.

The following discussion, therefore, will address two, only partially separable, objects: the actual marital patterns in Soviet society, and the images presented of them in sociology, literature, and art. Available data and methodology do not always permit a clear separation of actual behavior and its depiction, especially because their interaction in social reality is so constant.

When examining the different images and depictions of marital relations, another methodological consideration should also be kept in mind. This refers to the degree to which different individuals perceive in the likelihood of social change and the possibility of adapting behavior to become consistent with social values. Thus, the same image will be evaluated in different ways by different groups of people. A particular model of marriage may be viewed by some as ideal and attainable, reflecting an image of social reality somewhat unrestricted by concrete imperatives. Others may view it as desirable but only partially achievable, owing to various constraints in society. Still others may adopt more practical stances, supposing that life must be taken as it is found. (On the differences between images, see Rosenberg 1979, pp. 38–45.)

With respect to marriage, the majority of Soviet people operate with the more practical view of conjugal relations. They oppose these to the official concepts of marriage. In other words, the structures of marital relations, as creations of the spouses, are adapted to practical concerns in most cases, and few are now bound by moral prescriptions of appropriate behavior in married life.

STABILITY VERSUS PASSION

The acceptance of a pragmatic model of marriage in Soviet society should be attributed directly to the steady increase in the divorce rate, which rose from 0.6 per thousand people to 3.3 per thousand between 1955 and 1982 (*Narodnoie Khosiastvo SSSR v 1979 godu*, p. 35; *Narodnoie Khosiastvo SSSR v 1982 godu*, 1983, p. 30). By the end of the 1970s, one out of three marriages ended in divorce. This has been one of the most consistent trends in Soviet history: almost without exception, the divorce rate has increased annually. Clearly, this trend is not compatible with the romantic ideal of marriage fostered under Stalin. In evaluating statistics, it must not be forgotten that they pertain only to officially registered divorces and obviously cannot include *de facto* separation, marriages on the verge of dissolution, or marriages in which one spouse, at least, entertains the idea of divorce.

According to data from a survey of Moscow, in no less than half of all the families, at least one spouse constantly considered divorce (Kiselieva and Rodzinska 1982, p. 78.)* The divorce rate, however, is very differnt in various regions of the country.

The most salient feature of the pragmatic approach to marriage is its emphasis on the durability of the relationship, in contrast to the romantic model's orientation toward emotions. In the hierarchy of values, love is subordinated to stability. This implies a rejection of the official dogma that the only morally justifiable marriage is rooted in undying love. As Kharchev, one of the principal supporters of the pragmatic approach, emphasizes, "there has been a certain shift of emphasis from factors determining the necessity of conjugal alliance itself (love, mutual affection) to factors guaranteeing its durability and stability" (1979, p. 200). In praising the pragmatic model, generally Soviet sociologists have cited all the functions of the family, except emotional ones (i.e., reproductive, educational, economic) seeking to emphasize that these, rather than romantic love and sexual pleasure, constitute the *raison d'être* of marriage and the family (see Iankova 1979, pp. 105–7).

Significantly, a central element of the new pragmatic model is its emphasis on marital fidelity. This blend of the value of fidelity with the virtual denial of sexuality is one of the more interesting characteristics of the model. The similarity, in this regard, to the old conservative dictates on marriage proclaimed by the church before the Revolution (recall Tolstoy's *Anna Karenina*), as well as to fundamentalist religion in the West, is quite obvious.

The spread of the pragmatic approach to marriage has brought to the foreground new issues relevant to the preconditions of a stable relationship. Couples now focus on factors such as psychological compatability, the distribution of domestic chores among members of the family, and common leisure interests, as central to the durability of marriage. These are the

---

*It is highest in the major cities of the Slavic and Baltic regions. Here are some comparative divorce rates for 1981:

National	3.3	Moscow	5.3
Riga	6.0	Omsk	5.3
Leningrad	5.7	Tallin	5.3
Odessa	5.7	Baku	2.3
Kishinev	5.3	Tbilisi	3.0
		Erevan	1.8

(Source: *Vestnik Statistiki* 1983, no. 11, pp. 56–57)

issues also stressed by managerial sociologists in the elaboration of an official alternative to the romantic image of marriage.

In their efforts to substantiate the prominence of the pragmatic approach, Soviet sociologists have presented a variety of data documenting that marital happiness depends largely on the degree of equality between spouses in decision-making, the readiness of husbands to undertake domestic chores, and the inclinations of both spouses to spend their free time together. All of these may be viewed as manifestations of a certain measure of psychological compatibility between spouses.

Relatedly, the social psychologist Gozman argues that the "creation of psychological comfort and mutual support of each other is now the most important function of the family." To substantiate his view, he cites data from his own study that show that for the majority of single people, aged 25 to 50, whom he interviewed, the desire to escape from loneliness was the principal motivation for marrying (see Andreieva and Dontsov 1981, pp. 212–13).

The classification of respondnets as happy or unhappy in their marriages, based on self-evaluation, is a widely employed technique in Soviet sociological studies. Iurkevich's (1970) study of Bielorussia is typical in this respect. And, although his data are not actually representative of the Bielorussian republic, or even its capital, Minsk, Iurkevich argues that sociological research supports the adoption of the pragmatic model of marriage.

For example, Iurkevich's study found that in families where decision-making is controlled by the husband, only 28 percent of respondents considered themselves happy. This was true of 60 percent of respondents from families where both partners participate in decision-making. Similarly, in marriages where spouses shared equally in domestic chores, 60 percent of respondents claimed to be happy, as against only 22 percent in situations where women performed all domestic tasks. The same pattern is found with regard to shared leisure time. Among couples who entertain together, 50 percent were classified as happy, compared to 20 percent of couples who engage in separate leisure activities (Iurkevitch 1970, p. 128).

Shilova's data on shared leisure activities reveal similar patterns. Among happy families, 90 to 96 percent go to movies together, about 70 percent take trips together, and up to 90 percent meet together with friends. In unhappy families, 62 to 82 percent see movies together, 38 to 53 percent travel together, and 48 to 59 percent visit together with friends (1978, p. 133).

THE SIGNIFICANCE OF CHILDREN IN MARRIAGE

While children play a special role in the pragmatic model of marriage, variation exists in Soviet society as to the importance of children in the lives of adults. While some place little importance on having children, and are likely to remain childless, others exhibit the greatest devotion to their offspring.

It is interesting to discover the significance of children to Soviets who choose to have families. In a study of Leningrad parents, respondents were asked to rank twenty implications of having children. Two alternatives received the greatest number of votes. "A child gives meaning to life" was chosen by 61 percent of women and 54 percent of men. "Joy in the home" was selected by 61 percent of women and 48 percent of men. All other alternatives came much further behind. "A child strengthens the family and the relations between spouses" was chosen by only 33 percent of women and 30 percent of men (Boiko 1980, p. 79).

The same study found respondents divided on the importance of children to a happy family life. When respondents were asked what the principal factors in a happy family life were, only 42 percent of married people indicated children (Ibid., p. 105).

When considering the importance of children to Soviet couples, it should be indicated that, especially as aspirations for upward mobility have increased in recent years, many parents delegate to their children the task of achieving the goals they could not themselves attain. Although this appears a nearly universal human trait, it is especially pronounced in the Soviet Union.

The point is that present Soviet society combines relatively high intergenerational social mobility and rather low intragenerational mobility. Adult Soviet workers or peasants have very little chance to change their social status. Even more than in U.S. society, they do not have the chance or even the illusions of leaving the assembly line before retirement or of having a small business or something else that will change their lives. For workers who have reached their thirties, or worse their forties, the probability of advancing to the level of an engineer is very low.

A representative study of the workers in cities of the Russian Republic found that only 2.3 percent have a chance of becoming engineers. Moreover, a considerable number of workers even lower their status by moving to a job with lesser qualifications. Thus, in 1976, 23 percent of the most qualified workers in Orlov, a Russian regional center, moved down (Kotliar 1982, pp. 92–98). At the same time, the children of workers have a very good chance of obtaining a higher education and of climbing to more prestigious social strata.

To some extent, the role of children for many professionals is the same. The conservative, stagnating character of present Soviet society shatters the hopes of many intellectuals for creative work, with broad recognition of its social importance. So they also assign to their children the realization of their unfulfilled ambitions.* Of course, a few intellectuals, mostly among successful actors and musicians, want to transfer their skills and positions in society to their children.

A very interesting survey was conducted by a Leningrad sociologist, A. Baranov, and his colleagues in Leningrad and Al'metievsk (a middle-sized city in Bashkiria).† The workers were asked whether they wanted their children to follow their lives; only 14 percent of Leningrad respondents and 27 percent of Al'metievsk (a middle-sized city in Tataria).† The workers were city and 23 percent from the second wished for their offspring the same job or place of work as they had (Baranov 1981, p. 103; see also Faisulin 1978, p. 39).

The overpowering desire to see children moving up the ladder of prestige pushes Soviet parents to make sacrifices to ensure their offspring the best education and best jobs. In this respect, probably only Japanese parents can compete with Soviet ones. Parents in both countries spare no expense to provide their children with coaches and tutors to prepare them for university entrance examinations. Indeed, the Soviet press regularly complains about the coach mania that has been sweeping a growing number of parents. The complaints have had no effect, however, simply because one-third of those who graduate from secondary school can continue their education without interruption, and because no less than 80 percent, despite this, want to go to a university immediately after high school. Anxious for a career for

---

*In the 1960s, in the family of a fairly liberal scholar in the academic town of Novosibirsk, the traditional toast during a party to celebrate the birth of a baby was: "May we outlive them," which meant that there was taken to be no chance of reform with the current leaders. In the 1970s, when under Brezhnev torpor reached its peak, the toast became: "May our children outlive them."

†In another study conducted by G. Slesarev, respondents were asked what was the social status they desired for their children. Only 10 percent of the workers wanted their children to inherit their social position. Sixty-seven percent wished their children to become professionals. All groups, and the professionals themselves, thought in the same way (Slesarev 1978, p. 214).

their children, many parents are not afraid to resort to various illegal methods that can open the door to a good college, a prestigious research institute, or the Party apparatus. In fact, one of the most widespread forms of corruption in the Soviet Union is that connected with the settling of children's affairs.

Bribes as a means of overcoming the negative results of entrance examinations are very broadly used in the USSR. Even under Brezhnev, who did not like to publicize negative phenomena in the country, there were a number of trials in which defendants were professors from Soviet institutions of higher education (Simis 1982, pp. 229–42). Along with bribery, the patronage of children and nephews is also one of the best known manifestations of corruption in Soviet society. Parents and uncles, quite often with some risk, use their positions to ensure the younger generation of their families the best place in society. Social connections are important in Soviet society, as in other socialist countries, and there is nepotism on a full scale.

Developing networks of mutual assistance in promoting children is one of the most important goals of interaction between people. Of course, this is much more relevant to the bureaucracy and the intelligentsia than to workers, peasants, or white-collar workers; however, even the masses are drawn into the nationwide fuss about the promotion of children.

The record belongs to Georgia, where corruption in higher education has practically nullified any role for the entrance examination. Because of this, one of the targets of the anti-corruption campaign launched by Shervanadze, when he was appointed First Secretary of the Georgian Communist Party in the early 1970s, was higher education. A number of trials of bribe takers in institutions of higher education ensued at the beginning of this campaign, and various measures were instituted, such as giving parents access to entrance examinations in order to ensure public control over results. However, by all accounts, there is no evidence that the new leadership considerably diminished the scope of corruption in this or other spheres of Georgian life.

Along with promoting their children by all means, legal and illegal, Soviet parents also use them as instruments for demonstrating their social status and wealth, as another manifestation of conspicuous consumption. This selfish motive is quite often combined with parents' readiness to pamper their little ones and to cater to their wishes.

Of course, in many societies children are dressed and fed better than their parents. But Soviet society must be among those in which this difference is greatest, a condition that has been noted by many foreign observers (Smith 1976, Chapter 6).

The growing material aspirations of Soviet citizens have strongly stimulated the inclinations of parents to provide children with the most luxurious clothes and gadgets of all kinds, as well as with expensive trips and other forms of entertainment. For example, it has been found that practically all urban families with tape recorders (40 percent of all families in cities) have children. In addition, families with children are the first who buy color television sets, the best record players, books and magazines (*Literaturnaia gazeta*, October 26, 1983, p. 14).

Moreover, expenditures on children often do not correlate with the incomes of parents, a fact partly traceable to the role of the "second economy" in which influence and connections are more important than money. Soviet parents do not hesitate to buy American jeans or sheepskin coats on the black market for their offspring, although the price of these prestigious clothes in the USSR may be one month's salary, a fact that has been much discussed in the Soviet mass media (Zhukhovitskii 1976; Shlapentokh 1977a; Matskovskii 1981, p. 74). A survey conducted in a school in Evpatoriia shed light on parents' ambitions in a small provincial city: 115 senior students were asked about the gifts they had been given on their last birthday. To the great amazement of their teachers, only three children received flowers, and only five received books. Twenty students had been given money, and one-third of the girls something gold. However, even more surprising was the average value of the gifts—92 rubles (*Pravda*, April 18, 1983). (The average monthly salary of Soviet workers is 172 rubles, and average per capita income is much less (*Narodnoie Khosiastvo SSSR 1922–1982*, p. 420).*

The growing preoccupation of Soviet parents with the fate of their children has impelled some Soviet sociologists and demographers to advance the concept of "the quality of children" to explain and justify the decline of the size of families through the growth of expenditures on children (Volkov 1977, p. 47; Baranov 1981, p. 77; Rogovin 1980, p. 179).† This concept is organically

---

*The fact that these data are in an article published in *Pravda* is also remarkable. The author of the article, a teacher from Evpatoriia, writes, "some mothers, using the school as an arena for demonstrating their material well-being, encourage their children to show off their ultra-fashionable dresses in class. At a very early age, the girls start to flaunt gold jewelry. All of this engenders unhealthy competition among children."

†The same process has been going on in the United States. According to the

connected to the model of pragmatic marriage and is especially backed by those scholars who, like Vishnievskii, of all the attributes of this marriage puts the emphasis on "the role of happy parents" and on "social recognition and the elevation of parental feelings" (Vishnievskii 1982, pp. 190–97; see also Rogovin 1980, p. 187).‡

It is curious that none of those ardently advocating a high birthrate uses the argument that children are a help to aged parents. The situation is just the opposite. Provided, by Soviet standards, with a good pension, Soviet grandmothers and grandfathers continue to help their children and grandchildren to the day they die. According to the data of Vladimir Shapiro, the best Soviet expert on this subject, whereas two-thirds of older working parents materially help their children's families, only in one in ten families does material help flow in the opposite direction. Even one-quarter of the retired, without income other than their pension, continue to give money to their children (Shapiro 1980, p. 129). (According to one Soviet joke, parents who do not help

---

Bureau of Labor Statistics, the direct costs of raising a child to his majority in 1959 came to $20,000; in 1980 the costs were estimated to be between $80,000 and $100,000 (Veevers 1980).

‡This conception is opposed by those sociologists and demographers who stress not the "quality" but the "quantity" of children. These thinkers contend that a family that has only one child creates not better, but worse conditions for the development of this one child who, deprived of brothers and sisters, is likely to grow up as an egotist or even an asocial being. Mikhail Matskovskii gives his article in *Literaturnaia gazeta* (1981) the maudlin title, "Why a Man Needs a Brother." The same view was developed by the most famous Soviet demographer, Boris Urlanis. He, with eloquence not typical of Soviet scholars, described the dangerous fate of an only child: a heavenly body, a sun, around which revolve plants in the persons of mother, father, numerous aunts, grandmothers, etc. To parents of only children, he promised terrible problems (Urlanis 1977, pp. 5–6). In arguing for large families, some Soviet authors try to play on the feelings of women longing for a stable marriage. It is suggested that a marriage with many children is difficult to dissolve. Women are also urged that the postponement of child-bearing (the only child is often born when the mother is over 30) endangers a woman's health, because this postponement assumes a number of abortions undergone by the woman in her twenties, and because complications often accompany the labor of older women (Kisilieva 1979, p. 75).

Some authors try to persuade young people that children help to alleviate the decline of communication that comes from moving from an apartment with a common kitchen and bathroom, and with close relations between residents, to a self-contained apartment and very casual contacts with neighbors. Children are also described as a way of escaping from troubles outside and inside the family (Boiko 1980, p. 60).

their children up to the children's retirement are real scoundrels.)

Of course, those advocating high birthrates resort to an assortment of social arguments—the negative consequences of the low birthrate for the economy, above all. One of them, Anatolii Antonov, bluntly rejects the concept of the "quality of children" and refuses to see "any positive aspect" in the decrease of the number of children in families. He demands that the average Soviet family return to having three or four children (Antonov 1980, p. 265). As a special argument for the stable family, whatever other reasons might be against it, adherents of pragmatic marriage use the fact that children in broken families are much more likely than their peers in normal families to be involved in delinquent activity. According to various surveys and studies, one-third of all teenagers who have broken the law have lived in an "incomplete" family, i.e., a family without a father. According to K. Igoshev, the author of a book on juvenile delinquency, 42 percent of lawbreakers between 18 and 25 lacked one or both parents, while only 23 percent of young people committing no crimes were without at least one parent. Among young under 18, the difference is even greater (Igoshev 1971, pp. 125–26).

The survey carried out by N. Iurkevich, Z. Iankova, N. Grabovskaia, and N. Gavrilova brought similar results: among young lawbreakers, the proportion not raised in two-parent families was never below 55 percent (Kharchev 1979, pp. 299–302; Kharchev 1982, p. 22). The defenders of pragmatic marriage require from parents not only that they forego the possibility of divorce to keep their children from slipping into the criminal world, they also demand that they not drink and that they maintain a good relationship between themselves. Kharchev, an indomitable defender of pragmatic marriage, whatever the price, alarms readers of his book with the prospect that even when parents stay together, but drink regularly or bicker with each other, the children also have a good chance of winding up in jail.

He cites results of a survey conducted in sixteen high schools of Riazan, a city near Moscow. Only 13 percent of children in unhappy families possess a good combination of two qualities—socially approved activity and a strong will—whereas 95 percent of children in happy families have this combination (Kharchev 1979, pp. 304–5; Kharchev 1982, p. 99).

Advocates of the pragmatic approach offer one further argument relating to the happiness of children. Some data suggest that children raised in "incomplete" families are more prone to divorce in their adult years than children from two-parent families. Emme Tiit's study of Estonian families found that nearly half of divorced adults had come from broken families and had been raised by only one parent (*Literaturnaia gazeta*, May 11, 1983).

Additionally, Tiit found that people who divorce have a negative perception of the marriage of their parents twice as frequently as married people as a whole (Tiit 1978, p. 139).

SCIENCE AND MARRIAGE

It is notable that proponents of the pragmatic marriage have used, besides sociological surveys, a number of modern scientific arguments. Thus, if the old prerevolutionary marriage was sanctioned by the authority of the church, the new version of conservative marriage presumably gains its credibility from scientific evidence.

The importance of this credibility should not be underestimated because science is a social value highly respected by the Soviets. This respect can be traced not only to the worldwide prestige of science and the special role of science in Marxist ideology, but also to atheism as a fundamental element of the Soviet vision of life. Thus, all hope for the solution of any problem is usually placed by the Soviet intelligentsia, and even by the masses, in science.* It is not surprising, therefore, that defenders of pragmatic marriage have systematically used various arguments borrowed from science and have even tried to present the model of pragmatic marriage as a pure result of scientific research.

Two branches of science have been chiefly referred to by proponents of pragmatic marriage—social psychology and, even

---

*It should be remarked that the 1950s, and particularly the 1960s, were periods when science was especially glorified in Soviet society. At first, science was opposed to Stalin's despotism, then to Khrushchev's "voluntarism." In both cases, the elite sought to exploit the prestige of science and their allegiance to it to gain popular support in the first period of their ascendency to power. In both cases, Soviet scholars could not help using this favorable climate for the development of those branches of science that had been stifled before. In Khrushchev's time, cybernetics was among the principal beneficiaries, in the early days of Brezhnev's rule, it was molecular biology and sociology.

more, cybernetics. Social psychology has provided advocates of this type of marriage with an array of ideas about the structure and dynamics of small groups. Under the influence of sociology and social psychology, the Soviet intelligentsia has believed that science could discover ways of mitigating conflicts within existing small groups and even of working out guidelines for the creation of virtually ideal groups.* Since the family can be regarded as a small group, it appeared that these sciences had the answers to cardinal questions about happiness and stability in marriage. The title of an article in a book devoted to marital issues is very typical: "The Efficiency of a Family Group" (Ruzhzhe *et al.* 1982, p. 71).

Hence, Western studies of the family that applied the entire apparatus of small group theory, especially the concepts of "role" and "role conflict," found almost ecstatic support in the Soviet Union. Even Talcott Parsons's approach to the analysis of the family became dominant, if some authors who employed Parsons's theories were sometimes ignorant of their actual origin.†

The optimism of Soviet sociologists about the potential of science as a powerful factor in the amelioration of social problems spread among the intelligentsia, through various channels, and contributed to the creation of a new model of marriage that presumably could be supported by recent research. The concept of "psychological compatibility" that underlay many sociometric

---

*Sociometric studies were very popular in the 1960s. Relationships between colleagues, subordinates, and superiors were investigated *à la* Moreno in hundreds of offices, factories, and research institutes (see for instance, Shubkin 1970). These studies, which continued, if on a smaller scale, in the 1970s and early 1980s (see for instance, Kronik 1982), have lead to the proposition that psychological climate is one of the most important factors influencing the efficiency of any production unit. Yet, in the 1950s, everything that smacked of the "human relations approach" was castigated as a typical manifestation of "bourgeois ideology" trying to argue that relations, antagonistic by virtue of their class nature, could be transformed into harmonious ones. Later, in the 1960s, with the growth of the pragmatic component in ideology, followers of Elton Mayo have ceased to be standing objects of ideological denunciations, and not only sociologists, but even Party officials have engaged in reflection and even investigations on the role of good relations between people.

†Parsons has always been a "bad guy" to Soviet officialdom, and no fluctuation in Soviet ideology has ever changed that. "Parsonsian" has remained a dangerous label that a Soviet liberal sociologist seeks to avoid. As a result, many Parsonsian ideas have been used by outstanding Soviet sociologists, their disciples and colleagues in various fields of sociology (family sociology is only one example) without indication of the source of these ideas.

studies was transferred to the analysis of marriage and was taken to be crucial for long conjugal coexistence.

Cybernetics also made an important contribution in the shaping of the pragmatic model. The 1960s were times of real idolatry of computers and mathematics in the Soviet Union. The belief that mathematical models, based on computerized information, could make breakthroughs in every sphere of science and life had been all but transformed into an official dogma, though on occasion conservative ideologues made attempts to counterattack the mathematical intrusion into social science. Soviet cyberneticians, with their Western and especially American counterparts, left no field of life beyond their attention. And marriage and the family seemed to them an area in which their approach could be very fruitful.

As a starting point for their incursion into marriage, cyberneticians used the theory that psychological compatibility was the principal precondition for a stable conjugal life. Since compatibility could be regarded as much more suitable for quantitative measurement than, say, romantic love, the road for the intrusion of mathematicians and computer programmers seemed open. It is quite natural that it was cyberneticians who initiated the discussion on dating services in the Soviet Union, for their prestige at the time provided them the leeway to raise controversial issues for discussion. Some fields related to cybernetics, such as systems analysis and management, also helped create an image of marriage based on scientific principles ("rationalistic marriage" as it was labeled by Sergei Golod).

One of the most brilliant attempts to apply refined scholarly concepts to marriage was made by the eminent Estonian physicist, Naan. Having derogated all lay and traditional explanations about the instability of the modern family, he insisted that the problem became extremely clear if it was treated in the terms of the second law of thermodynamics, which predicts the increase of entropy, or disorganization, with the aging of any system. A member of the Estonian Academy of Science, and an eloquent publicist, Naan contended that modern marriage constituted a normal complex system, whose reliability is just as difficult to guarantee as, for instance, that of a television set, automobile, or transister radio. In order to save the family, if it is possible, spouses have to have special knowledge of "safety rules" that can allow them to grapple with the complexity of modern marriage produced mostly by the emancipation of women (*Literaturnaia gazeta*, September 15, 1976; see also Blekher 1979, pp. 68–70).

WOMEN AS THE MAJOR CONSTITUENCY OF THE PRAGMATIC MARRIAGE

The most active supporters of the pragmatic marriage can be found among Soviet women. However, the attitudes of Soviet women toward a value like marriage, or more specifically, toward alternative images of marriage, are apparently contradictory. Such a contradiction can be entertained only because two images and related values have been confounded—the "ideal" and the "practical" marriage. Very meaningful in any domain of life, this distinction is also of pivotal importance here.

With reference to the ideal marriage, women reveal themselves, as sociological data show, as adherents of the romantic image of love. But as they move from the imaginary world, where there are no contradictions between different needs and values, and no constraints or insurmountable obstacles, they begin to modify their ideal image and transform it into a "normal," "practical" one.

Soviet women's understanding that there are deep differences between the two images of marriage—the ideal and the practical—is a recent development of Soviet history. Again, it is obvious that unconsciously, many women have been aware of this primary distinction; but only with the growing impact of public opinion, the appearance of literary works and sociological publications in which family problems could be illuminated more or less freely, could Soviet women draw clear lines between what is most desirable and what can be achieved within the actual framework of marriage.

With a much higher level of education than before and a growing feeling of self-respect, Soviet women since the mid-1950s have put emphasis not so much on their professional progress, as on achievement of real equality in the family. Two aspects of this equality are of special significance—the distribution of domestic chores and participation in decision-making within the family.

I will return to these issues later. Another merit of pragmatic marriage is, from women's point of view, the stability of the family. It is well established that women appreciate stability in their relations much more than men do. This asymmetry in attitudes about this element of marriage accounts for much of women's greater support of the pragmatic model of marriage.

If aspirations for equality in the family can be ascribed to the rising level of women's education, the rise in the rate of divorce accounts for stability taking a place as one of the most desirable features of the "normal" marriage. The rise in the rate of divorce, despite Soviet women's more active role as initiators of divorce, is, to their mind, largely unfavorable for them. The rate of remarriage is much lower for women than for men, and hence divorced women mostly replenish the army of single women. Soviet women regard divorce not only as a threat to their own normal lives in a country where the prestige of marriage remains high, but also as a blow against their children.

There is little doubt that in the system of personal values of men and women, children as such play different roles, and it is women who give them more weight. Because of this, the stability of marriage as a value in women's minds is strongly correlated with another value—children—and consequently takes on additional importance.

In this regard, women are much closer to the official ideology than are men. The state and Soviet women are united in the belief that children in a family without a father are much more prone to deviant social behavior than are children in a "complete" family, not to mention the other deficiencies, emotional and material, of children from broken homes.

HOW IMPORTANT IS THE SOCIAL STATUS OF THE GROOM?

Stability of marriage based on psychological compatibility, common cultural interests, and children is preferred by many women not only to romantic love, but also to two other things that determine the "quality" of the partner—his social status and prosperity. It is not that these two things do not at all affect women's preferences; however, the majority of women are usually satisfied with the groom's social status if equal to their own and do not consider marriage as a vehicle for material progress.

The point is that two factors determining social status in the USSR—position in the social hierarchy (boss or non-boss) and sphere of activity (the Party, the KGB, the army, science, industry, agriculture, commerce, education, and so on)—cannot exert much influence on the choice of a groom, because most men are still quite young when they marry. Usually they are students or are taking the first steps in their career. The bride can only have some expectations about the future social status of her chosen partner. Therefore, at the outset of their conjugal life, both spouses, if they have the same education, have practically the same social status.

The differences emerge later, usually ten to fifteen years after the wedding. During this period, the husband and wife may move up the ladder at different speeds. Usually it is the man who is out in front. Divorce on the man's initiative is a typical implication of the new situation in the household. Certainly, as women get older (most older women in search of a spouse are divorced), the social status of a potential mate is more important, because the range of such status is larger than when she was younger. Yet, even at this point, the role of this factor should not be exaggerated. Given that the two most prestigious strata of Soviet society—the creative intelligentsia (authors, scholars, artists) and the bureaucracy—are relatively small and therefore not to be plentiful sources of mates, social status does not have a great impact on the public image of the "ideal" husband.

The issue of a spouse's economic well-being plays an even more modest role in the public image of desirable mates. Some evidence of this is found in the low prestige of "wheelers and dealers" in the second economy. Those who have become rich through various illegal activities (embezzlement of state property, bribery, deception of customers) are not regarded—at least outside of Central Asia and the Caucasus—as enviable catches.

The minimal role of economic well-being in the formation of the image of the desirable "practical" marriage can be traced to three interconnected factors: 1) the relatively low prestige of the value of affluence; 2) the shortages of consumer goods (which make money less important than connections in obtaining such goods); and 3) the relatively modest differences in living standards among the population (except, of course, for the elite and "entrepreneurs" in the second economy).*

WOMEN AND PSYCHOLOGICAL COMPATIBILITY

Forced to prefer stability and equality to the love they so highly appreciate, Soviet women look for compensation in the

---

*To some degree, this is a result of a very peculiar social policy of the Soviet leadership. Preserving the scope of their own privileges, Soviet rulers have at the same time been pursuing a course aimed at decreasing differences between the living conditions of the different strata of the Soviet population, first of all between the intelligentsia and the workers. Whereas before the Second World War, engineers earned twice as much as workers, today the incomes of these groups are now practically equal (*Literaturnaia gazeta*, February 2, 1983).

psychological and cultural spheres.* Soviet sociologists who advocate the pragmatic model and who accent compatibility and common interests are, to a considerable degree, influenced by the views shared by many Soviet women.

This reorientation of Soviet women from a romantic marriage to a pragmatic one can be documented not only with data cited before, but also with findings on the Soviet woman's image of the ideal partner, as well as data on attitudes toward husbands. Thus, Estonian studies established that future brides assign the greatest importance to positive psychological traits of grooms (Tiit 1978, p. 24). These results are consistent with data from the survey of women in Zaporozhe in the Ukraine. In evaluating the positive qualities of their husbands, 47 percent cited consideration and attentiveness, 46 percent fidelity, and 43 percent fairness. Among their husbands' negative features, 46 percent cited callousness, 39 percent dishonesty, 38 percent jealousy, 35 percent egoism, and 32 percent irascibility (Korenevskaia 1972, p. 54).

In a Leningrad survey, married people were asked about factors that make a couple close. The women put spiritual values in second place, whereas men put them fifth (Kharchev and Golod 1971, p. 137).

In a more recent study in the same city, married people were asked what conditions are necessary for "a happy family life." Women put "mutual understanding" first (57 percent), ahead of "children" and material factors (a "one-family apartment" and "material prosperity"). The men in this sample were much more materially oriented: they put first both of the material factors (49 percent) and put "mutual understanding" in third place (38 percent). For the men, "material factors" outranked even "children" (38 percent) (Boiko 1980, p. 105).

All new developments in family life affect the grounds for divorce. With the growing significance of psychological compatibility, this factor has come to the forefront in divorce. Today it is second only to alcoholism as a cited cause of divorce. Various Soviet data ascribe about one-third of all divorces to psychological incompatibility (Zvidrin'sh 1981, p. 119; Sysenko 1981, p. 167; Chuiko 1975; Batanov 1981; Sysenko 1982, p. 101.)†

---

*In this context, psychological and cultural qualities of marriage are opposed to love because they are merits under the control of well-intentioned human beings, whereas love is unwilled and for this reason is more difficult to manipulate.

†Iuri Riurikov, perhaps the best analyst of new trends in human relations in

Of special interest are data produced in an experiment staged during the study of attitudes of the Soviet intelligentsia toward dating services. The sensational and unprecedented publication in *Literaturnaia gazeta* in 1976 of two fictitious marriage advertisements—one on behalf of a man, another on behalf of a woman—and the avalanche of responses—about ten thousand—was the immediate trigger for the new research.

Both advertisements were composed by a journalist inspired only by common sense and intuition. In presenting the self-image of the alleged authors of these advertisements, along with their wishes regarding potential partners, this journalist put emphasis almost exclusively on aspects of temperament and on leisure pursuits like reading, movies, music, and travel. With no mention of emotional factors or of material status in these advertisements, we sociologists were sure that advertisements composed by real seekers of marital partners would be very different. To check this hypothesis, a question was inserted into a questionnaire, asking respondents to appraise the content of the ads and to tell us what kind of information they lacked.

The answers truly stunned us. Only 17 percent of all respondents expressed dissatisfaction with the mode of description of the self-image of the author and of the image of a desired partner. Asked to indicate what additional information would be helpful, respondents again put psychological qualities in first place, ranked second a mention of leisure pursuits, and then, information about occupation—which is, by the way, also relevant to interpersonal communication; and finally, appearance. Informa-

---

Soviet society, managed to publish an article in *Pravda* in a style absolutely alien to this stuffy Soviet newspaper. In this article, Riurikov sang a hymn to the ideal family as a haven against life's big storms and petty worries. Discussing the role of the family in the past, Riurikov writes, "Over many centuries, the family was an economic unit for the satisfaction of human material needs and for raising children. Spouses needed each other in the first place as assistants and only then as human beings, personalities. The family was largely a sort of agency for everyday material necessities. Such a family is too "small" for real people, it presses on them and they break out without understanding very often why they are discontent. As a result, a radical transition, very slow, is going on—from a family "as an agency for material, everyday necessity" to a family as "an agency for the satisfaction of spiritual needs, demands of the soul."

In his desire to underscore the psychological function of the family, Riurikov goes so far as to state that the new family is principally for the happiness of adults and not for that of children. "The family has to be," continues Riurikov, "a rest home for nerves, an oasis for soul. As people used to say in the past, a good family is a haven during a tempest, and a bad one a tempest at haven" (Riurikov 1983).

tion about income and housing conditions were mentioned as important by only a very small part of the sample (Shlapentokh 1977b).

PRAGMATIC MARRIAGE FOR ME AND FOR OTHERS

Women constitute the largest group of supporters of the pragmatic model of marriage. Besides them, we can cite other groups, some overlapping, like the single and the divorced. The two groups are made up of people disappointed, to various degrees, with love as a basis for marriage. Strikingly, however, divorced people rarely cite the eclipse of romantic love as a reason for divorce. As for single people, especially women, again their unanimous support for the idea of dating services reveals that they put their hope in such marriage. I shall return to this matter.

Along with the thoroughgoing advocates of pragmatic marriage, there are others whose support of this model of marriage is limited in one way or another. One group encompasses those who profess their perspective on the pragmatic model as appropriate for others but not for themselves. This elitist approach is shared by those who regard themselves as the chosen because they have been exceptionally endowed by fortune with a stable romantic marriage, though others must acquiesce in a pragmatic one, or because they can afford themselves other patterns of marriage, including sexual diversity.

Along with those who assume that pragmatic marriage is a proper model for the masses, but not for them, there are others who think quite the opposite, assuming that pragmatic marriage is *just* for them but *not* for others. This is the stance of some of the middle-aged and many of the elderly. As people grow old, they put less and less emphasis on the emotional aspects of their marriage and find justification and consolation in other functions of marriage in line with the recommendations of the pragmatic model. Some empirical evidence for this can be drawn from a survey conducted by Maia Pankratova. In this somewhat unique study, she asked inhabitants of villages near Moscow to express their opinions on the importance of different functions of marriage and the family. An advocate of the pragmatic model, she did not include in her questionnaire alternatives directly related to love or even to the emotions. Among the alternatives she offered, an alternative like "having a close friend whom you can trust" is probably the best indicator of the importance of feelings in the mind of the respondent. Thus, 63 percent of men under 30 and 56 percent of women of the same age chose this alternative as against 44 percent of men and 31 percent of women over 41. At the same time, the degree of support for the statement, "help is necessary in misfortune, illness, and old age" increased with age. This alternative was chosen by 7 percent of men under 30, by 5 percent of women of this age and by 23 percent of men and 12 percent of women over 40 (Pankratova 1972, pp. 120–21).

ETHNIC CONFLICTS AND MARRIAGE

In light of the growing significance of psychological compatibility, the impact of the ethnic origin of partners comes to the forefront. On the one hand, there is little doubt that the extensive territorial mobility of the Soviet people, the growing role of the Russian language, and the increase in education (as well as the exposure of all Soviet people to the same ideology, mass media, literature, and arts) have been contributing to the diminishing influence of ethnic origin as a factor in the choice of marriage partners.

On the other hand, however, there are trends that exert the opposite influence, most importantly the upsurge of nationalism in all parts of the country. In addition, some studies show that in many cases, nationalist feelings rise in intensity with increased education (see, for example, Arutiunian 1973). The growing role of psychological and cultural factors in family life is, by all accounts, one of those things that resist the process of ethnic homogenization of Soviet society in this domain.

In any event, the ethnically homogeneous marriage continues to be the more frequent type of alliance between men and women than those between ethnic groups. In 1979, the proportion of mixed marriages was only 14.9 percent, a modest increase over 1959 when the figure was 10.9 percent of all marriages (*Vestnik Statistiki* 5, 1983, p. 75; Kozlov 1982, p. 281). It is characteristic that, as a rule, members of non-Russian minorities, even if they live in regions where Russians prevail in numbers (meaning that, theoretically they meet more Russians than members of their own nationality), more often than Russians prefer to marry within their ethnic group. The Ukrainian demographer, Chuiko, computed a special index of homogeneity of marriage, which takes into account the number of people of different nationalities that individuals can meet. It emerged that the probability that Georgians will marry within their ethnic group is 80 percent, roughly the same for Estonians (79 percent), and 68 percent for Lithuanians. Corresponding measures for Armenians and Ukrainians, who live in all parts of the country, are 33 and 34 percent, respectively (Chuiko 1975, p. 76).

It is natural to assume that the greater the intergroup animosity, the lower the probability that people will marry members of those "hostile" ethnic groups. Again, with the growing role of psychological and cultural compatibility, this factor is rising in importance. Jews are an excellent example. Living as a tiny minority, and quite strongly culturally assimilated to the majority (only 14 percent of Jews in 1979 regarded the Jewish language, either Yiddish or Hebrew, as their native language), Jews still prefer to marry each other. In Latvia, only one-third of all male Jews married people of other nationalities, as against 77 percent of Ukranians and 68 percent of Poles (Kholmogorov 1970, pp. 86–92). In Moldavia, the proportion of Jews who live in all-Jewish families is 62 percent, in Bielorussia, 77 percent, and 66 percent in the Ukraine (see Fisher 1980, p. 239; Chuiko 1975, p. 49).

Another fact is also characteristic. Intermarriages between Armenians and Azerbaidzhanians, two Caucasian peoples whose hostility toward each other is almost legendary, are extremely rare, although they live in the same areas and often in the same cities. The probability of such marriages, according to Ter-Sarkisiants' computations, was only .001 in 1969, or 4310 times lower than the theoretical probability (Ter-Sarkisiants 1973).

The analysis of the constituency of the pragmatic model of marriage leads to a curious conclusion. Under Soviet conditions, this model is backed by social groups that are usually conservatively oriented—women and the elderly. It is hardly accidental that between such values as romantic love and social change, there exists a conspicuous correlation that made itself manifest in the revolutionary period of Russian history, as well as during the student movement in the United States in the late 1960s.

SUMMARY

The pragmatic marriage is the leading model of conjugal relations opposed to the official image of marriage. This concept of marriage sacrifices passion and sex for stability. It also promises gratification from the psychological and cultural proximity of spouses. The greatest beneficiary of such a marriage are children, who are fostered in the most favorable climate.

The most ardent advocates of this concept of marriage are women, and of all unofficial models of marriage, only this one enjoys the tacit support of the political elite who sees in this model some antidote against the growing rate of divorce. Because of this, "managerial sociologists" who attack love as the basis of marriage, emerge as the most active theoreticians of this type of marriage.

6

Permissive Marriage ────────────────────────

Pragmatic marriage is one of the marital patterns that are contrary to the official romantic model of marriage; but, unlike other new models of marriage, the pragmatic model is supported by the political leadership, which reasonably sees in this model an acceptable alternative. Now I shall turn to those models of marriage that are condemned by official ideology and supported only by certain groups of intellectuals. As with pragmatic marriage, each of these other patterns has its own constituency among the Soviet population.

THE EROSION OF IDEOLOGY AND SEX

Two things account for the drastic increase in the role of eroticism in Soviet life—one "subjective," the other "objective." The first is a by-product of the process of the general demoralization of Soviet society since 1953. The decaying acceptance of Soviet ideology in various ways has stimulated eroticism in Soviet life. Since romantic love and romantic marriage have the status of official values, they, too, have been victimized as parts of an ideology despised by a growing number of people (I discussed this issue earlier). It is interesting that while in the 1920s, immediately after the Revolution, eroticism and sexual pleasure were regarded by young Communists as a direct challenge to the old morality and almost as pillars of a new ideology; now they have come to be treated as something that challenges the hypocrisy of official morality and ideology. This can clearly be seen in the songs of Soviet bards like Alexander Galich or Vladimir Vysotskii.

A famous song by Galich describes the adventure of the husband of a high official, Paramonova. In this famous satire, Galich derisively depicts how a love affair of Paramonova's husband was discussed at a Party meeting, where "all the details" were exacted from the "defendant"—all the details of his relations with a voluptuous niece of the barmaid in the office of his big-shot wife. Of course, the songwriter's and his audience's sympathy is with the husband, who has to repent and return to his repellent wife, "Citizen Paramonova."

The lie, as an all-encompassing phenomenon of Soviet society, plays a special role in the growing looseness of sexual practice. The system forces practically everyone in the Soviet Union to lie many times a day, to his or her superiors, colleagues, subordinates, editors, children, and so forth. Because of this, it is so easy to lie to a husband or a wife, for everybody wants to conceal a new affair from the current partner, spouse, or lover. Without the institutionalization of the lie in Soviet society, the present character of relations between the sexes would not have developed.*

---

*The cause of the demoralization of Soviet people, in particular in the sphere of sex, is the subject of fierce debate among Soviet intellectuals. If Westernizers emphasize the lack of democracy as a principal cause of all failures of the Soviet system, in the domain of morals or elsewhere, Slavophiles make the West account for the moral degradation of the Soviet people. They go so far as to treat urbanization as a negative phenomenon inevitably generating this process. Writers of the so-called "rural prose," such as Vasilii Shukshin, Fedor Abramov, and Valentin Rasputin, describe rural life, including the relations between men and women, as based on fundamental moral principles, principles that wither away in cities where, among other things, sexual wantonness flourishes.

Moreover, some Slavophiles sometimes even directly accuse the intelligentsia and the Jews of being responsible for the sexual indulgence and debauchery spreading in the country. Thus, the critic, S. Borovik, by all accounts far from liberal (he is something of a Slavophile), attacking recent Soviet "women's" prose for the promiscuous behavior of its heroes, entitled his caustic article, "We Are Only Acquainted"—an allusion to a song about a couple who have sex when they've barely been introduced. Assailing not only little known women authors, but also a prominent writer like I. Grekova (for her novel, *Department*), Borovik still recognized that the permissive style in the relations between the sexes described in the novels, "reflects some objective reality."

Barely holding back on his hatred of intellectuals and Jews (almost all the authors criticized are supposed to be Jews or related to them), the critic accuses these writers of portraying only the intelligentsia as continuing to follow romantic images of love and friendship in their behavior, while all "simple people" wallow in depravity and vice (see Borovik 1980). Such accusations against the intelligentsia are easy to find everywhere, from Khomeini's Iran to the United States. See, for instance, *Capturing the Middle Ground* (1982), in which the authors, Brigitte and Peter Berger, exactly like the Russian Slavophiles, attack professors, students, and

EROS AND WOMEN'S PROFESSIONAL ACTIVITY

There is an important development that goes far to account for the growth of eroticism in Soviet life. This is the increased role of women in occupational, especially professional, activity. It has generated radically different sexual relations between men and women. With her professional life, the Soviet woman does not need to be involved in love affairs with hapless milkmen or plumbers. She can find a partner for extramarital sex among people who are equal to her in all respects, or even among those of higher social status.*

Women's prominence in the work world has led to the creation of an erotic zone in almost every office, shop, and plant.† Consequently, men and women constantly compare their spouses with their coworkers. If we keep in mind, besides the drastic growth of the number of potential partners for emotional relations that this entails, the attractiveness of new experience, it will be evident how much the relations between the sexes have changed since the day when the notion of the eternal union of two faithful spouses took hold.‡

---

students' parents for their disrespect of the family and all values traditionally related to it and glorify ordinary people as true upholders of these values.

*In considering the dramatic increase in the sexual activity rates of Soviet women, one very important variable must be taken into account: the woman's appearance. Of course, many unattractive women are still quite successful in sex, but the attractive Soviet woman is, on the average, much more involved in new emotional adventures than her less alluring counterpart. As in many other areas, inherited or acquired personal traits exert a tremendous impact on human relations, compared to the influence of such "objective" factors as social status, education, income, and so on.

Female beauty is an important social factor in Soviet life, as elsewhere. It significantly affects the fate of women and men in various ways. It is noticeable that the concentration of attractive women in Moscow is much higher than in the provinces, and that the number of attractive, well-groomed women decreases as one moves from the West to the East, and from the North to the South of the country.

†There is no question that sex plays a significant role in U.S. offices too (see, for instance, P. Horn and J. Horn 1982). U.S. public opinion is very concerned with sexual harassment in the workplace, and this is a frequent topic in the mass media. However, the U.S. office cannot really compare with the Soviet one—sexual relations between Soviet officemates are much more intense. Nearly every Soviet novel pays some attention to this aspect of everyday life. And Soviet superiors much more actively exploit their status in order to get sexual favors than do their U.S. counterparts.

‡The Soviet intelligentsia is not familiar with the famous Desmond Morris book, *The Naked Ape*. But many of the book's ideas have long been ingrained in to their mentality.

Soviet sociological data indicate that partners in sexual relations (including spouses) do not meet each other so much near their homes but in various public locations where new prospects appear frequently. For example, among newlyweds, only 10 to 15 percent found their mates among neighbors, while 30 to 40 percent did so at entertainment or vacation spots (Tiit 1982, p. 29; Zvidrinsh and Lapin'sh 1979, p. 66). In the West, people are more likely to marry those who live near them (see Peach 1974).

Data describing networks of human communication show that colleagues and workmates more and more supplant relatives and neighbors as those with whom the individual is in regular contact, a development that influences sexual relationships. A study in Moscow in the mid-1970s showed that 77 percent of respondents met informally with colleagues and workmates several times a week, while 53 percent met as frequently with neighbors, and only 19 percent met with relatives that often (Iankova and Rodzinskaia 1982, p. 52).

Kolpakov and Patrushev conducted an international comparison of ways in which people spend their time. In Pskov, one Soviet city studied, married men averaged 6.2 hours per weekday in the presence of coworkers, while women averaged 5.4 hours. Time spent with neighbors, friends, and relatives amounted to only 0.3 hours, among both men and women. Thus, both sexes spent 18 to 20 times as much time with coworkers as with neighbors, friends and relatives. By contrast, in the U.S. national data studied, men spent only 2.6 times as much time with coworkers as with neighbors, friends, and relatives, and women only 1.8 times as much time (1971, p. 178).

It is remarkable, too, how the Soviets like to spend their vacations. Asked about their preferences—to have vacations with children and with their spouse, to have it with their spouse alone, or to take it all by oneself—only a minority (less than one-third) of Leningraders opted for a holiday with their marital partner. No less than half said they would rather take their vacation by themselves (Boiko 1980, p. 70).*

Of course, there are many reasons that Soviet couples try to avoid common vacations, but it is no secret that hopes for sexual adventure play a not insignificant role in their decision. Soviet

---

*It is also characteristic that the married respondent set a fairly high value on "independence, freedom" in family life: 10 percent of the women and 17 percent of the men found it important. As can be supposed, this factor is much more highly valued by the unmarried (Boiko 1980, p. 105).

novels, movies, and plays are replete with romances begun during vacations—for instance, Gerasimov's *A Gap in the Calendar* (1983). Some of these romances continue after the end of the holiday and lead to marriages, divorces, or long affairs.

A significant number of spouses want not only to spend their vacations apart, but try to avoid each other weekdays and weekends. According to a Moscow study (1976–77), in up to one-fifth of families, separate leisure time is the norm. The study in Taganrog discovered that 50 to 70 percent of the outings of married men were without their wives (Soloviev 1981, p. 30).

Soviet men quite often postpone their return home after 5 o'clock as much as possible. Making a survey of letters sent to *Pravda*, in connection with a debate on the problems of modern family life, the reviewer Mikhailova, a woman herself, recognized that "numerous responses confirmed that the situation of 'a home without a man' is not at all atypical and is rather widespread." One woman, an author of a letter to *Pravda*, writes, "I married many years ago. However, I do not remember an instance when the members of our family went to a movie or theater or out on the town together." (*Pravda*, October 9, 1983)

Even more interesting is that the predilection to separate leisure time increases with educational level. Of married couples with little education, 90 percent like to go out together; among people with a higher education, the figure drops to 76 percent (Iankova and Rodzinskaia 1982, pp. 56–58). The tendency is especially strong among women. Analyzing data collected in Estonia in the 1960s and 1970s, the Estonian sociologist, Iarve, notes that, "with the rise of their educational level, the desire of women to spend their leisure time outside the home increases drastically." The correlation coefficient he refers to is relatively high at .45 (Iarve 1977, p. 149).

SOVIET SEX HUNTERS

Each of three hedonistic values—consumerism, alcohol, and sex—has its own "constituency," and it is possible to single out three groups of Soviet people predominantly inclined in their daily life toward one of these values: those whose major source of pleasure is the acquisition of prestigious material goods, those for whom life is divided into three periods—before drinking, drinking, and after drinking—and those for whom life seems worthwhile only when they are having an affair with a new partner.

The boundaries between the three groups are blurred and they often overlap. Alcohol is in many cases a stimulant necessary for the elevation of the contact between a man and a woman to the sexual level. And the hunt for prestigious goods is not rarely combined with the desire to attract a prestigious lover. For all this, there are people who have clearly "specialized" in one of these three hedonistic values.

Each group's content depends very much on age, sex, social status, ethnic origin, and other factors. The sex-oriented are younger rather than older, more often men than women, and more non-Moslems than Moslems, more city than country dwellers, more people living in big cities rather than small cities, more educated intellectuals than nonintellectuals, more women regarded as good looking than as unattractive.

Soviet society knows a number of types who are absorbed in love affairs. Some of them, of course, can hardly be regarded as an invention of Soviet society. Here are some possible descriptions:

No. 1—A professional woman between 25 and 40 years old. Married. Children; no more than two, of course, usually only one. Values her husband and her marriage very highly, but cannot live without regular flirtations with other men. Sometimes, but not always, goes to bed with them. Affairs usually brief. Is afraid of long, intimate relations that could threaten her marriage. The ideal for her is to have three men around—a husband, a man ready to marry her if she should divorce, and a lover; all handsome or prestigious.

No. 2—A woman. The same age as above, any occupation. Dislikes or even hates her husband, but deems it necessary to preserve the marriage for the children's sake. Looks for love outside marriage. If she finds a man who fits her image of a lover and who responds to her, she is very much involved and will be faithful to her lover. Separation from her lover a terrible tragedy to her.

No. 3—A woman. Highly flirtatious, usually attractive and sensual. In her thirties. Her main goal in life: adding to the number of admirers and lovers. She looks for them everywhere—at the office, in resort hotels, at parties, at business conferences, and even on the streets and on public transportation. Sometimes she changes not only lovers, but also husbands. Searches particularly in literary milieu where a more prestigious spouse could raise her social status.

No. 4—A man. A Soviet Don Juan. Practically any level of education. For him, sex is a kind of sport. He persists into his sixties in increasing the number of his victories over women. Often a good family man, loves his children, and may not even be hostile to his wife.

No. 5—A man. Hates his wife. Wants love and compassion. Does not avoid adventures, but prefers a stable relationship with a woman who loves him and whom he can trust.

HOW TO COMBINE A STABLE MARRIAGE AND EROS

Among those for whom love and sexual pleasure constitute the main part of their life, only a minority are opponents of marriage as an institution. Moreover, by all accounts, most of them do not often or even ever divorce and they are proponents of stable marriage. In the opinion of this majority, love and passion cannot persist—the framework of marriage and the exposure to temptations on the job makes love last even more briefly. But those who adhere to the permissive model, besides holding that love and sexual feelings are very important, do not believe in lasting love but do believe in lasting marriage. They find that only such marriage can meet their needs for children and bring happiness, that only stable relations based on a long, common life can provide partners with the mutual help and relaxation so necessary in this tempestuous world.

The obvious conflict between two values—intense emotional relations, which by definition cannot endure, and lasting marriage—can be resolved only if extramarital relations are regarded as a normal, even desirable, phenomenon.

We have seen that extramarital sex is important for many Soviet people but not always because they look for new strong emotions or sexual diversity. There is another factor of great psychological importance. In many cases, people yearn for love affairs, not because their love for a partner has withered, but for the opposite reason: their love is too strong compared to that which they receive in return from their spouses. This is especially true if their partner starts to look for amorous affairs. As a result, a chain reaction is triggered: the spouse, faithful up to that point, also seeks to take part in extramarital promiscuity. As the Soviet author, Rozhanovskaia, suggests, adultery is most often a result of a spouse's desire to assert themselves "on the side" (1981, p. 115).

Soviet novels abound with descriptions of cases when a spouse, especially a wife, becomes a lover to an "outsider" because she was hurt by the infidelity of her partner. Lida Muliavka, a heroine of Belai's novel, *Line*, loves her husband very much. However, over the years, she as become convinced that her husband does not respect her and that he had enjoyed great success among women more sophisticated than she. So, as we read in the novel (written by a nonprofessional writer who works as a foreman in a Moscow construction project), "she becomes too afraid that a long and hopeless jealousy will make her diffident and incapable not only of attracting someone else, but also of being attracted to someone other than Muliavka. This ambition pushes Lida to repay Muliavka in his own coin. She must have a lover; she wished and waited for it." Then the author continues, "she became Andreiev's [another married man] in the first night. When he asked to drive her home [after their first meeting in the office], she nonchalantly said to him at the porch that her husband had left for his next mission—she was happy that she could speak and think about Muliavka's missions [she supposed that her husband betrayed her with special activity there] with a light heart—and led Andreiev into the empty, childless apartment" (Belai 1983, pp. 57–58).

PERMISSIVE MARRIAGE: HOW IT WORKS AND HOW IT IS JUSTIFIED

The permissive model should not be confused with U.S. "swinging." There is a crucial difference between these patterns. The Soviet model entails that both spouses follow certain rules of conduct. The assumption is that extramarital relations should be hidden from the spouse as well as from other people. It is thought to be in very bad taste to parade these relations or to tell any but the closest friends. A spouse must do everything to conceal these relations from his partner. It is not acceptable, at the same time, for anyone, including best friends, to inform one of the spouses about the unfaithfulness of the others.

Moreover, the principles underlying this kind of marriage suppose that the best approach for a spouse in case he or she encounters evidence of infidelity is to pretend to know nothing.*

---

*On the role of jealousy as a motive for crime, the Soviet expert on criminology, Boris Volkov, cited Voltaire, who suggested that "wild jealousy committed more crimes than self-interest or ambition." Volkov added that "now jealousy does not play such a role as a source of crime. As a motive for crime, jealousy yields to many other motives." (Volkov 1982, p. 59)

This characteristic of the permissive marriage is rooted in the fact that, however common it may be, this model is not granted any type of public acceptance. The official support for the romantic and pragmatic models, which are both based on the assumption of fidelity, does not extend to permissive marriages—the same is true of public opinion.

The permissive marriage has only the status of a cathectic value. The same rules are applied to it as to power, wealth, drinking, and other values that no one praises but that constitute objectives for many people. These values, as far as they are not supported publicly, function as values "for me and not for other people," and those who are absorbed by these values advise others to ignore them.

Until recently, the permissive model has been so inimical to the dominant values, that no one in the Soviet Union has dared to defend it openly. However, the situation has been changing, and a first attempt to legitimate this model has been made. As justifications of this model, arguments apprehensible to Soviet ideologues were used—the necessity of coping with the problem of single women and the decline of the birthrate.

The first of these arguments was used by a prominent Soviet journalist and writer, Leonid Zhukhovitskii (1977, p. 12), the second by the leading Soviet demographer, Boris Urlanis (1980). The logic of Zhukhovitskii's article was watertight: it is impossible to help all single woman have husbands, let us not hinder them from having lovers and, at least in this way, make their lives more tolerable. As to the wives of these lovers, they should acquiesce in this situation, because otherwise their husbands might leave them for the other woman.

Urlanis put the accent not so much on the quality of single women's lives, as on their role in reproduction. He insisted that the social importance of this issue is so great that it is necessary to encourage single women to bear children and support them.*

---

*Recently, *Literaturnaia gazeta* (April 13, 1983) made a new attempt to launch a discussion on "permissive marriage." It began with a recounting of a case of a certain nice and noble single woman, Zhenka, who, at 35 and without prospects of marrying, took to visiting her very sick coworker, Valentina, and helping her family. Valentina's husband, Nicolai, was very devoted to his wife in her long and seemingly hopeless illness. Zhenka and Nicolai fell in love with each other. Zhenka decides never to visit again, though without her the order and good atmosphere in the family, which are so important for the sick woman, will disappear. After some hesitation, Valentina calls her friend and asks her to keep coming—completely aware of what that means. Readers were invited to express

How many people regard the model of permissive marriage as "a value for me" in the Soviet Union? Certainly, the fact of the publication of the two articles mentioned is indicative in itself. Taking into account the resistance of Soviet ideology to change in this sphere, only the strong pressure of real life could have forced editors and censors to allow such unconventional articles to appear in the Soviet mass media.

Soviet literature and art can also be regarded as an important source of evidence that permissive marriage is perceived by a growing number of people as a normal phenomenon for themselves and, more and more often, even for others. Of course, novelists and playwrights keep a certain distance from their heroes who carry on intimate relations with two women—they do not grant them their open approval, but these heroes are not at all objects of rebuke; on the contrary, they arouse compassion among readers and spectators.

The wanton sexual life of the Soviets, predominantly the professionals, is tellingly described in various novels by Iuri Trifonov, one of the best Soviet writers. In his novel, *Preliminary Review*, all his heroes are involved in love affairs, hampered by a lack of apartments to meet in. The novel, *A Gap in the Calendar*, mentioned above, is very typical. The author, Iosif Gerasimov, describes the life of the scientific intelligentsia. All conflicts in the novel originate in science and are the result of the different attitudes of the main characters to their roles as scholars. Their family life is depicted only as far as is necessary for their professional behavior to be understood. But, by all accounts, the author intentionally gave very prominent treatment to the sexual relations of his heroes. The lives of five couples are at the center of the novel. There is not a single alliance in which the dominant morality is not violated in the most conspicuous way. One couple lives together though not married; in all the other couples, at least one partner is having, or has lately had, an affair. No less remarkable is that the author paints the sex lives of his characters as perfectly normal and does not show anybody among them condemning the fact of conjugal unfaithfulness. And spouses who learn about their betrayal by their mates are in a hurry to forgive and to continue their life as if nothing serious had happened (Gerasimov 1983).

---

their views on this case. However, perhaps because of a preemptory shout from above, the *Gazeta* stopped right there. Nothing further has been published about the case.

In another recent novel, Nabatnikova's *Daughter*, all heroes are involved in extramarital affairs, including the old father of the heroine, who brings women to the kitchen in his daughter's apartment (where he lives, having left his wife in the village). The reviewer of this novel, Vladimir Sukhnev, does not call into question the plausibility of any of the events in this novel. He only rebukes the author for not explaining why "people ran into such a life" (*Literaturnaia gazeta*, November 2, 1983).

V. Shmit and G. Zelms, two authors in *Literaturnaia gazeta*, sought to analyze how Soviet writers, especially those in their own Latvian republic, treat the modern Soviet marriage. They found the results of their investigation to be frustrating: "As soon as a writer touches on the issue of marriage, conflicts with hysteria, betrayals, and divorce emerge immediately." The authors of the article strained their memories, but could not remember a novel or story about a happy family or where the spouses were faithful to each other. This survey of literary heroes and heroines found that nearly all of them were betraying their spouses or preparing to do so for the first time. As Martyn', a typical character in one story declares, "The marital bed is not a temple, but a scaffold of love. An individual feels himself much better, not in his marital bed (let the hypocrites praise it!), but in those of his neighbors" (*Literaturnaia gazeta*, February 29, 1984).

Pavel Basinskii made another attempt in the same newspaper to survey the "love theme" in recent Soviet literature. His evaluation also turned out to be distressing. First, he was struck by the monotony of love plots in the novels and stories of his compatriot-writers. He could detect only two types of love affairs: those on business missions and those at the workplace. Basinskii was even more amazed by the utterly uninhibited nature of the relations between literary characters on short missions. They leap into intimate contact with one another almost immediately, as soon as they have found attractive sexual partners. And they change partners as soon as they tire of one. Among those who initiate the affairs, according to the article's author, they completely ignore the marital status of their prospective partner. Basinskii suggests that heroines are much more sexually aggressive than men in these literary works. Many of these "Soviet amazons" literally abduct grooms from their weddings and nearly rape them. Basinskii laments that "writers seemingly forget that love is a lofty feeling and a psychologism, and the feeling of ideals is necessary in the portrayal of love." Rebuking these writers for their retreat from the style of classic Russian literature, reknowned for its descriptions of passionate and romantic love, he does not accuse them of distorting reality; he only begs them not to ignore ideals (*Literaturnaia gazeta*, March 21, 1984).

In Soviet movies, heroes regularly commit adultery without rousing the ire of film producers or spectators. The very positive heroine of the famous *Moscow Does Not Believe in Tears* maintains a sexual relationship with a married man. The moral anger of the movie is not to blame this woman, but to condemn her partner, and not for his unfaithfulness to his wife, but for his craven behavior toward the heroine: he has always been afraid he would be caught by his wife, and because of this he has always spoiled all the heroine's pleasure in being with him. We find, more or less, the same accent in another movie, *The Autumn Marathon*, in which the hero is shown as having a difficult plight—he cannot be everywhere at once, with his wife, his mistress, and his colleagues.

THE MAGNITUDE OF EXTRAMARITAL SEX

Although the study of sexual relations is virtually prohibited in the Soviet Union, some scant data published by Soviet sociologists attest to the magnitude of the phenomenon of extramarital sex. Four kinds of data are of paramount interest in this connection, which, while often indirect, provide some indication of how widespread such activities are. First, there are some direct indicators, but also there are data on the rates of illegitimate births and on the rate of abortion among unmarried women. Finally, there are data on public attitudes toward single mothers, which will be discussed later. Again, we should point out that such behavioral indicators are utilized in an attempt to grasp the personal values of the Soviet people.

Direct indicators in this area are particularly scant. In one small survey of married women in Leningrad, Kharchev found that 40 percent of respondents considered it acceptable for married people to have sex outside marriage with people they like (1979, p. 199). Meanwhile, a national survey in the United States in 1974 found that 73 percent of respondents answered that extramarital sex is "always wrong" (National Opinion Research Center 1974).

Probably more remarkable and meaningful are data on 1200 respondents gathered by Svetlana Burova, who inquired into the causes of divorces in Minsk. Unlike other Soviet investigators of this problem, she paid special attention to the extramarital sex life of men. She could establish, with more or less certainty, the absence of such relations in only half of all cases considered by the courts, despite the fact that the courts judged that there were such relations in only one out of ten of the cases (Burova 1979, p. 81). If we recall that the annual ratio of divorces to marriages is 1:3, and that the courts grant almost one million divorces per year, this suggests a rather widespread phenomenon.

The data on the proportion of divorces ascribed to infidelity deserve some special discussion. Using these measures as indicators of values is problematic, for they are difficult to interpret. It is clear that, in most cases, infidelity in itself does not lead to divorce. But, on the other hand, Burova's data indicate that people tend not to claim infidelity as the cause of divorce when appearing before the courts. This underreporting may reflect either people's reluctance publicly to reveal the existence of infidelity in their marriage, or it may reflect the degree of permissiveness in marriage, such that people do not divorce simply because of infidelity. Given these difficulties in interpretation, we shall address the role of infidelity in divorce in more detail.

By all accounts, the number of divorces traceable to infidelity does not reflect the true role of sexual conflict in marriage. The point here is that the image of the ideal marriage still assumes the fidelity of spouses. While this image may be declining in significance, it continues to be highly influential in the conceptions of the Soviet people and the formation of their self-images.

Thus, in dealing with others and with their own self-concepts, many people are unwilling to ascribe the failure of their marriages to their infidelity, or even more, to that of their spouse. The erosion of love is a more acceptable justification for divorce for both the unfaithful spouse and the spouse who has been the victim of infidelity. To admit to infidelity as the cause of divorce is to accept responsibility that certain actions, which should have been avoided, were at fault, resulting in negative appraisal by both society and self. The erosion of love, on the other hand, is much more vague and more difficult to lay at the feet of a certain person.*

---

*Only this phenomenon, a combination of the rationalization and coping mechanisms, explains why surveys consistently show the vast majority of respondents claiming to be more or less happy in their marriages, even while the divorce rate is so high. In our 1968 survey of *Pravda* readers, we found no more than one-fourth of respondents willing to express dissatisfaction with their marriages, even including those who avoided answering the question. In a more

Nonetheless, further examination of Burova's data suggests that it is probably the greater permissiveness about infidelity, rather than reluctance to admit to it publicly, that accounts for the small proportion of couples viewing unfaithfulness as grounds for divorce. Burova found that in Minsk the proportion of divorces where infidelity was cited as the principal grounds has diminished. Although 16 percent of divorces in 1965 were officially traced to infidelity, this figure dropped to 14 percent in 1966, 11 percent in 1971 and 10 percent in 1975 (1979, p. 22). Given the seeming relaxation of sexual morality during this period, it is unlikely that concerns for public and self-image pressed individuals increasingly to avoid the admission of infidelity. It is more plausible that the reverse is true: more open practice of infidelity diminishes its significance as grounds for divorce.†

EXTRAMARITAL SEX AND ILLEGITIMATE CHILDREN

The numbers of children born out of wedlock is also an indicator of the changes in sexual morality. However, using this indicator in the estimation of extramarital sex is not without its difficulties. One problem is that the measure cannot distinguish births resulting from premarital sex from those resulting from extramarital relations. Thus, while the mothers of these children are, of course, single, we cannot say anything about the marital status of the fathers (further, not all extramarital liaisons result in pregnancy and birth).

---

recent survey, spanning the years 1972–73, the Estonian sociologist, E.M. Tiit, found 80 percent of young wives evaluating their marriages as happy (1982, p. 31), even while other data show more than one-third of marriages breaking up in the first years of marriage.

A similar contradiction is found in the United States. While more than one out of three marriages ends in divorce, research by Angus Campbell and his colleagues found that 87 percent of women and 91 percent of men reported virtually never thinking about getting divorced (1976, p. 324).

†The substitution of one cause or motive of an action for another is one of the most interesting methodological problems—a problem that can be solved somewhat only if sociologists are aware of the social context that forces respondents to substitute one kind of explanation of their behavior with another. The existence of rationalizations of this kind (each real reason having another reason covering it) has been established in various areas of Soviet sociology: turnover of industrial workers, migration, choice of profession, mass media, and so on (Shlapentokh 1973).

At present, it can be said that between 10 to 15 percent of all children in the Soviet Union are born to single women* (Larmin 1974; Tolts 1974). After a period of decline, this rate has begun to increase as the balance in the distribution of the sexes began to normalize, recovering from the effects of the war (Bedny 1980, p. 13).

What proportion of illegitimate births can be traced to extramarital relations? We can begin to sketch the outlines of an answer with data collected by M. Tolts (1974). First, he shows that 40 percent of illegitimate births were by women over the age of thirty. This figure can be compared to another, showing that 31 percent of women, aged 40 to 44, giving birth were unmarried. Moreover, this proportion had risen from 22 percent in 1959 (1974, p. 154).

Now, given that in the early 1970s, among the Soviet population over the age of thirty, single women far outnumbered single men—and especially since men are more likely to be older than women in love relationships—the probability is high that the fathers of a large proportion of these illegimate children were married.†

Not all illegitimate pregnancies result in birth. Indeed, pregnancies among single mothers are probably somewhat less likely to come to term, especially given that abortion is one of the principal means of birth control in the USSR.† Between the ages of 15 and 49, Soviet women average between five to eight abortions each (Vasil'eva 1981, pp. 33–34). Thus, data on abortion can help us further grasp the scope of extramarital sex.

---

*In contrast, according to recent data, the proportion of children in the United States born out of wedlock rose from 10.7 percent in 1970 to 17.0 percent in 1979. Among whites, the percentage of children born to single mothers increased from 5.7 to 9.4 over this period, while for blacks, the proportion rose from 38 percent to 55 percent (New York Times, October 26, 1983).

†This is the opinion of Bednyi, one of the leading Soviet experts in demography. According to his recent survey, 80 percent of all mothers of illegitimate children deliberately made a decision to have a child without an official father. He also found that the majority of women who choose to become single mothers now fall between the ages of 30 and 40, while in the past the typical age was 17 or 18. Frequently, when asked why they had not registered the marriage with the father of their child, the women replied that he was already married. Bednyi's survey also revealed another important discovery: more than half of all single mothers had themselves been born out of wedlock (Nedelia, 15, 1984, pp. 16–17).

Of each 100 pregnancies in 1967 (more recent data are not available) only 20 percent resulted in birth; the rest, in abortion. (see Boiarinova et al., 1983, p. 182).

According to data from Sadvokasova (1969) and Boiarinova *et al.* (1983) about half of all abortions (48 percent in cities; 52 percent in villages) are performed on unmarried women. It is reasonable to assume that the age distribution of women getting abortions is similar to that of those giving births. If this is so, these figures are further, though indirect, evidence of the frequency of extramarital relations in the Soviet Union. A crude guess might be that 20 to 25 percent of illegitimate pregnancies result from extramarital sex.

Despite the shortcomings of these data, they can be regarded as solid ground for asserting that permissive marriage is regarded by a large number of Soviet people as acceptable, at least for themselves. Of course, such infidelity continues to be strongly disapproved, even among some who practice it. These people may remain supporters of romantic, or at least pragmatic, marriage for everyone else, including their children, friends, and colleagues.

SUMMARY

The growing role of hedonism in Soviet life has led to the relatively broad acceptance of permissive marriage. This type of marriage intends to combine sexual diversity, love, and passion with a stable marriage. In this case, married people are tolerant toward the sexual activity of their partners outside of marriage, if only the veneer of respectability is preserved.

To a considerable degree, the emergence of this type of marriage is a result of women's occupational roles and the involvement of both men and women in mutual flirtations at work. Separate leisure time and vacations also play an important role in the permissive sexual behavior of partners in Soviet marriage.

Attitudinal as well as "hard" behavioral data (for instance, the number of children born out of wedlock) show that the scope of extramarital sex in Soviet society is very high. Public opinion is very tolerant toward it and the affairs that abound in Soviet novels and films are only rarely condemned by the authors or film directors.

Serial Marriage ————————————————

PASSION AS A BASIS FOR MARRIAGE

Some part of the Soviet population continues to adhere to a certain romantic model of marriage as relevant to them, as an image not only for others but for themselves as well. This romantic model, though, is less similar to that advanced under Stalin, and more like the image proclaimed by the Revolution and backed by the founders of Marxism: marriage is only worth retaining if it is permeated by romantic, passionate, sexually charged love. Should such love decay, marriage loses its *raison d'être*.

The high and growing rate of divorce is partly traceable to the persistence of this image in the Soviet mind. Like all other models of marriage, however, this one is supported more among specific groups in the population. The young and the well educated and particularly men are more likely to support and pursue this pre-Stalinist version of the romantic marriage.

This image of a marriage imbued with passion rejects both infidelity as a normal feature of conjugal life, and the idea of a life long marriage. It proceeds from the assumption that passion and fidelity are incompatible with a life long marriage and sees the resolution of this problem in the regular change of marriage partners. Agreeing with those who deny passion a long existence, modern advocates of the alliance of love and marriage consider divorce a normal phenomenon. The incorporation of divorce as a normal element in current life is probably the most salient feature of this concept of love and marriage.* The most substantial evidence of the existence of a serial model in the Soviet mind is data on the scope of remarriage.

According to various investigations, no less than 36 percent of men and 22 percent of women remarry after divorce. Of special interest are data on the number of marriages that preceded the given divorce. In one study, it was found that more than one-tenth of all divorces were granted in the second, third, and consecutive marriages, and that the proportion of such divorces has been rising (Burova 1979, p. 7).

The following data, which evidently surprised the demographer Viktor Boiko, suggest how common among Soviet people the idea of possibly changing marital partners is. In his study of married couples in Leningrad, Boiko included "confidence in the stability of marriage" on a list of requirements of a "happy family life." Asked to indicate which requirements were most important, only 16 percent of the respondents chose this alternative (1980, p. 105).

In another study, an Estonian sociologist asked Estonians (1972–74) how married people should behave if they fall in love with someone outside their marriage. About half of the city dwellers did not support leaving the marriage. Only in the countryside did the majority take the old conservative view that the married should stay within their families whatever their emotional inclinations (Arutiunian and Kakhk 1979, p. 51).

Each model of marriage involves certain attitudes regarding the well-being of children. The model of serial marriage is built on some widespread ideas on this matter. First it is assumed that, for children, life with a step-parent, or even with only one parent, is preferable to life in an unhappy family. Second, advocates of serial marriage argue that a child, especially many children, is not necessary to a happy marriage and may even be incongruent with it. This latter notion is apparently rising in popularity in the Soviet Union: more and more, couples are opting for no children or are limiting themselves to only one.

WHY WOMEN DO NOT WANT A SECOND CHILD

People who want to have only one child represent a special case in this regard. The growing number of one-child families is

---

*According to the last census of the Soviet population in 1979, among single women between the ages of 20 and 29, more than one-third had been divorced; between 30 and 39, more than one-half had been divorced. (Volkov 1983, p. 15)

one of the most alarming demographic phenomena in the USSR and the major cause of the decline of the birthrate.

By the end of the 1970s, of all Soviet families with children under 18, fifty-two percent were families with one child. (In the U.S. the figure was 37.7 percent.) In the cities, the proportion of these families was 61 percent, in the countryside 44 percent (*Deti v SSSR*, 1979, p. 9; *Vestnik Statistiki* 1983, 2, p. 69).

The rate of children born per 1000 women 25 years old and older dropped drastically over the last two decades: by 24 percent for women 25 to 29, 36 percent for women 35 to 39, and by 51 percent for women 45 to 49. At the same time, the figures for younger women, who were usually giving birth to their first child, rose: by 35 percent for those 15 to 19 and by 8 percent for those 20 to 24 (Perevedentsev 1982a, p. 13).

In evaluating the data demonstrating the decrease of the number of children in the Soviet family, it must be taken into account, as indicated earlier, that Soviet women rely mostly on abortion as a means of controlling the birthrate. One survey found that even in Moscow in 1976, some 80 to 90 percent of women have no real knowledge about contraceptives (Antonov 1980, p. 131). Moreover, birth control devices and medications tend to be both in short supply and often less than satisfactory to use. According to the opinion of one of the best Soviet demographers, Leonid Darskii, "a considerable number of children born have not been planned by their parents," which implies that were contraceptives more available, second and third children would be even fewer.* He refers to data obtained by him and Valentina Belova, according to which 77 percent of all the women who already had one child considered a subsequent pregnancy undesirable. For women with two children, the figure is 97 percent (Belova and Darskii 1972, p. 128).

No doubt a significant number of men and women do not want to have two or more children only because having a big family implies privations that people today do not wish to bear. Data show, as would be expected, that the addition of more children contributes to a declining standard of living among families, as measured by per capita income. A 1978 survey in Moscow found that, among families with two children, 59 percent fell into the lowest per capita income category (below 75 rubles per

---

*As a cause or motive leading to the birth of the second and third child in their families, 53 percent of married women in Moscow and Vilnius (1976) indicated a combination of "circumstances" (Antonov 1980, p. 174). This implies that the decision was not completely of their own free will and was the result of some social or official pressure.

month). Only 23 percent of families with one child were in this category (Khorev and Kisilieva 1982, p. 88).

The attitudinal data are quite consistent with the "hard" behavioral data. Viktor Boiko asked Leningraders why they chose not to have more children. They cited material factors (housing conditions and per capita income of the family) as the most important. Among all motives cited by all respondents, 36 percent were material conditions, whereas 22 percent were "difficulties in rearing children" (Boiko 1980, p. 157).

The concern about housing conditions is a reflection of the shortage of adequate space, especially in urban areas, in Soviet apartments. Floor space tends to be quite limited, and it is only the more fortunate who do not have to use their living room as a bedroom for some member of the family. A survey of women workers in Bielorussia in 1978–80 also established the important role of material conditions in making the decision on family size. Forty-one percent of all respondents cited inadequate housing conditions as preventing them from having more children than they already had (Buslov and Chigir 1983, p. 25).

However, for all the importance of material factors, Soviets today avoid having a second child quite often simply because they do not believe their marriage will last, even after the most dangerous period—the first five years—has passed. The young are much more inclined to divorce than the old and they are the ones mostly responsible for the procreation of a new generation. The point is that two or more children make divorce less likely. One child is not regarded as an insurmountable obstacle to separation either for a man or for a woman. Under Soviet law, fathers with one child pay one-quarter of their salary in child support—a tolerable sum, even if he is going to have a new family. But if a man with two or more children divorces, child support goes up to as much as half his salary, which, in view of the average individual income, will make his life even as a bachelor quite hard, let alone the life of a new family and new children.

One child is also an optimal number for a woman who does not want to exclude the possibility of divorce and a new marriage. Two circumstances are of key importance in this respect. First, a single woman with one child can have a more or less comfortable life by Soviet standards. Her salary and her child support from her former husband make up a considerable sum—sometimes a per capita income higher than that of a household with a husband. Second, although generally speaking a woman with one child has less chance of getting married than her childless counterpart, the chances are still fair that she will find a new husband. But the odds drop catastrophically for a woman with two or more children. It is rare that such a woman will find a man ready to be a father to her children and to those they would have together. Although this problem is hardly unique to Soviet society, we have seen that keeping large families is particularly difficult in the Soviet Union. The average family size in the Soviet Union is 3.5 people, a social norm that few people (outside the Moslem republics) care to violate. Thus, one child is an acceptable number for both men and women who wish to preserve a little leeway in the matrimonial domain and not burn their bridges behind them.

The results of a survey conducted in Moscow are consistent with these ideas. Kisilieva and Rodzinskaia explored the influence of the psychological climate of families on the number of children couples had and planned to have. Marriages in which relations between the spouses were bad were termed "unstable," and those with good relations "stable." It was found that in "stable" marriages, 65 percent of such families had two or more children, while only 35 percent of "unstable" marriages had more than one child. Among couples married less than ten years, the difference is even more pronounced: among unstable marriages, the probability of having two or more children is one-third that in stable cases. And in families where spouses had considered divorce, only 12 percent had more than one child, as against 41 percent in families where divorce had not been contemplated. Data on family plans of couples are consistent with the figures above. In young married couples where relations are good, both spouses plan for a second child in 80 percent of the cases; but if their relations are strained, only 44 percent have such plans.

Summarizing the results of their study, the Moscow sociologists state that "the second child has a very small chance of coming to a marriage when relations are strained" (Kisilieva and Rodzinskaia 1982, p. 79).* This opinion is shared by other sociologists and demographers. Borisov observes: "procreation is now not so much influenced by divorce as by relations between the spouses before it" (Borisov 1976, p. 94; see also Volkov 1977, p. 50).

---

*Kisilieva and Rodzinskaia make a very apt observation about the correlation between the age of the second child and the atmosphere in the family. The younger this child at the time of the survey, the more probable that the couple lives in harmony: relations seem to deteriorate from the time the second child is born. Indeed, of all families with a second child younger than 3, only 18 percent are

Perevedentsev formulates the problem even more bluntly. Conflicts in young families and the high rate of divorce are by themselves very important factors accounting for the small number of children. Numerous divorces among acquaintances, neighbors, and relatives negatively affect a woman's decision to have another child. Childlessness directly encourages divorce, for with only one or two children, it is easier to divorce than if a woman has more children (Perevedenstev 1982b, p. 87).

The number of children from broken marriages confirms the attitudinal data above. Of all the divorced couples in Kiev, only 19 percent had more than two children; in Lithuania, 17 percent; in Latvia, 10 percent (Chuiko 1975, p. 146; Solov'ev 1977, p. 121). Data on the proportion of remarried women among those who have two or more children bear witness to the same effect. Only 6 percent of Moscow women with that many children were not in their first marriage (Khorev and Kisilieva 1982, p. 84).*

In a recent Leningrad study of family life, sociologists singled out five types of families according to the professional and social activity of the spouses. Of course, the families in which both wife and husband were successful in both spheres of life were declared by the researchers to be the most ideal: 70 percent of all families of this type were happy. It turned out that the number of children in such families is lower than in any other group: 61 percent have only one child.

These "exemplary" families were contrasted to others—especially to those in which both spouses, though good workers, were very passive in their social lives. These families, the authors

---

unhappy, with a child between 3 and 7, 24 percent are unhappy, with a child over 7, 35 percent are unhappy (1982, p. 80). These sociologists discard the alternative theory advanced by Antonov (1977, p. 32), which proposes to consider the number of children in the family not as a dependent but as an independent variable and which hypothesizes that the absence of a second child is a *cause* of tension in a family.

*The growing orientation of the Soviet people toward the one-child family has aroused a lively discussion with a diversity of views not commonly found in the USSR after the 1960s, on the role of children in human life. Of all the participants of the discussion, Leonid Darskii has, in my opinion, developed the most interesting conception. According to him, it is necessary to make a distinction between "reproductive behavior" and "family needs." In a time when people can control births, the number of children is determined by their role in satisfying these needs. Today, with the significant modification of these needs, children are necessary mainly as objects of "altruistic concern and tutelage." However, for the fulfillment of this need, one child is often enough (Darskii 1979; see also Antonov 1980, Vishnevskii 1982, Borisov 1976).

say, are the most dissatisfied with their family life. It would be hasty to attribute this fact to social inertia. It is much more likely that the number of children plays the crucial role here. These families have more children than other families: 69 percent of them have two children (Suslov and Lebedev 1982, p. 151).

The "enmity" of women to children steadily increases (as in other societies) with the rise of education. The correlation between these two variables is, of course, to be attributed to a considerable extent to the woman's desire to pursue her career and not to be afraid of divorce or of living alone, a desire that strengthens with the growth of education. If we put the average fertility of Soviet women at 1.00, the figure for women with secondary education is 1.16, and for those with elementary education it is 1.53 (Sifman 1976, p. 58; see also Bondarskaia 1977, p. 16).* Of course, it is only to be expected that there will be this inverse correlation between the involvement of women in professional life and the number of their children.

Using the Soviet republics as units of analysis, available data clearly show this correlation. The Latvian republic, which has the highest proportion of women among the employed (1979), had the lowest birthrate—54 percent and 13.7 births per 1000 people, whereas the Tadzhik republic had the lowest proportion of women employed and the highest birthrate—39 percent and 37.8 per thousand (*Narodnoie Khosiastvo SSSR v 1979 Godu*, 1980, pp. 38–39; *Vestnik Statistiki* 1980, No. 1, p. 71).

Though many women are against having a second child because it will restrict their possible options in case of sharp family conflict, I do not want to ignore that a considerable proportion of women (about one-third, see Antonov 1980, p. 174) were moved to have a second child by an exactly opposite reason—to bind their husband to them and to defeat any hope of the husband to leave easily. For many women for whom the status of being married is of extraordinary importance, children are, under Soviet conditions, an efficient weapon against a husband's desire to leave his wife. Again, here, as in many cases, the same phenomenon can play diametrically opposite roles and serve two opposite purposes.

---

*Doubtless the relationship between fertility and the education of women is not simple. In many cases, education affects birthrate indirectly through a number of variables—age of first marriage, place of residence, income, use of contraceptives, role of the husband in the household chores, and so on (see Kharchev and Matskovskii 1978, pp. 175–80; Antonov 1980).

It is extremely indicative that it is Soviet women (as is probably true in other societies) who are much more strongly against having two or more children. All Soviet data show that women want significantly fewer children than do their husbands. A very representative nationwide survey conducted by Valentina Belova showed that the average number of children Soviet men want to have is 18 percent higher than that of Soviet women (Belova 1975, p. 116).

One investigation was conducted in Lithuania in 1976. Families begun 12 years before were the object of this study. Couples were asked how many more children they wanted to have. Of the wives, 79 percent said "none"; but only 67 percent of the husbands did. Only 11 percent of the wives were agreeable to having one more child, but 18 percent of husbands were (Barshis 1982, p. 54). Similar results were produced in a recent Leningrad study (Suslov and Lebedev 1982, p. 57).*

People who are not planning to have children are the real constituency not only for the concept of serial marriage, but also for the rejection of the idea of marriage at all.

SUMMARY

A large number of Soviet people reject the official concept of marriage, as well as the new models, such as pragmatic or permissive marriage. They stick to the image of romantic marriage as it was proclaimed at the time of the Revolution. They want a marriage based on strong mutual passion and prefer divorce and the formation of a new alliance to lifelong marriage, with its possibility of stagnation.

The growth of the divorce rate is a direct result of the increasingly high mutual expectations of spouses and their

---

*A study carried out in Leningrad by Boiko discovered relatively small differences in men's and women's attitudes toward children. Respondents—200 engineers, married and with children—were asked to evaluate on a five-point scale their relations with their children on a questionnaire containing 36 items. Men in one-child families put their attitudes toward children at 3.4, women put their attitudes at 3.6. Scores of men and women in two-child families were the same—3.8. The differences in readiness to have various contacts with children were more pronounced: in one-child families, 2.7 for men and 3.4 for women; and in two-children families, 3.2 and 4.0 respectively (Boiko 1980, pp. 65, 68).

unwillingness to tolerate an erosion of emotion in the family. The instability of marriage strongly influences the birthrate. Since many young people do not believe in the longevity of their marriage, they prefer to have only one child.

8

Life Without Marriage ───────────────────

DISAPPOINTMENT WITH MARRIAGE AS AN INSTITUTION

As noted in previous chapters, marriage as a social institution still enjoys the support of most of the Soviet population. However, there are reasons for thinking that a growing number of people have been growing disappointed with marriage as such and are moving toward the hostile attitude toward marriage that was widespread in the 1920s.

The antimarriage model, of course, reflects the growing hedonistic aspirations of the population, people's unwillingness to submit to any restriction in the emotional sphere, and their determination to preserve the possibility of changing partners at any moment without any legal implications. At the same time, divorce is an undesirable event that can damage one's career, arouse moral condemnation, and so on.

There are some general objective factors that allow people to spurn marriage as an institution. First, there is the independence of women, traced to their role in the labor force. Women start to work at about the same age as men. By all accounts, women earn less than men (although the gap is relatively small). But, considering a greater tendency among Soviet women to be more responsible with their money and seemingly to adapt better to the various difficulties of life, it may be suggested that single Soviet women have living standards no lower than single men. Thus, as in the West, the greater involvement of women in the occupational world, the less they must be dependent on men.*

───────────────

*Wesley Fisher's (1980) attempt to explain variations in the frequency of marriage in the Soviet Union, using Becker's economic model, appears to have

Other developments have an impact on the independence of men. The mechanization of domestic chores and the growing availability of various facilities (cafeterias, laundries, cleaning services, and so on) has to some extent freed men from their dependence on the domestic labor of women. Of course, these services in the USSR are much worse than those in the West. Nonetheless, the Soviet bachelor today is in a much better position than his predecessor of, say, forty years ago.

When discussing this alternative approach to relationships, it is necessary to make a distinction between those who reject the idea of marriage as absolutely insuitable for them, and those who try to postpone marriage as long as possible, i.e., between the consistent adversaries of this institution and opportunists who want to exploit the advantages of both marital statuses.†

The resurgence of the postrevolutionary negative attitudes toward marriage is so serious that it has become the subject of discussion in sociological literature, despite the great reluctance of Soviet ideologues to recognize a fact that testifies to the rejection of a value strongly supported by the system. "Some boys and girls," according to one author,"think that the family is not necessary now that marriage is not an ideal form of alliance between men and women" (Soloviev 1962, p. 116; see also Savenkova 1966, p. 130). Twenty years later, A. Kharchev also speaks of the dissemination of opinion on "the withering away of the family," even if he consoles readers that this opinion is a phenomenon not of "scientific," but "everyday" theory (Kharchev 1982, p. 24; see also Bestuzhev-Lada 1981, p. 126).

In his article about negative attitudes toward marriage, a prominent Soviet demographer and economist, Michail Sonin, cites the letter of a man with a Ph.D., 42 years old, who flaunts his reluctance to marry. The man begins his letter with the descrip-

---

missed this crucial point. He predicted that rising incomes of men and women would encourage increased marriage rates, as individuals seek to maximize their material position by combining their incomes. The prevailing situation in the USSR appears quite the opposite. In regions like the Baltic republics, where women earn the most relative to men, the proportion of single women is larger than in area (e.g., the Moslem republics) where the income gap is wider.

†Andrew Cherlin's statements about the behavior of U.S. young people are applicable, with some modifications, to Soviet youth. In the past, he argues, young men were more apt to live at home and not to marry until they had saved enough for a down payment on a house. Now they wait until their middle twenties because staying single is more enjoyable. Once they do decide on marriage, whether they will remain married depends on how they compare the constrictions of marriage with the freedom of their bachelor days (Cherlin 1982).

tion of his rather high standard of living, and then puts the question and answers it: "Why don't I marry? Simply because I don't want to," and advises other men not to. "I may ask myself whether loneliness oppresses me. I answer no, because there are always women around who are ready to brighten up my life." He ends his letter: "Times change. Before, married people lived better than bachelors in every way. But now, everything is different. Freedom and love—that is my ideal. Man's ideal, I mean."

It is notable that Sonin does not deny the man's major thesis, that the life of the bachelor is better than that of a family man who cannot afford himself pleasures so accessible to bachelors. Sonin's major criticism is that these egotistical people decrease the birthrate and deprive many women of a "good mood" which in turn diminishes their productivity in the economy by 15 to 20 percent (Sonin 1981, pp. 189–93).*

Most problematic in this respect are not so much the attitudes of adults (whatever their influence on the divorce rate), but the stance of young people who are entering the period of crucial decisions. One study that sheds light on this subject produced some shocking results, despite the understandable attempts of their authors to mitigate their alarming character.

This survey was carried out in the Azerbaijanian city of Lenkoran in 1982, among students in their last years of high school and among students in professional schools. In evaluating data from this study, it is necessary to take into account that, in this Moslem republic, marriage is much more respected than in Russian or Baltic regions of the country. However, as the authors of the study rather reluctantly state, only "23.3 percent of all urban students, and 40 percent of rural ones, share the opinion that marriage is a valuable social institution," even though few directly supported the obviously loaded alternative that "marriage is an obsolete form of relation between men and women" (3.3 percent among urban students in high schools and 1.6 percent among students of professional schools).

The subsequent data explain why young people even in Moslem culture are so lukewarm about marriage. The urban young people, as can be expected, are especially hostile toward

---

*Here Sonin's article greatly differs from an article by A. Kositskii in the same collection devoted to demographic problems. Kositskii discusses the numerous illnesses that beset the solitary lives of unmarried men. Having no Soviet data, he profusely cites Western authors, mostly from the medical world. Of course, if he were a sociologist, he would refer to Durkheim's studies of suicide, which so eloquently demonstrated the danger of solitude (Kositskii 1981, pp. 108–12).

marriage because they are less exposed than their counterparts in the countryside to the influence of traditional values. Thus, 36.7 percent of students in the city suppose that marriage curtails "male activity." Almost the same proportion point out that marriage increases the female domestic workload (Mansimov and Foteiva 1982, p. 129).

A letter from a young girl, presumably Russian, published in *Pravda*, is quite consistent with the results of the study described above. She writes: "In recent times, many people think about the family. I am 19 years old, but I do not have the slightest desire to marry. Women are overloaded. Music, theater, books—all this is available only before the wedding. All the more if you do not have a mother. And then the subjects of conversation of married women—husbands and children. Perhaps those who do not need more really are happy." (*Pravda*, November 13, 1983).

It can be suggested that people who oppose the institution of marriage are a good sample of those who believe that any social values whose pursuit may require effort or sacrifice are not "for them," only "for others." The majority of adherents to this antimarriage model are men,* but the supporters also include women with feminist orientations.† This latter category deserves some comment.

As was indicated, the majority of Soviet women see their ideal life as one involving a combination family and a pleasant, prestigious job. Moreover, most women are far from advocates of the revolutionary idea of complete sexual equality, or of the more modern feminist concept of the transcendance of gender in society.‡ However, it is evident that many Soviet women focus more on their independence and professional lives and are no less disposed against having domestic problems than are men. They may be hostile toward marriage, or at least try to postpone it as long as possible.

---

*In the United States, as in Soviet society, men are more likely to be the proponents of the antimarriage model, and their numbers are growing. From 1970 to 1980, the number of men who have "never married" grew by 118 percent, but by only 89 percent among women.

†Although women are less likely to take antimarriage views, men's behavior may compel them to remain single by default. Although initially forced to live alone, many single women adapt to the situation and may even become opponents of marriage, either sincerely or as a justification for their situation.

‡Perhaps the most outspoken Soviet feminist, Larisa Kuznetsova, remarked that if women from the 1920s and 1930s were to read current Soviet publications on women's issues, they would be startled by the positive treatment of things that would have been condemned in their own times (Kuznetsova 1980).

HOW MANY PEOPLE ARE AGAINST MARRIAGE?

There are a number of indicators that can shed light on the number who support the anti-marriage model in part (postponed marriage) or completely (marriage–never). First of all, there are the data on remarriage—especially among men. Referring to such data, Viktor Perevedenstev affirms that a growing number of people are rejecting marriage as a social institution. The divorced, says this famous Soviet demographer and sociologist, do not want to enter a new conjugal alliance because they have been disappointed, not so much with their former partner, as with marriage as such (Perevedenstev 1982a, p. 25; see also Perevedenstev 1975). According to the calculations of the young Soviet sociologist Alexander Sinel'nikov, in 1926, of 100 divorced men, 59 married again; for women the figure was 40. By 1969–70, the figures were 36 and 22* (Sinel'nikov 1978, p. 169). The number of the divorced and the number of those who enter a second marriage have been growing apart. In 1973, the figures show 679,000 newly divorced people and 369,000 divorced people entering second (or subsequent) marriages. In 1979, 951,000 people obtained divorces and 453,000 divorcees remarried. Thus, the ratio of divorcees to the remarried rose from 1.84:1 in 1973 to 2.09:1 in 1979. The most recent data show that even those who divorce when young (under 30 years of age) still very often do not remarry—only 48 percent of men and 41 percent of women. M. Tolts noted that the proportion of remarriages among all marriages in a given period has not increased over the last hundred years despite the tremendous growth of divorce and a low death rate. About 15 to 19 percent are remarriages for men and 13 to 14 percent for women (Tolts 1979, pp. 45–46). Data on the number of men in their middle and old age who have never married are also of interest. Results from the 1959 and 1970 census can be compared to show the increase in the rate of never-married men in different age groups. Table 8.1 provides such data for the urban population of the Russian Republic.

It can be seen that this rate increased in all age groups, with the largest increases in the younger groups. In the nation as a whole, the rate increased for the group 30 to 39 by 45 percent (only slightly under the Russian rate of 50 percent in the table above),

---

*The proportion of remarried is much higher in the U.S. than in the USSR. Among U.S. women who get divorced in their twenties, over three-quarters remarry (Hacker 1982, p. 38).

TABLE 8.1: Never–married men
(per 1000, by age group)

	30–34	35–39	40–44	45–49	50–54
1959	87	52	38	45	45
1970	127	81	62	55	51

Source: Compiled from data in Gerasimova, I. 1976. *Struktura Sem'i.* Moscow: Statistika, p. 98.

and by 14 percent among those 25 to 29. This smaller increase in the youngest group reflects the relatively late average age of marriage in the USSR, such that large numbers of men are still single anyway at that age.

Along with data on the number of unmarried men, there are data that demonstrate that the growing proportion of single people, especially women, can be attributed not only to the demographic composition of the population, but also to purely cultural factors.

The number of unmarried women varies directly with the degree of Westernization of a region. Thus, in 1970, the relative number of unmarried Estonian women was five times greater than that of Tadzhiis women. (Bondarskaia and Il'ina 1979, p. 16). Even more illustrative are data on the duration of marriage. Estonian and other Baltic women born in 1918 to 1922 had 12.2 years of married life behind them when they reached 35. Women born in 1928 to 1932 had, by the same age, been married 11.0 years. For women in the Moslem republics, the figures were 14.2 and 15.0. In other words, while the length of time a Baltic woman is married decreased, for a Moslem woman the length increased. It is notable that Slavic women (Russian, Ukrainian, and Bielorussian) follow largely the Baltic pattern (Bondarskaia and Il'ina 1979, p. 33).

The same is true about men. Among Estonian men in 1970, 13 percent of the men 40 to 45 had never married, against 6 percent in Russia (Laas 1982, p. 72). It should be added that the probability of a man of this age marrying for the first time is no more than 5 percent—and for women it is only 2 percent.

COHABITATION: AN EMERGING INSTITUTION?

The growth of antimarriage sentiment has been accompanied by an increase in unregistered cohabitation, something of a throwback to the 1920s. Viktor Perevedentsev asserts that "there are many unofficial marriages," but that without special investigation, their precise number cannot be established. As indirect evidence, he cites the fact that in the 1970 census, 1.3 million more women than men reported being married. This rather remarkable discrepancy may be partially explained by the greater reluctance of women publicly to admit to cohabitation. For men, the social pressures and derogation associated with "living together" are less severe, making them more likely to report being unmarried. Theoretically, then, cohabitation may be fairly widespread. Perevedentsev also suggests that some portion of the increase in the numbers of single men may be traced to cohabitation (Perevedentsev 1982a).

In Soviet law, as in many nations, cohabitation without official registration of marriage is illegal. But in the Soviet Union life can be particularly difficult for those who opt for this type of relationship. Couples will not be able to obtain formal permission to live in the same apartment (the so-called *propiska*). On vacation, they will not be able to occupy the same hotel room or even to visit each other's rooms after 11 P.M. And, of course, many other privileges are not available to such couples, such as a person's access to his or her partner's fringe benefits from work.

It is likely that if these restrictions were removed, and cohabitation legalized, the number of people who would choose this lifestyle, at least for a while, would increase remarkably. Moreover, there is good reason to assume that if cohabitation were officially sanctioned, promiscuity would diminish drastically. The absence of the officially recognized "half-way step" between being single and being married pressures couples into wedlock before they are truly ready, increasing the likelihood that dissatisfaction and infidelity will result. However, such official recognition would be too revolutionary to expect that it will occur too soon. Even in the United States, where nearly two million adults shared a residence with an unrelated person of the opposite sex (Glick and Norton 1977) and condemnation of "living together" seems to be decreasing, no official recognition is likely.

However, in Soviet society, some first signs of the change of attitudes toward "unofficial marriage" can be detected. When the authorities are preparing to allow some novelties in Soviet life, they give permission to translate some foreign books that treat the subject positively. Recently, a review on the book of Yugoslavian author, Bosanats, *Extramarital Family*, appeared in *Sotsiologi-*

cheskiie Issledovaniia, the Soviet sociological journal. Moreover, the reviewer did not condemn the discussion of extramarital relations and suggested to readers that the "extramarital family" is an institution deserving attention, and even a place, in socialist society (*Sotsiologicheskiie Issledovaniia* 4, 1982, pp. 491–93).

THE ISSUE OF SINGLE MOTHERS

A growing number of women not only prefer to remain single, if they cannot find a suitable mate, but even choose to have an "incomplete family," one with children but no husband. The proportion of women living alone with children has grown steadily, if not rapidly.

In 1959, the number of single women with children constituted 11.9 percent of all urban families in the country; in 1979 the figure rose to 12.5 percent (*Vestnik Statistiki 2*, 1983, p. 70; Darskii 1978, p. 47). These include not only divorcees who cannot remarry under existing conditions, nor only women deceived by men promising to lead them to the altar, but more and more women who deliberately conceive a child out of wedlock, having no desire to establish a family with the child's father.*

Gone are the days when a woman conceiving a child out of wedlock was regarded virtually as a leper. Now a single woman who decides to conceive a child may even be viewed as a heroine: she has vowed to raise a son or daughter alone, without anyone's assistance. Official ideology and public opinion, no longer insisting on the conditions under which a child may be conceived, are united in encouraging the single mother and to lending her moral and material support.†

Advocating this stance toward single mothers, Igor Bestuzhev-Lada, a well-known Soviet sociologist, exclaims, "And to a women with a child, who lives alone without a husband, or if she has acquired a child alone—in any case: Thank you, mother, for your difficult work in bringing up a future citizen and for the creation

---

*This same process is occurring in the United States. During the 1970s, while the number of "non-standard" households (i.e. those without a married couple present) as a whole rose by 25 percent, the number of single parent households headed by women increased by 72 percent.

†The first Soviet film that portrayed the fate of a woman who gave birth to a child out of wedlock was *A Man Was Born*, starring Olga Bgan. In the late 1950s, this movie made a great impression on the public, still terrorized by Stalinist bigotry.

of the fundamentals of the future economy and culture of the country!" (*Literaturnaia gazeta*, September 14, 1983). And in the Soviet film, *Moscow Does Not Believe in Tears* (1980), the single mother is portrayed with understanding and sympathy.

It is notable that the lenient public attitudes toward women with illegitimate children continue to encounter opposition from part of the Soviet population, which maintains that such attitudes favor wanton sexual lives and encourage irresponsibility among young people. However, these attempts to restore the traditional hostility to such women do not receive the support of either the mass media or the general public (see *Literaturnaia gazeta*, November 30, 1983).

PREMARITAL SEX IN THE SOVIET UNION

It is also important to clarify the role of premarital sexual relations in connection with our exploration of anti-marriage attitudes (although, of course, premarital sexuality need not imply rejection of marriage). Obviously, when premarital sexuality faces official restrictions and hurdles, antimarrige attitudes are more difficult to translate into behavior. Indeed, many couples may be driven to marry largely because this makes it possible for them to have privacy: living with parents, especially in relatively crowded apartments, provides few opportunities for couples to be alone. But as official—and more important, public—attitudes toward sexuality in general have relaxed, it is more likely that a part of the population (especially men) will be able to translate their reservations toward marriage into practice.

As noted, Soviet sociologists have very limited opportunities to study sexuality, let alone publish the results of research they may have been able to conduct. Thus, as in other situations, the available data are scarce. As we explore what information there is, we will continue the pattern of treating attitudinal and behavioral measures separately.

Beginning with attitudinal data, the information available suggests that Soviet people support a fairly high level of permissiveness in premarital sexuality. The most serious investigations of this issue were those of Golod (1977) and Kharchev (1979) conducted in the 1960s when sexual freedom was more restricted than now. According to Golod's study of workers in Leningrad, only 24 percent of men and 34 percent of women expressed disapproval of premarital sexuality. Sixty percent of the men reported that they would have sex with a woman even if they did not love her. Only 14 percent of women, however, would engage in premarital sex (Golod 1977, p. 49).

In Kharchev's study of students and engineers in Leningrad, even greater tolerance for premarital sex was found. Among students, only 16 percent of men and 27 percent of women expressed disapproval. Interestingly, among engineers, fewer women (7 percent) than men (14 percent) disapproved of sex before marriage. And it is notable that, of all students and engineers expressing disapproval, only about one-quarter of men and one-third of women cited moral considerations as important to their decision (Kharchev 1979, pp. 193–95).

Perhaps even greater tolerance still is revealed in a study in Estonia, conducted in 1972. Women who engaged in premarital sex were disapproved of by only 11 percent of male, and 12 percent of female, respondents. When men's premarital sex was at issue, only 5 and 6 percent of men and women respectively indicated disapproval (Tiit 1978, p. 14).

As is true with many of the attitudes examined, different degrees of support are related to educational levels, as well as age, of respondents. Data from a survey of the Ukrainian city of Chernovtsy, conducted in the late 1970s by Nemirovskii (1982, pp. 119–21), show somewhat less approval of premarital sex among the less educated. Only 39 percent of this group gave unqualified approval of sex before marriage. It is notable, however, that more than one-third of those expressing disapproval based their decision on pragmatic, rather than moral, grounds. Among the students in higher educational institutions, Nemirovskii found levels of approval consistent with those of similar students in other cities.

Some other data make regional comparisons on this issue possible. The survey of high school students in the Azerbaijanian city of Lenkoran, cited above, reveals that young people in a Moslem republic are not very different in their permissiveness from students in the European part of the USSR. Asked about premarital sex, only 15 percent of urban students and 18 percent of rural students expressed disapproval (Mansimov and Foteieva 1982, p. 130).

While these studies are suggestive, the Soviet data on sexual behavior (which are treated officially almost as military secrets) are scant, and it is difficult to make valid international comparisons on attitudes toward premarital and extramarital sexuality. I would gingerly speculate that, though "ahead" in extramarital relations, the Soviets are still "behind" U.S. society in premarital sex.*

We can now turn from studies of attitudes to behavioral data. In the early 1960s, one of the first surveys on sexuality in Leningrad found that 88 percent of male, and 46 percent of female, respondents had had premarital relations (Kon 1967, p. 152). A more recent study, conducted in Estonia, revealed that 82 percent of men and 71 percent of women had had such experiences (Tiit 1978, p. 142).

In the 1960s, Kharchev and his colleagues conducted a unique survey based on in-depth interviews with women in Leningrad. The results showed more than half the respondents had begun their sexual lives before marriage. Many of them, however, had done so with their future spouses, probably the most common pattern. The study also gathered information on the age of the respondents at their first sexual experience. The largest group (44 percent) had their first experience at age twenty or twenty-one. About 12 percent had a sexual encounter between age 15 and 17, another 22 percent between 18 and 19, and 8 percent at 23 or 24. Only 14 percent waited until age 24 or later (Kharchev 1979, p. 196).

The number of children born before marriage, while obviously an underestimator of premarital sex is probably the best "hard" indicator of its scope. According to data cited by Kon (1982, p. 118), the proportion of children in Leningrad conceived before marriage has been increasing. In 1968, 23 percent of all births were conceived before marriage, 28 percent in 1973, and 38 percent in 1978. Tolts's study in Perm found one-fourth of married women gave birth to their first child within five months of the weddings (*Literaturnaia gazeta*, December 21, 1983). These figures include children born at any point before this five-month mark, even before the marriage itself.

Other indirect measures suggest the increasing frequency of premarital sex. We can use data on the numbers of children born to women between 15 and 19 years of age, since only 3 percent of 16 to 17 year old women are married and only 19 percent of those

---

*By Soviet standards, the sociological data demonstrate a considerably relaxed sexual morality among Soviet youth. Yet, data imply even greater tolerance in these matters among their counterparts in the U.S. In a study from the early 1960s, before the "sexual revolution," no more than 14 percent of young women condemned sex before marriage. Among young men, the figure was naturally lower at 5 percent (De Lamates and MacCorguodal 1964, p. 90).

between 18 and 19. Perevedentsev shows the number of children born to these young women rose by one-third over the last two decades (1982a, pp. 13 and 20).

As was indicated in the discussion on extramarital sex, data on unwed mothers cannot distinguish between pre- and extramarital sexual activity. All available data identify only the marital status of the mother and tell us nothing about that of her partner. While it is unlikely that all partners had the same marital status as the survey respondents, we can assume that as the age of such mothers decreases, the probability is higher that her child was the result of premarital sexual activity.

This also alerts us to the unsurprising fact that there are similarities between the antimarriage model and the model of permissive marriage. Both rest on a basis of less restrictive sexual morality, manifested in the reluctance to equate "legitimate" sex with the institution of marriage. Adherents of these lifestyles, then, consider sex outside of marriage as acceptable, at least for themselves if not for others.

Nevertheless, when comparing these two models, it must be pointed out that their statuses in Soviet society are not equivalent. Given the dominant official values and the support of marriage as an institution, the permissive model is more commonly regarded as acceptable for "me" but not for "others." As we have seen, only rarely have attempts been made to legalize this marital pattern and raise its status to a model legitimate for all "others."

While the antimarriage model cannot be praised widely in mass media or literature, at the private level, defense of the single life is not viewed as an infringement of official morality. Although marriage is avoided, this model does not violate the principles of marriage. All in all, the differences between these patterns does not seem greatly to influence the results of surveys on sexuality. Respondents are no more sincere in discussing premarital contacts than extramarital ones.

CHILDLESS FAMILIES AND ANTIMARRIAGE SENTIMENT

I have already discussed the role of the number of children in the modern Soviet family, emphasizing the significance of having more than one child. Let us now consider couples who have no children at all.

A growing number of Soviet families are childless, a fact that frightens both Soviet demographers and the authorities. In some way, a childless family can be regarded as a prototype of relations between a man and a woman outside marriage; or, to put it otherwise, the number of childless families today may be a good predictor of single people tomorrow for it implies a changing meaning of the significance of marriage.

We have two kinds of data on this subject—the proportion of families without children and the proportion of people who do not want children. In 1970, 21 percent of families had no children, with the proportion being roughly uniform in urban and rural areas (20 and 22 percent, respectively). Of course, many of these families are young couples who have not yet had their children. Nonetheless, regional differences in these figures suggest that childlessness involves not only a delay in having children among young couples, or some physical inability to conceive by one or the other spouse, but also a special pattern of behavior that excludes children from married life.

Regional comparisons show the higher the average level of education, and the more urbanized and Westernized the region, the higher the proportion of childless couples. The table below shows three areas, arranged in descending order of education, urbanization, and Westernization:

TABLE 8.2: Percentage of Childless Families in Three Regions by Residence (Urban or Rural), 1970

	Urban	Rural
Latvia	25	33
Bielorussia	18	25
Uzbekistan	15	10

Source: Compiled from data in Riabushkin, T. (ed.). 1978. Demograficheskiie Problemy Sem'i. Moscow: Nauka, p. 67.

We find the same pattern is controlled for age of the wife. Among families with wives aged 25 to 39, 9 percent of Latvian families were childless, with 5 percent in Bielorussia, and 4 percent in Uzbekistan (Riabushkin 1978, p. 67).

Of special interest are data related to women 35 to 39 years old, an age at which few women begin to procreate. According to Zoia Iankova, 6.8 percent of women at this age were childless (1979, p. 35). It is interesting that this figure is almost identical to that for U.S. women of the same age (see Pankhurst 1982, p. 498).

Turning to attitudinal data, we tend to find that quite a few survey respondents actually claim steadfastly that they will never have children. But when assessing Soviet data on this issue, it is important to remember that having children is highly respectable in both public opinion and official ideology.

L. Chuiko found that almost the same number of Kiev brides and grooms (20.9 percent and 21.5 percent) declared at the moment of the official registration of their marriage that they did not want children at all (Chuiko 1975, p. 107). Of the students in Tartu University, 12 percent said that children did not have "any importance" in marriage (Blumfelt 1971, p. 107). Only 7 percent of village dwellers in Bashkiria considered children the main condition of a stable and happy marriage (Nafikov 1974, p. 84). The survey of working Leningraders brought forth an even more remarkable figure: 26 percent of men and 28 percent of women disagreed with the statement that children are necessary to family happiness (Dmitriev 1980, p. 63; see also Antonov 1980, pp. 174–75.

In addressing this subject, young childless marriages are of special interest. Among these marriages we must single out those couples who simply postpone having children, those who plan not to have any, and those who are uncertain because they are not sure of the stability of their union.*

The first two categories postpone propagation, or even reject the idea of having children altogether, because they are unwilling to endure the privations that come with the birth of a child. The mounting material aspirations of the Soviet people have also contributed to the increase in the number of families with no children, or with only one child. It takes many more resources— material and emotional—and much more time to bring up a child today than it did a few decades ago.

As Valentina Belova, a well-known Soviet demographer states, children have become too expensive, especially under the conditions of urban life: "Too expensive, and not so much in the material sense, as psychologically, emotionally. A child is becoming a luxury not only because it is difficult to keep him

---

*According to a Leningrad study, fewer than one-fifth of all respondents think that the young couple should immediately have a child (Boiko 1980, p. 71). A survey conducted in Vilnius reveals that only 15.3 percent of couples felt that newlyweds should have children in their first year of marriage. About one-third (32.3 percent) felt that a child should appear in the first one to two years, and another 19.2 percent proposed that couples should delay having children for three or more years (Katkova 1978a, p. 222)

materially, but because it is necessary to spend a tremendous amount of time and emotional effort" (Belova 1972, p. 9; see also Kozlov 1982, pp. 180–81).†

I have mentioned before that many Soviet parents actively take opportunities to lavish money and time on their children, as well as to use all their connections to assure for their children the most prestigious school or job. And, because so much energy can be spent on children, a significant number of people try to postpone the appearance of their heirs as long as possible, or even to forego it altogether. Again, the dialectic is at work when a child is born into a family. In some cases, the birth fortifies the marriage and distracts the attention of husband and wife from previous bickerings and struggles for power, time, and prestige.* But in many other cases, the same event produces the opposite effect because it forces a happy couple to divide their new domestic workload and drastically reduces their entertainment, their studies, and all other activities more pleasant than washing diapers and running around getting special food for the baby (see Boiko 1980, p. 60). Data obtained by Z. Fainburg in a large survey of Soviet workers in 1970–75, shows that people's evaluations of their life is inversely correlated with the number of children in the family (see Table 8.3).

Similar data were obtained in a Moscow study (Iankova and Rodzinskaia 1982, p. 51). So, women, for all their stronger "parental instincts" (or because of them), feel themselves much better off when they do not have to be preoccupied with children.

The same Moscow survey produced some data that partially

---

†Velikanova and Balaian in an article published in *Literaturnaia gazeta*, "Seventy Million Families and the Thousands of Problems that Worry Them," cite the results of a sociological study (they do not indicate the researcher). "A child costs a great deal in our times, and as he or she grows, the cost of up-bringing rises significantly. While maintenance of a small child demands about fifty rubles a month, 64 percent of all families spend 100 rubles a month on a teenager, and 32 percent over 120 rubles. Two working spouses spend one-third of their income on one child." The average monthly salary in 1982 was 177 rubles (*Literaturnaia gazeta*, October 26, 1983, p. 14).

*In a recent Soviet movie, *Remember to Forget* (1983), the heroine, Nina, in order to retain a prestigious husband, decides to bear a child. Then she gets the terrible news that the child has died soon after birth. She, however, does not want to forego her plan and she secretly adopts a child abandoned by its parents and presents it to her husband as their own. Learning that her own child is, in fact, alive, she decides to forget about it and does not put her marriage to the test.

TABLE 8.3:   Percentage of married people who evaluate their current life situation positively, by number of children

	Men	Women
No children	40.4	48.8
One child	30.2	33.9
Two or more	32.2	34.6

Source: Compiled from data in Fainburg, Z. 1981. "Emotsial' no–Kul' turnyie Faktory Funktsionirovaniia Sem'i." *Sotsiologicheskiie Issledovaniia*, 1, p. 146.

explain the figures cited in Table 8.3. Parents with children can spend significantly less time on culture and sports than childless couples. Thus, women with two or more children go to the movies 18 percent less than childless couples; the theater 44 percent less; sporting events 30 percent less; take trips 73 percent less; read books and magazines 24 percent less. The difference for men is of the same order—44 percent, 65 percent, 24 percent, 55 percent, and 18 percent.

The third category of childless young couples differs radically in the motive of their behavior from the other two. In these marriages, the couple does not want to have even one child simply because they suppose that they may break up soon. The experience of their peers, along with well-known statistical and sociological data, suggest to them that their tension and quarrels are likely to lead to separation and divorce. Indeed, Soviet studies show that about 11 percent of all marriages break up within a year of the wedding. And almost one-fourth of couples will not have a fifth wedding anniversary (Perevedentsev 1982a, p. 24).

It is natural that with such a vision of the future, young marrieds, wives especially, try to defer the appearance of the first child. Moscow sociologists asked women about what influenced their decision about having a first child. The quality of relations between the husbands and wives turned out to be the most important factor—83 percent of all respondents mentioned it. Other factors were health, 74 percent; material well-being, 66 percent; availability of an apartment, 61 percent (Khorev and Kisilieva 1982, p. 94). Other studies also suggest that a lack of confidence in the stability of the marriage accounts for absence of children in a family (see Fedotova 1977, pp. 146–55).

The demographic behavior of the Soviet people, in this case their attitudes toward the birth of their first child, again shows the importance of psychological variables in the explanation of people's lives. People living in the same social and cultural milieu choose different types of behavior in various domains. In this case, different perceptions of the importance of the stability of marriage, by women with the same demographic and educational traits, are related to different decisions about the size of the family.*

SUMMARY

The growth of hedonistic aspirations accounts for the increase in the number of those who postpone marriage either temporarily or forever. People with strong egotistical inclinations do not want to bind themselves with any kind of marital ties. The opponents of marriage and the family are mostly men; however, the number of voluntarily single women is also growing.

The scope of this phenomenon greatly bothers Soviet authorities who, in various ways, try to dispel antimarriage attitudes among young people. At the same time, the number of "extramarital" families is growing: cohabitation among young people who have not formalized their relationship, as well as single mothers.

The rejection of marriage is naturally combined with the wide scope of premarital and extramarital sex. By all accounts, Soviet people's attitudes toward premarital sex, especially the young, is quite permissive, and not dissimilar to the attitudes of young people in the United States.

---

*Two American authors, Sharon Houseknecht and Jerry Pankhurst, studying attitudes of Americans toward children, also maintain that the pure "structural approach," with its stress on such factors as educational level, women's occupational activity, health, and other factors related to urbanization, cannot account fully for the dynamics of demographic variables, such as family size. They refer particularly to the role of changes in the cultural environment, which has strong influence on the choice of family size (see Houseknecht 1982; Pankhurst and Houseknecht 1983).

9

The Single Woman, Courtship, and Soviet Ideology: "Love has to be Spontaneous"

In the conflict between different images of ideal and actual marriages that have prevailed in the Soviet Union, the mechanisms of meeting and courtship have come to be of very sensitive importance. Each model of marriage assumes its own image of how both young people should start on their way to the altar.

The official romantic image of marriage supposes that the first meeting of the future bride and groom should be spontaneous. It strongly and persistently rejects the idea that this meeting can be arranged by someone who thinks that the given pair could create a happy matrimonial alliance.

This remarkable allegiance of Soviet ideology to spontaneity—especially when they tend to be opposed in most other domains—can be imputed to the circumstances under which the romantic model of marriage was born. Engels once remarked that if the bourgeoisie had been atheistic, proletarian ideology would have had no other choice but to be religious. This remark gives us a clue to understanding this devotion of Soviet officials to spontaneity in the courtship process. The point is that bourgeois marriage was condemned by the founders of the new ideology for its "mercantilism" and disregard of romantic love as the sole moral justification of marriage. Therefore, any forms of matrimonial prearrangement, any devices used to get two people acquainted with the prospect of marriage, were regarded as dictated by mercantilist considerations—and thus, Marxists declared all such devices to be incompatible with the new morality.

Matchmaking, which was broadly the custom in prerevolutionary Russia, had become, after the Revolution, an object of special criticism and derogation. This service became a symbol of the mercantile approach to marriage, a symbol of the hostile attitude of the old morality to love and to the rights of young people to choose partners for themselves. As a result of the long deprecation of matchmaking services in the mass media, literature, and film, the negative attitude toward it was deeply entrenched in the Soviet mentality. For practical purposes, this institution ceased to exist in the majority of Soviet regions, except for the Moslem republics.

In the mid-1960s, Soviet intellectuals launched an offensive designed to create a new matchmaking service based on the achievements of modern science. This initiative of Soviet intellectuals constituted one of the elements of a general upsurge of social activity by Soviet scholars which, as it is known, occurred in the first period after the coup of October 1964. The matchmaking problem seemed to be a worthwhile object of scientific attention. The point is that by that time, the real magnitude of the social problem of the plight of single women drew the attention of the public. Only then did the public mind become aware that this issue concerns about 28 million women.*

THE PLIGHT OF SINGLE WOMEN

The media, in particular *Literaturnaia gazeta*, began to discuss the plight of single women in the late 1960s. Very soon it became clear that single women constitute an enormous group of the population who feels itself deprived of one very important precondition for a happy life—a normal family.

---

*According to the census of 1970, the percentages of unmarried women in each age group were surprisingly large, as the table below illustrates:

Age	Percentage	Age	Percentage
20–24	44.1	40–44	21.0
25–29	16.3	45–49	28.1
30–34	14.7	50–54	39.7
35–39	16.1		

Source: Kharchev and Matskovskii 1978, p. 102

Irina Gerasimova, in a special demographic investigation in Kostroma, found that in 1969 and 1970, one-third of women aged 30 to 55 were unmarried. About 10 percent had never been married and more than 20 percent were divorced (1976, p. 100).

In Stalin's era, with its pathos of selflessness and self-sacrifice, with its complete and officially proclaimed subordination of the interests of the individual to the common cause, the interests of society and the state, the plea of single women for help would have been absolutely incomprehensible. It would have been treated as a direct challenge to the official ideology and an attempt to divert the attention of those toiling to build the new society.

Since 1953, however, the role of the individual has been gradually moving forward, and by the mid-1960s, the individual's prosperity came to be regarded as a goal of almost the same importance as the strengthening of the state. It was even proclaimed at the 25th Party Congress that increase in the standard of living was a major objective of the Soviet state (Brezhnev 1976, p. 44). With this evolution of Soviet ideology, the problem of single women was legitimized by Soviet authority, and thus, intellectuals could approach it publicly.

THE FIRST DISCUSSION ON DATING SERVICES

After the first contact with the problem of single women, intellectuals decided that a solution to the problem lay in addressing the difficulties women had in meeting potential partners. Rapidly, a particular image of the problems of single women took shape in the public mind. Typically, such a woman is in her thirties and divorced with one child. She works in a women's collective and her child goes to kindergarten. After work, this woman must pick up her child, take the child home, and provide care and nurturance in the evening. She must tend besides, to various chores, including shopping for food—a task that will require spending a number of hours standing in lines. It becomes clear that this woman has little chance of meeting new men and developing relationships that might lead to marriage.*

Consistent with the atmosphere of the period, as Soviet intellectuals began to discuss the plight of single women, they

---

*Although close relations between people are much more frequent in Soviet society than in the West, many single women in the Soviet Union suffer from a lack of intimate friends, which makes their plight even more bitter. As a rule, these women do not go to church and cannot find consolation in confession or in other contacts with priests, a fact that explains why the loneliness of these women is often so desperate.

encompassed the problem with a technocratic, scientific vision of the world (characteristically, the discussion was initially advanced in *Literaturnaia gazeta*, largely by cyberneticians and computer specialists). While common among certain strata in the West, the Soviet version of this vision was reinforced by the spirit of the planned society. In this context, nothing could be more natural than the application of the full might of science to the problem of these millions of women. Activists in this cause were convinced that officials would recognize the potential of a scientific approach and would lift the ban on dating services. Clearly what the advocates did not have in mind was the old, greedy, prerevolutionary matchmaker, roving from one house to another trying to sell her living commodity—a voiceless girl yearning secretly for a nice boy. (About "dating services" in prerevolutionary Russia, see Zhirnova 1978; Fisher 1980.) Indeed, it is indicative that single women themselves tried to argue for dating services by reference to the progress of science. One-third of those who participated in the first exchange in 1969 insisted that nowadays science has made it possible to avoid the sufferings that befall single women.

The initiators of the discussion regarded the "dogma of spontaneity" as strange and illogical, not only because it was incompatible with science; they also pointed out that such a dogma was at odds with the practice of the Soviet state. Indeed, on the one hand the Soviet state was inspired by belief in its unlimited right to interfere in any aspect of private life; on the other hand, the same state rejected the idea that people could be helped by society in their search for a partner, even when the people themselves asked for this help. Soviet intellectuals could not help being irritated by this pretentious and preposterous delicacy of a state known for its cruelty toward the individual.*

Whatever the intellectuals' contempt for the ideological opposition to dating services, they could not ignore it. Initially

---

*There was another aspect of the controversy about the role of society in matrimonial affairs. A number of people, mostly young and self-confident, regarded outside aid in searching for a partner as something encouraging individual weakness, inertia, and feelings of inferiority. About 30 percent of the participants in the 1969 exchange in *Literaturnaia gazeta* who were against the idea of dating services advanced such an argument and contended that a self-regulating marriage market could provide everyone with a partner if he or she was ready to exert energy and persistence. This debate is reminiscent of the eternal argument between proponents and opponents of a laissez-faire policy of economics (Shlapentokh 1971).

they tried to manipulate official values in order to show that the proposed innovation would not be in opposition to any Soviet ideological dogma. Thus, in the mid-1960s, the advocates of dating services persuaded vigilant officials that their proposal would not undermine traditional methods of meeting partners and would be applied only to a fraction of the population. This clarification was necessary because the Soviet mentality tends to assume that any alteration in the existing order has to be immediately implemented by the state everywhere.

It was no less important to persuade officials that dating services were not directed against love. Partisans of dating services did not spare efforts to convince ideologues that the relationships generated by this service would be regarded by both individuals as extremely preliminary and that managers of the services would not drag the partners immediately to an office where marriages were registered. It was particularly essential to convince officials that dating services did not have to be regarded as an egregious enemy of romantic love, that in an interval between the first contact of two persons and the wedding, if it took place, love could develop at any moment.

For all these reasons, the role of dating services only as a tool to accelerate first contacts between single persons was the predominant theme in the first discussion in the late 1960s. Two-thirds of the participants in the discussion held this view.

In letters to the *Gazeta*, 31 percent of the writers remarked that the style of contemporary life made it very difficult to find an opportunity to meet a new person. Eighteen percent underscored the fact that many people worked in strictly female or male collectives and were, therefore, deprived of a very important chance of meeting someone of the opposite sex. This is important because sociological data show that up to one-half of all people are introduced to their future conjugal partners at the office, factory, or university (Kharchev 1979, p. 215; Kharchev and Matskovskii 1978, p. 73).

Moreover, one-fifth of the letters pointed to the problem of shyness and feelings of inferiority among women facing these difficulties, further underscoring the need for some kind of service.

Initially, in the mid-1960s, advocates of the dating services tried to present themselves as consistent with the official image of romantic marriage still steeped in the Stalinist perspective. By the late 1960s, however, they allowed themselves to deviate from this image and gravitated toward the pragmatic model of marriage, thereby stressing the practical merits of married life rather than love. This approach stressed the presumed importance of distinguishing between "a priori love" and "a posteriori love," i.e., between love that emerges before, and thus leads to marriage, and love that develops after the wedding. Emphasis on the second type of love bolsters the argument favoring dating services in connection with the pragmatic image of wedlock. It was in this second stage, in the late 1960s, that *Literaturnaia gazeta* began this discussion, referred to above, inviting readers to send in their viewpoints on dating services.

It can be noted that the *Gazeta* played a special role in the 1960s. As a product of the post-Stalin political thaw, this publication gradually developed into the official mouthpiece of liberal intellectuals. During this period, *Literaturnaia gazeta* was publishing the most controversial articles of any Soviet journal, raising issues that were considered taboo,* and in the process gaining remarkable popularity among the intelligentsia.†

The decision of the *Gazeta* to initiate public discussion of dating services was an undertaking to which ideological purists shut their eyes. The discussion lasted more than a year, during which time the newspaper received about five hundred letters. The content analysis of these letters, done in 1970 by my sociological unit, found that three-quarters of the letter writers were in favor of the creation of dating services. One-quarter were more or less in

---

*In the first survey, respondents (subscribers to *Literaturnaia gazeta*) were asked an open question about which kinds of articles and discussions most attracted their attention. Extraordinarily, 79 percent of respondents answered this question; usually in Soviet surveys a question like this would elicit responses from no more than one-third of respondents.

It is worthwhile to note that articles and discussion about issues of morality were read by 84 percent of respondents, while only 51 percent read articles less critical and controversial on the economy (Shlapentokh 1969, p. 175).

†Before our first survey, the editorial boards of all Soviet national papers were convinced that their newspapers were read by people from all walks of life, including the editors of *Literaturnaia gazeta*. The survey, carried out by my laboratory on the sociology of the media, the Siberian Section of the Academy of Science, revealed that in 1968, four-fifths of all subscribers to the *Gazeta* had a college education. Scholars constituted 17 percent of subscribers, engineers about 16 percent, students 16 percent, and secondary school teachers another 12 percent. People in literature and the arts made up 6 percent of the audience and physicians about 3 percent (Shlapentokh 1969, p. 146). According to some calculations, subscribers to the *Gazeta* represented as much as one-fifth of all scientific workers in the country (Sheinin 1980, p. 80). We can estimate that about half of all Soviet scholars, and a considerable part of the rest of the intelligentsia, read *Literaturnaia gazeta*.

opposition to the services. The most vocal advocates of the services were, as would be expected, single women between the ages of 30 and 50. The youngest letter writers, while not necessarily enthusiastic about the idea, generally took no firm stand against it. Those most hostile to dating services were the oldest contributors.

Conservative attitudes on the question were not only related to age but also to level of education: college-educated contributors objected to dating services much less often than those with only an elementary education. And people from small towns tended to be more conservative toward these services than those from larger cities, especially from Moscow and Leningrad. While 43 percent of small-town contributors voiced opposition to the services, only 14 percent of big-city ones did so.

From the very beginning, the discussion acquired a significance transcending the role of dating services and even the plight of single women in the country. Enthusiasts and foes of dating services alike realized that each argument for and against a form of matchmaking bore additional meaning: for or against the dominant ideology. Putting forth the advantages of dating services, its proponents targeted the official image of marriage as one of the typical hypocritical products of Soviet ideology because this image supposed, against all evidence, that all Soviet marriages (unlike bourgeois ones) were based on love and were free of any mercantile calculations. But the recognition of hypocrisy in any field of Soviet life would have been a notable blow against the entire ideological construction and would have fostered a further erosion of Soviet ideology.

IDEOLOGICAL DENUNCIATIONS OF DATING SERVICES

If the political course of the elite had not drastically altered after the invasion of Czechoslovakia in 1968, and the process of the modernization of ideology ceased, the discussion about the dating service would have continued. However, by coincidence, the political atmosphere underwent significant changes just at the end of the discussion. Among the most indicative events witnessing the stark shift to the right were political trials and attacks against Sakharov and Solzhenitsyn; the dismissal of Tvardovskii from the position of the editorship of *Novyi Mir*, a paper more liberal along the political spectrum of that time than *Literaturnaia gazeta*; the deposition of A. Rumiantsev, a "legal" leader of the Soviet liberals from all his posts; and the dismissal of the directors of some Institutes of the Academy of Science who were regarded as "Rumiantsev people"; the ruthless purge carried out by M. Rutkevich, the new director of the Sociological Institute; and "the Levada case" (the persecution of a famous Soviet sociologist for his book). Also to be noted are numerous cases of victimization of the people who, during the 1960s, signed various letters of protest against the political trials and the restoration of the cult of Stalin.

It would be wrong to compare the discussion of dating services in its political meaning with all these events just mentioned. However, the logic of the ideological struggle, at least in socialist countries, has been such that when a political campaign is launched, it has a spontaneous tendency to extend itself into new areas, if only because people get the possibility of demonstrating their political loyalty or squaring accounts with their enemies and rivals, or simply of giving expression to their previously repressed desires.

In any case, six days after my article containing the major results of the analysis of the content of the letters came out in *Literaturnaia gazeta, Pravda* published an article, under the rubric "Rejoinder," rudely reprimanding me and *Literaturnaia gazeta* for our liberal attitude toward dating services, which in *Pravda's* opinion was incompatible with Soviet morality.

"Who is not aware," the article said, "that only the deep, inspiring and elevating feeling of mutual love, trust and respect unite and bind together a man and a woman and bring genuine happiness to a family? Yet, it is strange that literally not one word about love can be found in a long article by Dr. V. Shlapentokh that was published in the last issue of *Literaturnaia gazeta*." The author of the rejoinder continued, "What did this 'analysis' offer those who are burdened with loneliness and the dream of finding happiness in marriage? Nothing less than an omnipotent, super-efficient, electronic matchmaker—a marriage bureau employing the largest equipment. . . . Could this learned sociologist, and with him the editors of the newspaper, really believe that the public activity of Soviet people can find worthy application in fussing over the arrangement of a marriage bureau with an electronic matchmaker ejecting a mechanical list of the virtues of an optimal partner? Incredible! *Literaturnaia gazeta's* discussion, useful in intent about marriage and family, can hardly be said to have ended in the best way. *Literaturnaia gazeta* should hardly have used its columns to propagate an idea alien to our Soviet moral outlook, the idea of arranging marriage and family by calculation or even electronic matchmakers." (*Pravda*, June 16, 1971)

It was obvious, with all its rough and impertinent style, that this article could not have come out in the second half of the 1960s,* at a time when liberalism was still alive. *Pravda*'s article was perceived by the public as another ominous signal of the new trend in Soviet political life.†

The most ignoble aspect of the rejoinder of *Pravda* was presenting the case as if the author of the article in the *Gazeta* had expressed only his positive opinion on dating services, though

---

*The rejoinder of *Pravda* was published at the direct command of the Central Committee. The editors of *Pravda* were reluctant to publish it because they were sure that criticism of the discussion of marriage would be received by the public with disgust and derision as a symptom of the restoration of Stalinist customs, and they were not mistaken. Even conservatives were furious about the *Pravda* snub. Nor did foreign radio stations miss an opportunity to deride Soviet ideological purism, which challenged the usefulness of the computer, at least in one field.

The editors of *Pravda* also had one special reason not to be very enthusiastic on this subject. The problem was that the first survey of readers of *Pravda* had been finished only a year earlier, and I had been the head of this survey. *Pravda*, then, would be taking a position against someone who had had its confidence and who communicated frequently about business matters with all the leading figures of the paper, including its editor-in-chief, Zimianin. This fact lent the *Pravda* rejoinder a further sinister color in that it showed that only very high officials, at the level of the Politburo, could have made the editors of *Pravda* do what they did. Among Soviet leaders, who exactly interfered is even now not known.

†The editors of *Literaturnaia gazeta* were especially confused. The qualifications of a Soviet editor are measured first of all by his presentiment of danger emanating from above, by his skills in foreseeing the reaction of leaders to published materials. Having allowed my article to be published without apprehensions, the editors of the newspaper seemed for a moment to lose self-confidence. They tried first of all to decode the meaning of the signal: was *Pravda*'s attack directed against the liberal line of the newspaper; was it a personal attack against its editor-in-chief, Chakovskii, on the eve of the writers' congress due to begin its work at the end of June; or was this article aimed at Soviet sociology as a whole, or separately against A. Rumiantsev, as the director of the Sociological institute? Other hypotheses were related to my Jewish origins, political reputations, and my inadequate role in the mass media. As the following events showed, almost all the hypotheses advanced were wrong. The article in *Pravda* was really directed only against the idea of dating services as incompatible with Soviet morals.

Of course, there were some negative consequences for me personally (*Literaturnaia gazeta* could not publish my articles for six years, and in the first two years after this event, I incurred some restrictions within the Institute). However, they turned out to be much less serious than could have been expected. At the same time, as always happens in Soviet society when authority strikes against someone, the *Pravda* attack made me a kind of "hero" among intellectuals, a martyr suffering for the cause of unlucky single women. Even people ill-disposed toward me expressed their support and, at the peak of public recognition, I was for the first time in my life elected to the presidium of the trade union meeting in my institute.

in fact he had been simply conveying the attitudes of the readers. So, *Pravda's* statement was an insult to millions of single women who had expected from the discussion some positive steps that could alleviate their condition. In this way, the chief organ of the Central Committee declared that old and preposterous dogmas were much more dear to it than the quality of life of a great part of Soviet population.* The action of *Pravda* halted for five years any discussion on the dating service and problems about it.

THE RESURRECTION OF THE DATING SERVICE ISSUE

Further developments were extremely curious. They exemplified the general evolution of Soviet ideology and its adjustment to the practical interests of the elite. The elite supports ideological dogmas only as far as they are linked directly to legitimation of its power and as far as they do not tamper with the implementation of pragmatic policy. It is not to be overlooked that this ideological flexibility of the Soviet elite should in no way be attributed to a real intention to expand the freedoms of the individual or the quality of life. This flexibility stems exclusively from the elite's perceptions about what is expedient for strengthening its position. It is another matter that sometimes the elite's actions may be favorable for the country and the people.

It is very typical that not only sophisticated connoisseurs of the Soviet elite, but also ordinary Soviet people are completely aware of this. Analyzing arguments that were used by the authors of letters sent to *Literaturnaia gazeta* during the first discussion, we discovered, to our great surprise, that very often these authors, ordinary women usually very far from any politics, made references to the decline of labor productivity, the growth of population, and the increase of criminality as trends that could partially be countered if single women could have a normal family.

---

*With a shift toward political reaction, the early 1970s were, however, not similar to Stalin's times. Therefore, outraged by *Pravda*, many people sent angry letters to this paper and to *Literaturnaia gazeta* condemning the rejoinder. Some of these letters were addressed directly to me. Of course, not all these letters were accessible to me for analysis.

The public reaction against the main official newspaper in the Soviet Union was also a remarkable indicator of changes that had taken place since the times when an article in *Pravda* was regarded as the ultimate and unquestionable verdict on any problem.

Soviet single women seemed sure that such reasons could better convince Soviet leaders to give permission for a dating service than sentimental considerations about happiness, love of children, and so on.

The disbelief of Soviet single women in the genuineness of the authorities' intentions to help them was clear also in the second wave of letters to *Literaturnaia gazeta*, six to eight years after the first wave. Among those who were part of the second wave of correspondence were a number of single women who had taken part in the first debate. The letters were full of rebukes addressed to Soviet leaders for their unwillingness to settle such a minor problem as the establishment of a dating service for almost ten years. These women reminded them bitterly that now they were much older than when the talks about the dating service had begun. How long would they have to wait, they asked, for the implementation of the idea? Another few years and the issue would have no pertinence for them, they lamented.

This time the elite had been forced to back down under the pressures of demographic problems that had been growing worse in the mid-1970s. The decline of the birthrate had worried Soviet leaders for a long while. Probably, the Soviet leadership would have acquiesced to this, had the relatively low rate (17 to 18 births to 1000 people) not combined with other perilous trends, especially the rise of the mortality rate. The general death rate started to grow in the early 1960s and continued to do so during the next two decades.

But the Soviet leadership was upset even more by two other trends closely intertwined with the previous ones—the rise of infant mortality and the steady increase of the proportion of the Moslem population in the country.

The gravity of demographic trends forced Brezhnev to speak on them in his report to the 25th Party Congress in 1976 (Brezhnev 1976, p. 74). (About these trends, see Davis and Feschbach 1980; see also the report about the conference devoted to demographic problems on the USSR in *Vestnik Statistiki* no. 3, 1983, pp. 65–81.) The official worries about demographic problems paved the way for the reanimation of the public debate on dating services. But Soviet intellectuals no longer wanted to hold to their defensive line and to present dating services only as an auxiliary remedy for fighting single women's problems. Aware of the elite's concern with demographic trends, they decided to enlarge the subject of a public discussion and to debate the fate of the modern family as a whole. Intellectuals started the new offensive against official dogmas with the suggestion that a scientific approach to mating was necessary not only for those who failed to find a partner "on a spontaneous basis," but also for all people, because the growth of the divorce rate showed that traditional mechanisms of choice did not work.

The advocates of the dating service this time were not afraid to declare almost openly that stability and happiness in marriage depended not so much on love before or after the wedding, but on the psychological and cultural compatibility of the partners. This time the enthusiasts of dating services united with those sociologists who professed the pragmatic model of marriage.

From this new perspective, the purposeful search for a partner should be treated not as a remedy against loneliness, but as an efficient way of achieving a stable and happy conjugal alliance for everybody. (By the way, already during the first discussion, one-fourth of all participants had pointed out the role of science in fighting divorce.) Enlarging the number of arguments in favor of the new approach to the selection of partners, partisans of dating services more and more often drew attention to such things as data on how long people knew each other before they married. According to these data, up to one-third of all Soviet newlyweds had been introduced to each other less than a year before marrying (Kharchev and Matskovskii 1978, p. 74; Kharchev 1979, p. 217). At the same time, comparison of those who had divorced with those who continued to live with their spouses showed that the first group had known their partners for a much shorter period before they married.

Of the divorced, 71 percent had been acquainted with their future spouse less than a year, compared to 39 percent of those who had stayed married (Kharchev 1979, p. 217). Thus, showing how important familiarity with the personality of a would-be spouse is, sociologists and demographers insisted that scientific methods could also be very helpful in this domain of human life.

Editors of Soviet newspapers, who usually only rarely have an opportunity to raise in their columns any issue of genuine public interest, reacted to the change of mood "above" very quickly. In 1976 *Moskovskii Komsomolets* (Moscow Young Communist) and *Nedelia* (Weekly) almost simultaneously started a new series of articles about dating services and related problems. *Literaturnaia gazeta*, which regarded itself as the initiator, found itself outrun by other newspapers.

The desire to get the edge on other periodicals forced the

journalists of *Literaturnaia gazeta* to fabricate something that could bring the paper back to its leading role in this development. Anatolii Rubinov, the head of the social problems department of the paper, and one of the leading figures in journalism, who initiated the discussion in 1968, hit on a trick. Instead of starting a new debate, he published in one of the November issues of the paper two fake advertisements for partners. Rubinov, one of the best of Soviet journalists, and perhaps the leader in the number of innovations in Soviet mass media, had his reward. The notices turned out to be a sensation.* The reaction of the public was unexpected by Rubinov himself. During a single month, the paper received about ten thousand letters from single people who proposed their candidacy to the authors of the notices.

THE SURVEY OF ATTITUDES TOWARD DATING SERVICES

Invited to conduct a study,† I decided that this time we should not limit ourselves to a content analysis of letters, but we should try to discern the attitudes not only of those who were personally interested in dating services, but of all kinds of people. But *Literaturnaia gazeta* could not dare to conduct a poll encompassing the whole adult population of the country. Such an investigation can be undertaken only with the permission of the Central Committee, and the editors did not want to take the risk of asking for such approval. However, the editors could give their consent to a poll among readers of the newspaper. To our delight, they gave it.‡

---

*The first read: "Divorced woman, age 32, height 162 cm, has 6-year-old child, construction technician, wants to meet man who loves sports, is cheerful and does not drink. Voronezh."

The second notice was addressed to single women and sounded very similar: "Single man, age 48, height 166 cm, education in the humanities, home-loving, would like to meet blond woman under 35 who loves the theater and symphonic music, Moscow."

†This invitation was also an extraordinary act of courage on the part of the editors because I had been personally criticized by *Pravda*. Publishing the article with the results of the new investigation in November 1977 (it was my last publication in a Soviet paper before I emigrated), I found myself as perhaps the only person in the USSR who, criticized by *Pravda*, could publish an article on the same subject without recounting and recanting his faults.

‡The Soviet elite does not like nationwide sample surveys that can produce scathing findings. Therefore, any opportunity of doing such a survey has been regarded by professional sociologists devoted to their science as a gift from God.

The survey was performed on the basis of a model of nation-wide random stratified sample we prepared initially for the *Pravda* survey (see Shlapentokh 1976, Muchnik *et al.* 1980; Petrenko and Iarosnenko 1979). The size of the sample was 1600.*

The design of the study singled out three groups among the readers of the paper,† according to their personal involvement in the problem of dating services: the involved—the authors of letters sent to the newspaper; the potentially involved—unmarried people; the least involved—married people. It was supposed that

---

Usually they have tried to employ such an opportunity not only to satisfy sponsors, but also to obtain some information that would be valuable for understanding those social problems impossible to study directly.

As will be shown later, this time we did not miss our chance either, and we managed, despite all constraints, to detect a new trend in the Soviet mentality.

*This time we had very little money allotted to us by the editors of *Literaturnaia gazeta*, in contrast to the bounty of the 1960s when sociology was in favor.

In any case, we had to obtain representative data under conditions that did not allow us to hire interviewers, as we had done in conducting the surveys for *Literaturnaia gazeta* in the 1960s. The lack of resources compelled us to contrive some way to overcome this financial setback. We decided to exploit the enthusiasm of advocates of the dating service, the enthusiasm derided by *Pravda* in the rejoinder to my article.

Our stratagem was this. According to our model, we randomly sampled regions and then cities where the survey would be done. Then we looked through the letters that had been sent in connection with the marriage notices in order to pinpoint those from cities included in the sample. Then we wrote to authors of these letters and asked whether they would like to participate in our survey as interviewers. Without pay, of course. As we expected, the overwhelming majority of them (about 90 percent) immediately said yes.

It should be noted that these people were mostly college educated. Special instructions and copies of questionnaires were sent to each volunteer. Our representatives were on duty in the newspaper offices and answered the calls of our interviewers from various parts of the country. In Moscow we gathered our interviewers together and instructed them personally.

Taking into account the disposition of our activists in favor of dating services, we paid special attention to the "effect of the interviewer," warning the volunteers to restrain from expressing their personal point of view on this subject with respondents.

†The readership of *Literaturnaia gazeta* consists mostly of people with higher education. At the time of this survey, 64 percent of all readers had a college education, at least in part, and 30 percent had a secondary education. Forty-two percent were men and 58 percent women. *Literaturnaia gazeta* has been the most "feminist" paper in the country since men constitute the majority of the readership of Soviet papers. One-fourth of the readers of *Literaturnaia gazeta* were under 30. Other Soviet papers, except for those specially oriented to youth, are much less attractive to young readers than this one.

these three groups would differ in many aspects from each other and that the support of dating services would decrease from the first group to the third. The major hypothesis of the study was that the less people are engaged personally in the problem, the less they would back dating services and the more they would tend to be in consonance with official morality.

The content analysis of the letters revealed that support of dating services by people who suffered most from loneliness had increased even since the previous study. By the beginning of 1977, only one percent of them objected to the idea (against 20 to 25 percent in 1969).

The portrait of the average author of a letter was more or less the same as it had been eight years before—a divorced woman with one child, 25 to 40 years old, college educated. Men, as in the previous case, were in the minority (20 percent of all authors of letters). It was curious that the proportions of men and women in this population turned out to be rather close to estimates of the numbers on the marriage market.*

Both categories of readers—the married and the unmarried—attracted our attention for different reasons. Single people who sent letters with complaints about their personal life and asked for help were naturally mostly advocates of dating services. But what were the attitudes of married people who took little part in discussions organized by the paper? Would they treat those who resorted to the paper for help as having nothing in common with them and demonstrating their incapacity to find partners without "shameful" assistance?

It turned out, however, that against the hypothesis married readers of *Literaturnaia gazeta* expressed their support of dating services with almost the same intensity as did unmarried people (see table 9.1).

Thus, the survey revealed that the great majority of Soviet intelligentsia approved the idea and challenged official ideology in this regard. Respondents practically dismissed the ideological dogmas on romantic marriage and expressed their support of a pragmatic model of marriage. Many respondents remembered the *Pravda* article with its denunciations of dating services and expressed scorn for it.

But the survey brought us even more interesting data evidencing notable trends in the Soviet mentality. Soviet ideology, like any strong ideology, excludes the pluralistic evaluation of any

---

*According to the calculations of A. Sinel'nikov, there were 28 million unmarried women and 5.5 million unmarried men in 1970 (1978, p. 163).

issue. From its perspective, all should share one and the same views and values on everything.

Our survey discovered that there had been some important shifts in the Soviet mentality away from this. I tried to interpret data on attitudes toward dating services in terms of the distinction between "values for me" and "values for others." In the questionnaire, we included questions not only about the general evaluation of dating services, but also two other questions about the respondent's willingness to use the service for himself or herself, or to recommend it to his or her close relatives.

With the dominance of a "black and white" approach to values, the difference in the answers to these questions should be minimal. A person who declines to resort to the dating service for himself should be reluctant to advise others to do so. However, if value tolerance prevails, then we would expect that the figures should be aligned according to the requirement of a Goodman scale: the number of people who do not consider a dating service as relevant to them personally should be less than the number of those who approve the idea at an abstract level. At the same time, the number of those who are disposed to recommend this service to their friends should be between the two magnitudes.

The empirical data confirmed our supposition. They not only met the major demand—"yes, in general"; "yes, for people close to me"; "yes, for me"—but the difference between figures turned out to be very impressive, which witnesses the high degree of value tolerance. Here are the figures for all respondents:

Approval of dating service as an institution—90%
Positive attitude toward use of the service by close relatives and friends—75%
Readiness to use the service oneself—47%

Other data from the same survey confirmed our discovery of value tolerance among the Soviet intelligentsia in this area. As I have already mentioned, one-quarter of all unmarried respondents declared that the question about the application of dating services was beyond the competence of public opinion and society and was the private business of the individual.

In some sense, this was the most sensational result of our study. Making out our questionnaire, we conceived possible attitudes of respondents in the framework of a scale—approval/disapproval of dating services. We assumed that respondents would express their opinions as a positive prescription to others.

TABLE 9.1: Support for dating services, by sex and marital status, 1977

	Percentage Supporting
Women	
Divorced	91
Never Married	90
Married	89
Men	
Never Married	87
Married	86

Source: Shlapentokh 1977.

In other words, we perceived our respondents as participants in collective elaborations of a social norm, which should be regarded as a guide or a command for all.

However, about half a million of the readers of *Literaturnaia gazeta* took a stance against any moral intervention of society in the selection of a partner. According to these people, society should only provide its members with facilities they can use, or not use, at their own discretion.

Our survey also seemed to reveal a high level of altruism in a considerable part of the paper's readership: 21 percent of all the letters sent to the paper in 1976 we labeled "altruistic" because the authors of these letters spoke of the marital problems of "others"–their relatives and friends. Only 56 percent of all the letters were "egotistical," devoted solely to what were allowed to be the personal worries of the letter writer. The tendency to the "privatization" of life is combined in the mind of the intelligentsia with strong respect for collectivist actions really positive and beneficial for the people–a phenomenon related to the special role of the intellectuals in socialist society as the mouthpiece of the voiceless masses.

The survey was also intended to solicit opinions about various kinds of dating services. A majority chose the friendship club as the most suitable and effective form of this service. The special marriage bulletin was next, followed by the data bank about possible partners, and by the publication of advertisements in ordinary newspapers.

It is interesting that most respondents had reservations about verbal descriptions of marriage prospects, supposing that only face-to-face encounter is a real way of seriously getting to know somebody. Because of this, the idea of clubs had the support of the majority. It would be interesting to learn the reaction of these respondents to video dating services, an innovation they will have to wait long for, considering the pace of technological progress in the USSR.

THE PRECARIOUS INSTITUTIONALIZATION OF DATING SERVICES

In the mid-1970s, authorities became more tolerant of public debate and action on dating services and the problems surrounding them. By the end of the decade, they began to move in the direction of support of public initiative in this field.* Special decisions in favor of dating services were made at different administrative levels.† The number of "over 30" clubs where single people can be introduced to each other has grown.

The authorities have given the green light to many actions unthinkable only a few years ago. After a delay of five years, a number of Soviet papers started regularly to publish matrimonial ads. Riga, the capital of the Latvian Republic, which (along with Estonia and Lithuania) is more Westernized than other regions of the USSR, became the most active city in the country in dating services. Advertisements also began to appear in the newspapers of Dnepropetrovsk, Odessa, Alma-Ata, and other cities. (See, for instance the advertisement in *Vecherniaa Odessa* [Odessa Tonight], December 5, 1983.) At the same time, a majority of editors around the country remained resistant to the idea for fear of

---

*The radical change in the attitudes of Soviet authorities toward dating services allowed Anatolii Kharchev to join the ranks of its advocates (see for example, Kharchev 1978, p. 215). But he does not mention in his publications that, after the *Pravda* attacks on dating services in June, 1971, it was he who agreed to prepare an article for *Literaturnaia gazeta* that, according to Soviet ritual, had to recognize the correctness of this criticism from above. (*Pravda* plays the role of setting the lead for all other Soviet periodicals.) In this article, Kharchev not only derogated the idea of dating services, but also sought to minimize the importance of public opinion, downgrading the significance of letters sent by single people to the newspaper (*Literaturnaia gazeta*, July 3, 1971).

†There are only a very small number of other examples of Soviet authorities supporting the initiative of public opinion. Among them can be cited the decision to allow the mother of a child born out of wedlock to indicate the name of the father on the birth certificate and the cessation of publication in a newspaper of a notice of divorce before the court session.

exposing themselves to charges of "undermining" morality (Eremeiev 1982, p. 105).*

Moscow as well, with some delay, has become an arena for various activities seeking to strengthen the family and aid the plight of single people. There are now in Moscow seventeen "clubs for those who are older than 30," which bring together, however, only ten thousand people. The statute of such clubs was, of course, approved by the Soviet authorities (Severina and Zaikina 1983, pp. 89–90).†

It is curious and yet so typical of Soviet reality, that even in the domain of matchmaking, illegal private initiative has started to confront the state. As soon as the population had become aware of the tolerant attitude of the authorities toward dating services, people began to act at their own risk, posting their personal ads on walls and bulletin boards (*Literaturnaia gazeta*, April 2, 1980; *Komsomolskaia Pravda*, September 16, 1980). Some boasted of the results of their initiative and suggested that that was how they had found their mates.‡ Moreover, some industrious persons, with their contempt for the clumsy state machine, started to organize their own matrimonial bureaus, which aroused the wrath of the authorities who cannot tolerate competition in any sphere.

The legalization of dating services also allowed some Soviet scholars to begin researching this area without fear of being accused of disseminating "alien bourgeois morality." Thus, the Department of Social Psychology at Moscow University made a modest contribution in this direction and argued that their research "will make dating services completely acceptable morally and adequate to those norms and images of human dignity that

---

*Another sign that Soviet society more and more officially recognizes the problem of loneliness as important is the creation of a Moscow special telephone service—"Confidence"—to answer calls from people stricken by a bout of loneliness who need to pour out their sorrows.

The creation of this psychological emergency service is not without ideological implications. It is evidence that Soviet people have to address their woes not to the secretary of a Party committee, but to professionals—doctors and psychologists.

†The composition of these clubs' memberships is the following: 65 percent have higher education, 30 percent are widows and 50 percent divorcees (Severina and Zaikina 1983, p. 89).

‡A curious fact. *Literaturnaia gazeta* (April 13, 1983) describes the adventures of a rogue who got three thousand positive answers to his marital advertisement, with three hundred pictures of would-be brides. Among the women sending pictures were a Ph.D., a TV announcer, and a professor. The valise with all this material was "investigated" by one of his victims, who told the story to a journalist friend.

are admitted in our society" (see Andreieva and Dontsov 1981, p. 229).

However, when the Soviet authorities lifted the ban on dating services, the problem lost all the pleasures of forbidden fruit. As a result, the idea has not only ceased to attract public attention but has become an object of criticism, even if very mild, by Soviet intellectuals themselves (see, for instance, Bestuzhev-Lada 1981, p. 130).

This very peculiar turn of events only underscores the importance of the ideological meaning of the controversy that lasted almost a decade. This controversy, as it now becomes conspicuously clear, was not about the fate of single women but about the freedom to discuss publicly such problems as dating services, love, and marriage. Having won the possibility of discussing all these problems more freely than before, Soviet intellectuals have almost immediately begun to look at dating services more critically. The fact of the disproportion of the sexes on the marriage market, which went almost unmentioned in the late 1960s, has moved to the foreground.

Doubts have begun to be expressed on the value of information about a partner before personal contact has been made. Almost everyone has started to speak about the danger of illusions that the dating service could suggest to single people, especially women (Shlapentokh 1977; Perevedentsev 1982a; Sinel'nikov 1978).

SUMMARY

The history of dating services in the USSR is a good illustration of the rigidity of the Soviet system and its hostility to innovations that may even be useful to it. With the entrenched dogma that love can emerge only spontaneously, the Soviet authorities long resisted the creation of dating services in the country, despite the ardent interest of millions of single women and the support of this idea by the majority of the population.

Only the drastic deterioration of the demographic situation in the country prompted the authorities to allow the activities of the enthusiasts in this domain. However, when the Soviet intellectuals won, and dating services began to function, it became evident that the ability of this institution to ameliorate the plight of single women is very limited. It appeared that the exaggerated expectations about it were produced largely by the intensity of ideological confrontations around this almost seemingly trivial subject that, in the Soviet context, was turned into an almost political issue.

10

Angry Soviet Women Against Their Men——

The disruption of the dominant system of values, the sharp conflicts between often mutually exclusive desires, and the gigantic educational and professional advances of women—all this has destroyed the previous fundamentals of relations between the sexes in Soviet society. The conflicts between women and men are now among the most salient aspects of everyday life of the Soviet people.

THE IMPROVING EDUCATIONAL STATUS OF SOVIET WOMEN

There are many reasons for the reluctance of growing numbers of Soviet women to accept marriage proposals. Clearly, one of the most significant factors in this connection is the improving educational attainment of women.

As has been indicated, tremendous progress has been made over the last decades in the Soviet educational system, and women have benefited especially from this. In 1939, 41 percent more men than women had over seven years of education. By 1982, the gap had dropped to 13 percent. Today, 63 percent of women have at least a secondary education, compared with 9 percent in 1939. The proportion of women with higher education, including graduates of technical schools, is now 30 percent—even greater than the 25 percent among men (*Narodnoie Khosiastvo SSSR*, 1922–82, p. 43; *Vestnik Statistiki* 1983,2, pp. 71–72). Women also constitute a majority of the professional occupations at 59 percent, up from 36 percent in 1941 (*Zhenshchiny v SSSR* 1982, p. 10).

171

By all accounts, in the near future this trend among professionals will continue because today women constitute the majority among students in the higher schools and the technical colleges, and the proportion of females among students has grown unremittingly since the beginning of the 1960s: In the higher schools, this figure rose from 43 percent in 1960 to 52 percent in 1981, and in technical colleges from 47 percent to 57 percent (*Zhenshchiny v SSSR*, 1982, p. 13; *Vestnik Statistiki* 1983, 1, p. 74).

The same process is occurring in the United States, although at a somewhat slower rate. Among white college students in 1969, women represented about one-third. By 1980, the figure grew to one-half. Among black students, the proportion of women has grown only slightly, from 55.1 percent in 1969 to 56.6 percent in 1980 (*U.S. Statistical Abstract* 1981).

The higher level of education among Soviet women, coupled with rising cultural aspirations and their high representation in professional occupations, has contributed to a rise in the expectations women have of potential mates. In the past, when the overall educational attainment of men surpassed that of women, husbands were more likely to be better educated than their wives, a circumstance that apparently enhanced men's attractiveness. Now the situation is different: in many cases, women are more educated than their husbands.*

The rise in women's education and the proportion of women engaged in professional and skilled work has stimulated more socially and educationally homogeneous marriages.† Soviet data

---

*In some respects, Soviet matrimonial conflict is similar to that among blacks in the United States. According to Alvin Poussaint, the growing divorce rate among blacks is to be attributed to the fact that black women are more likely than white women to marry men with less education than they have, which leads to friction in relationships. Another researcher, Stuart Taylor, came to the same conclusion. As his data show, the divorce rate is about 10 percent higher for black women who are college graduates, and it rises to 15 percent for black women with college degrees and one year of graduate school, and to 19 percent for those with two years or more of graduate school.

As one black woman in a survey (conducted by Price Cobbs) said, there is "absolutely a smaller pool of black men to choose from" (*New York Times*, May 24, 1982, p. A17). The difference in the salary of black women and of black men with a bachelor's degree is also notable. The salary of the black woman with a BA is 8 percent above the average salary for a white woman with a BA; the salary of black men with BAs is 39 percent below the salary for a white man with a BA (see Fencks 1983, p. 34).

†Operating with such broad and heterogeneous categories as "workers," "peasants," "intelligentsia," and "clerical workers" allows some Soviet researchers

show that no less than two-thirds of all marriages are between people with the same, or nearly the same, level of education. For instance, 65 percent of all Kiev women with a higher educations chose to marry men with higher education. This figure is close to another: 67 percent of women with an elementary education married men with elementary education (Chuiko 1975, p. 95; about Estonian data, see also Tiit 1982, p. 28; about Latvian data see Zwidrin'sh and Lapin'sh 1979, pp. 64–65). Data from Saratov's survey are similar. Sixty-three percent of all brides with higher education married men with this level of education, or one close to it (technical college). Only 2 percent married men with elementary education. For all the desire of this survey's author to suggest that in selecting their partners Soviets do not pay attention to education, she was to acknowledge that the proportion of homogeneous marriages among the intelligentsia has been growing over the last twenty years (see also Iankova 1979, pp. 119–20; Sankova 1981, pp. 119–23).

If, in the past, men, and some women, were compelled to be satisfied with mates having less education and a lower social status than they, now they both prefer to have mates who are their equals. Clearly this requirement should significantly narrow the options for men and, especially, for women, as the marriage market for the latter has been always worse than for the former.

The analysis of ten thousand letters sent to *Literaturnaia gazeta* in response to the fake lonely-hearts ads bears out this thesis. The great majority of the authors of these letters, in one way or another underscored that similarity of education and of social status was of utmost importance for them.

Analyzing Estonian data, E.M. Tiit says, "The survey data show that men usually express a desire to have women with the same education as their own, or even somewhat less. As for women, they

---

to argue that the rate of marriage within social groups is high and increasing. But when they move to data on educational level, they must recognize, if reluctantly, that the situation is rather the opposite, or at least less pronounced.

These discrepancies are not difficult to explain. As an independent variable, education has turned out to be much stronger than occupational status categories, like those mentioned above (see Petrenko and Iaroshenko 1979). Education makes a greater impact on lifestyle than most other variables, and this is no less true with reference to marriage and family life. It is significant that the four occupational categories mentioned above can be fairly heterogeneous with respect to education. Among urban workers, about 45 percent have secondary or more education, and 10 percent have higher education. About one-fifth have only elementary education. Educational diversity among clerical workers is even greater (*Vestnik Statistiki* 1983, 4, p. 66).

assume that the man's educational level should be in no way lower than their own." Labeling the marriage of people with the same education "ideal" (60 percent of couples in her Estonian survey can be so labeled), she observed that "women with higher education have more trouble finding husbands." But she notes that marriages of people with higher education are the most stable, a fact that underscores the role of spiritual factors in family life (Tiit 1982, p. 28). The same view is shared by the Leningrad sociologist A. Baranov (1981, p. 90).

How differences in education influence the stability of marriage can be shown in the examples of women teachers in rural areas. Coming to the countryside at the age of 21 to 23, most of them have to look for a husband in the villages. Only 19 percent of them find a mate with higher education (in the cities the figure is 49 percent). The rest of those who marry (more than one-third do not) have to acquiesce to having husbands with less education than they have. Unfortunately, the fate of educationally heterogeneous marriages, in most cases, is not good. Female teachers tolerate mates who do not match them in education for no more than ten years: 64 percent of all the divorces among the rural female teachers were such "mixed marriages." Observing what happens to their friends who married men incapable of sharing their lifestyle, single women can be vindicated in their decision to stay single and not to betray their ideal of a husband (see Shenderezka 1979, p. 77).*

WORK AND MARRIAGE

Occupational activity is one of the most important values for contemporary Soviet women. In 1970, 82 percent of Soviet women of working age were employed compared with 42 percent in the United States and more than in any other country (*Naseleiniie SSSR* 1974, p. 173).

It is curious that the women's employment should reach its peak when Soviet attitudes toward women working have significantly changed. While feminists in the United States have been

---

*Various U.S. data demonstrate the existence of an inverse correlation between the educational level of spouses and the degree of marital disruption. However, Sharon Houseknecht and Graham Grenier (1980) discovered, in their analysis of a national sample, that the positive effect of female educational level on marital stability is especially strong.

struggling vigorously for the greater recognition of women in the work world to lessen their dependence on men, the viewpoint in the Soviet Union has been undergoing an interesting evolution.

In the 1920s and 1930s, official ideology conducted a strong campaign to recruit women into the labor force, enlisting their aid in the development of the economy. Thousands of novels, films, and paintings glorified women ready to make great sacrifices for their work in a factory, on a collective farm, or in a research institute. The propaganda was largely successful and the idea that all women, without exception, should join the labor force became firmly entrenched in the public mind (see Stites 1978; Lapidus 1978, 1982). In the last two decades, however, public opinion, as well as official ideology, has softened the stance on this issue.

An important factor in this change has been the general decline in the significance of work as a social value. Consequently, there is a growing opinion that women are not obliged to enter the labor force to serve the common good. Moreover, there is growing awareness that women's role in the labor force accounts, at least in part, for some of the undesirable demographic trends in Soviet society, such as the falling birthrate. (It is interesting that the softening of public opinion on women's participation in social production has occurred at a time when the Soviet Union has been experiencing a growing shortage of labor, which is one of the major causes of Soviet economic difficulties.)

In any case, as late as the mid-1970s, two Soviet authors could challenge the old dogma that the higher women's participation in productive activity, the better (Kotliar and Turchaninova 1975, p. 8). Since that time, public opinion on this subject has evolved so far that V. Boiko, the Leningrad demographer, could insert questions in his questionnaire about the negative consequences of women's involvement in work outside the home. He offered 11 items to be chosen by his Leningrad respondents. One item—the "intellectual degradation of women"—was completely rejected by women themselves, as well as by men. However, every other item gathered a great number of votes among both sexes. Men and women were almost unanimous that outside employment creates troubles in the household—95 percent of the men and 91 percent of the women indicated this. After that, they put women's domineering (72 percent) and neglect of children (57 percent) (Boiko 1980, p. 208).

The radical change in public attitudes toward women participating in social production has gone so far that *Pravda* deemed it appropriate to publish a review of readers' letters with the following symptomatic title: "I am a housewife. Is that good?" The question in the article is only rhetorical. The author of the article, Piskareva, does not hide her sympathy for the role of the housewife. Of course, she is not against women's working, but she supports the old, traditional (in her own words) perception of a woman's first duty—to run the house and raise children. To her it is obvious that society should not blame women who stay at home and are completely absorbed with domestic chores. Quoting from letters mostly in support of housewives, she says that very often housewives work much harder than women in industry. "I get up first at home and go to bed last," writes a woman from Kharkov, "there is no end to housework and I have become like a perpetual motion machine" (*Pravda* October 21, 1983).

In order to legitimize the social utility of domestic labor, some daredevils among Soviet scholars (such as Andrei Volkov) even insist on reconsidering sacred Marxist dogmas about labor and recognize "work related to bearing and raising children as socially useful activity" and on overcoming "negative attitudes toward family and family life as something which is against the interest of social production" (*Vestnik Statistiki* 1983, 3, p. 68). The paradox is that at a time when public opinion mitigated its attitude toward nonworking women, and when the authorities stopped pushing women into the factories, Soviet women are more eager to work than when the propaganda was strident about women's active role in the economy.

In 1972–74, 470 married women in Moscow were asked their major objective in life—a career or a home: 86 percent of all the respondents refused to single out one of these goals and said "both" (Iankova 1975, p. 48).* There are a number of reasons for such a reply.

---

*The eagerness of women to work is demonstrated especially convincingly by some other information. After the birth of a child, a Soviet woman can get one year unpaid leave, beyond four months paid leave. (Since 1981, the allowances have in some regions of the country been increased to 18 months.) The state has made such an allowance because of a shortage of preschools and, especially, because it has had to admit that the quality of existing preschools was rather low and the health of children in them poor (*Pravda*, November 21, 1983).

However, only a minority of women take the one-year leave. A study in Tambov found that 32 percent of new mothers do not completely avail themselves of the leave; 37 percent were off work only 6 months, and only 31 percent stayed with a new child a year or more (Katkova 1978a, p. 39).

In a recent *New York Times* poll, U.S. respondents were asked, "If you were free to do either, would you prefer to have a job outside the home, or would you prefer to stay home and take care of your house and family?" Forty-five percent of the

First, a woman's salary has become an essential part of a family's income. Although the standard of living of the Soviets has grown significantly since the war, aspirations have grown much more, and without the wife's contribution, very few families could make ends meet. About one-fifth to one-third of working women say that they work mostly for financial reasons. Thus, in 1978, 22 percent of married Moscow women with two children said that if their husbands earned as much as they earned together, they would quit their job (Sysenko 1981, p. 76). Other authors indicate higher proportions—one-third (Iankova 1975, p. 43) or even one-half (Kharchev and Golod 1971, p. 42).

Second, for many women, work constitutes a source of prestige and recognition, inside the family as well as outside of it. Although the social status of a woman is not her most important merit in the eyes of men, a man's decision to marry a certain given woman or to divorce her is to some extent influenced by her place in society.*

Third, work is important for women because the workplace provides opportunities for communication with other women, as well as with men. There, women are able to discuss issues of importance with each other. Of no less significance is the fact that the workplace is the major arena for affairs, and in this capacity, it seems to be even more important than vacation resorts, which attract many people of both sexes for the same reason. Soviet novels and movies are replete with adulterous liaisons developing

---

respondents opted to work outside the home, while 47 percent preferred to stay at home with their children (December 4, 1983). Age and occupational status were significant variables. Among women aged 18 to 29, 56 percent preferred to work outside the home; and among women classified as professionals and managers, 63 percent opted for a career over homemaking.

*The importance of the prestige of work rises with a woman's age. In their twenties and thirties, many Soviet women, especially among professionals, are strongly involved in emotional relations with men. Then, entering the period when their age diminishes opportunities for flirtations, women more actively look for emotional satisfaction in work and in the prestige related to it.

This prestige is a recompense of special importance for women who, for different reasons (because they are not attractive, for example, or because they are emotionally cold), cannot tap the pleasures of life from romantic affairs. In many cases, these women are strongly career-oriented. If they are divorced or have never married, they can be completely absorbed by professional or public activities.

Women in the Party apparatus are quite often recruited from among this type of women. The apparatus not only develops their ambitions but also their cruelty and mercilessness. These Party women are one of the most despicable and horrible products of the Soviet system (one of them was vividly portrayed in Balter's novel, *Farewell, Boys*).

among coworkers in all types of production units, offices, educational institutions, and so on.

Fourth, the major motive for going to work, especially among young women, is their desire to be independent of men. A woman considers her independence a precondition of her equality in the marriage—to her, being able to warn her husband that she can leave him if he does not meet her requirements. Material independence opens the possibility of changing partners, a possibility a woman often did not have before. Material independence also protects a woman if her husband should leave her and her children. The growing rate of divorce reminds a woman how vitally important a job is for her—a job that provides a decent place in society and the means of subsisting on one's own.

We can get some sense of the varying importance of these reasons for married women to work outside the home from a survey conducted in Leningrad (Kharchev and Matskovskii 1978, p. 156). Over half (54 percent) the women surveyed cited the necessity of their incomes to their family finances. The desire to be "part of the collective" was given by 22 percent, while 14 percent stressed a desire to take part in social production. The desire to be materially independent of their husbands was cited by 11 percent.

Of course, when considering survey data like these, we must recognize that respondents can rarely make clear distinctions between motives. Their choice of alternatives can be strongly influenced by prestige, ideology, or other circumstances. In view of this, it is possible to suggest that motives overlap and that the desire to be materially independent of a husband may implicitly lie beneath the other motives.

This supposition is borne out by another Leningrad study. Viktor Boiko offered to his respondents (married people) a list of possible positive effects of women's occupational life. "Emancipation"—really a synonym for "independence"—was chosen by three-quarters of all the women. "Prestige" was indicated almost as frequently (65 percent), as was "communication with other people" (57 percent). "The stirring character of work," a quality not deprived of some sexual flavor (in the Soviet context) collected surprisingly many mentions (74 percent) (Boiko 1980, p. 208). For all these reasons, the modern Soviet woman is far from being ready to sacrifice her occupational life for the sake of marriage, or even children. In the conflict between work and marriage, work often gets the upper hand.

As has been mentioned, the family with two children is regarded in the Soviet Union today as a big family. Only 9 percent of Moscow wives with two children are agreeable to quitting their job to bring up their children. But, two-thirds said they were prepared to have only a part-time job—a fact that testifies to the social importance of work for women (Khorev and Kisilieva 1982, p. 99; see also Shishkan 1980; Katkova 1978a).*

Because of this, many women looking for a job move to cities, where their chances of finding a husband are significantly lower than where they came from. Many women go from the country to the city even though they thus often diminish the chance of finding husbands.†

The proportion of single women under 50 is significantly higher in cities than in the country. In 1970, among women 20 to 25, 9.7 percent were single in cities and 4.2 percent in the country; among women 30 to 39, the figures are 3.7 and 1.6 (Dsarasova 1979, p. 47; see also Nauduzhas 1982, p. 64; Belen'kaia *et al.* 1981, pp. 118–19). In all large Soviet cities the proportion of married women under 45 is smaller than in small cities. But in big cities, of course, opportunities for finding a suitable job are the best (Khorev and Kisilieva 1982, p. 62).

In the mid-1970s, the proportion of women among all those employed in Leningrad was 56 percent (against 51 percent in the country). Among people with higher education, 54 percent of those employed were women and among those with secondary education, 65 percent (Baranov 1981, pp. 63–74).

Some Soviet women think it necessary that they go to a place like Ivanovo, for instance, where women constitute the greater part of those employed in the textile industry and where only 44

---

*In another survey of Moscow women, sociologists discovered another type of woman who, remaining in school into her thirties (for example, in university and graduate school), stays single and gives birth to children out of wedlock, earning the title, "lone mother" (Barbash and Glushkova 1983, p. 61).

†"The girl question," as Alexander Nikitin, a well-known Soviet journalist, formulates the problem, has somewhat suddenly joined the pack of worries that plague Soviet agriculture. "A new problem again," writes Nikitin in an article devoted to agriculture in Central Russia, "is the shortage of brides. This is a problem that, as it looks, will paralyze cattle breeding farms and, a little later, even plant growing. (*Literaturnaia gazeta*, October 26, 1983). As women leave the countryside in large numbers, men become all the more reluctant to devote their lives to agricultural pursuits, if this drastically lowers their chances of meeting women.

percent of all the women over 16 are married (Perevedentsev 1975, p. 122).*

Millions of women continue to choose such "female" professions as teaching in secondary schools or librarianship, though all know that they will thus be working in a kind of women's collective and thus significantly lower their chances of finding men who will please them.

The study conducted in the mid-1970s gives a glimpse of the fate of women teachers. In the Russian Republic, 10 percent of city women under 30 have not married, and 20 percent of country women. For teachers, however, the figures are 23 percent and 36 percent. This means that in choosing the profession of teaching, women increase their chances twofold of remaining alone, for the probability of marrying after 30 is very slight for women. Of all the women teachers in the Sverdlovsk region, only 63 percent were married (Shenderezka 1979, pp. 77–78).

THE DEGRADATION OF SOVIET MEN

Alongside requirements that have emerged with the rise of the educational and occupational status of women, there are other factors that have significantly whittled down women's options on the marriage market. One of them is the degradation of a considerable part of the male population of the USSR, mostly by alcoholism.

---

*Although the majority of women consider migration, in the first place, as a means of finding a good job, a part of the female population regards it chiefly as a way of finding a husband. Again, Soviet women are divided in opinion on the priority of job or marriage, though the majority yearn for a combination of both.

In many cases, according to Viktor Perevedenstev, the most perspicacious Soviet researcher on migration, Central Asia attracts women from Russian regions mainly because they can marry there much more easily than in their native cities and villages. He found a high correlation between the proportion of unmarried women in a given region and the size of migration to the Moslem republics. In regions where 54 percent of the women above 16 are unmarried, twice as many women go to Central Asia than go from regions where only 48 percent of the women are unmarried. And migrants move back much more often if they come to Central Asia from regions with a relatively low proportion of unmarried women (Perevedenstev 1975, pp. 122–23).

It is likely that the attraction of Central Asia for Russian women lies in the well-known fact that men from ethnic minorities (in this case, Uzbeks, Tadzhiks, Turkmens, Kasakhs) very willingly marry women from the dominant ethnic group, the Russians (Fisher 1980).

There is much evidence that vodka has been taking a growing toll of the Soviets. According to Vladimir Treml's computations, the annual consumption of pure alcohol per person, 15 years and older, rose almost two times in the last two decades, from 7.45 liters in 1960, to 15.25 liters (1982a p. 68).*

Grigorii Zaigraiev, a department head in the Academy of the Ministry of Internal Affairs, who is much more privy to the actual data on alcoholism than "civic" sociologists, cites figures on the rise of per capita alcohol consumption in the postwar period. In the 1950s, the annual rate of growth was fantastic, at 10.5 percent. It slowed to 6.7 percent in the 1960s, and to 3.2 percent in the 1970s. The Lieutenant-Colonel consoles his readers with the evident decline in this growth rate. But he cannot obscure the fact that the amount of alcohol drunk by the average Soviet citizen continues to increase, even if at a slower rate—perhaps because the current consumption of alcohol has nearly reached the human capacity to absorb it.

Zaigraiev also presents data showing that the Baltic republics and Russia are the leaders in alcohol consumption in the USSR. Per capita consumption in the Baltics is 124.3 percent of the All-Union average, while in Russia it is 116.9 percent of the average. The Caucasian republics are evidently the lightest drinkers, with a per capita average 46.7 percent of the national level (Zaigraiev 1983, pp. 97–102).

Data on the number of people addicted to alcohol as well as the number of those who are "only" heavy drinkers in the Soviet Union are unknown. Vladimir Kudriavtsev, the director of the Institute of Law and a prominent Soviet sociologist, dared to publish the only figures that, according to him, reflect the number of chronic alcoholics: "on average for the period from 1955 through 1975" (a really very rare case of the use of such averages). Kudriavstev contends that there were 4.9 to 5.0 cases of alcoholism per 1000 people, and that this is lower than that of the developed capitalist countries. With all this, he cites other data that show that more than three-quarters of all crimes are committed in the Soviet Union under the influence of alcohol (1983, p. 113). The available indirect data on alcoholism allow us

---

*Data on deaths from alcohol poisoning indicate that the number of such deaths almost tripled between 1968 and 1978 and reached a level that was more than a hundred times higher than in the U.S. (Treml 1982b, p. 488; Murphy 1983, p. 38).

Of course, alcohol poisoning occurs for various reasons; however, the dynamics of this indicator reflects quite clearly the growth of alcoholism in the USSR.

to suspect that the figures mentioned by Kudriavtsev do not give an accurate picture of the problem. That male alcoholism is officially recognized as the most important cause of divorce bespeaks the extremely great scope of the phenomenon.* According to Soviet sources, up to 50 percent of all divorces result from alcoholism (Chuiko 1975; Goldberg 1982; Kolokol'nikov 1976; Matskovskii and Kharchev 1982; Sysenko 1982).

With 945,000 divorces in 1979, for example, this means that 200,000 to 400,000 men have been declared intolerable drunks by their wives (Zaigraiev 1983, p. 98). Of course, people do not always cite their real motives for divorce; however, in the case of alcoholism, it can reasonably be supposed that the number of people who falsely use it as grounds is at least equal to the number of those who conceal it as the main real cause. If we may assume that the majority of alcoholics do not remarry and that the number of subsequent divorces of the same people for the same reason is not significant, then the army of alcoholics must be replenished each year with new contingents and totals many millions of men.†

Also of interest, information on the scope of alcoholism in the USSR comes from no other person than the Minister of Internal Affairs, Fedorchuk, who in an article in *Pravda* (June 12, 1983), certified that in 1982 more than 800 thousand drivers lost their driving licenses because they were drunk when stopped by police.

The monstrous social consequences of alcoholism are compounded by the self-perpetuating character of the phenomenon. The probability that children of alcoholics will become alcoholics themselves is high. According to Soviet data, 92 percent of hard

---

*It should be noted that in recent decades, Soviet women have enrolled in a "competition" with men in the domain of alcoholism. As various sources suggest, the proportion of alcoholics among women has been growing rapidly, a fact that probably accounts, at least in part, for the rise of infant mortality in the country over the last two decades (see *Literaturnaia gazeta*, December 20, 1978; Feshbach 1983, p. 225; Tiit 1982, p. 37).

Noting the growth of alcoholism among women, one Soviet author refers to data from all developing countries (hinting that the Soviet Union is among them), that reveal that in the beginning of this century, the ratio of male to female alcoholics was 10:1, whereas now it is only 6:1 (see Parygin 1982, p. 166).

According to Sysenko, data on Moscow (1978), problem drinking by the wife was mentioned as the cause of divorce by 4.5 percent of men who filed for divorce (1982, p. 101). According to Zaigraiev, only 30 percent of adult females in big cities do not drink alcohol (Zaigraiev, 1983, p. 97).

†According to Matskovskii and Kharchev (1982, p. 159), alcoholism as a cause of divorce is even more significant in the country than in the cities.

drinkers were brought up in families in which at least one parent was an alcoholic (Parygin 1982, p. 164).

According to data from a study carried out in Perm, more than 30 percent of children in the first three years of elementary school have already tasted wine. The author of the article in *Literaturnaia gazeta* who cites this figure exclaims, "What should be said in this connection of these who are in the last year of secondary school!" (*Literaturnaia gazeta*, December 21, 1983).

The radical change in the role of alcohol in Soviet life that took place in the 1960s is related not so much to the increase of chronic drunkenness, or to the decrease in the age when people start to drink, or even to the growth of female alcoholism—a phenomenon unknown in the past.* The change is that people have begun to drink on the job. The drinking area now encompasses not only home, bars, places near liquor stores, parks, and streets, but also factories, offices, research institutes, shopping centers, and all other places where people work. In the year of Andropov's rule, a special Governmental decree, perhaps the first in history, introduced special penalties for those who came to work drunk (*Pravda*, December 30, 1983).†

---

*The following data, from two rare studies on attitudes toward alcoholism, are characteristic. Responding to a question, itself heavily loaded against alcohol, only 35 percent of vocational school students across the country disapproved of heavy drinking as a vice (Sokolov 1981, p. 171). In another Moscow study of 2000 workers, the respondents were asked about their attitudes toward people who came to work drunk. It turned out that even at a verbal level, despite the loaded character of the question, 41 percent of all respondents did not condemn such behavior. Even a larger proportion of the workers (98 percent) did not disapprove of the extortion of vodka by supervisors who assign people to the most desirable jobs in the factory (Grechin 1983, p. 124–25).

†As Abel Aganbegian wrote in an article published in the Soviet paper, *Trud*, in many of the plants he visited, special brigades are set up to keep drunken workers away from complex and expensive machinery (*Trud*, October 17, 1981).

One recent Soviet publication (Lazarev *et al.* 1977, p. 57) allows us to figure the proportion of drunkards in a big Soviet enterprise, "Apatit," in the Murmansk region. In 1975, the shop committees gave careful consideration to 934 disorderly persons who, it is clear, were almost all drunkards. Various data to be found in this publication permit us to put the number of workers in this factory at about 10 to 15 thousand. This means that about 7 to 10 percent of the workers were the object of public denunciation. Since chiefs of any Soviet enterprise always try to minimize scandal of any kind, it would not be an exaggeration to suppose that the number of regular drunks was two to four times higher.

Another figure can also give us an idea of the scale of drunkenness in this enterprise. One hundred and seventy-seven people participated in the work of the special committees organized for fighting drunkenness. This means again that a high proportion of employees were involved in an activity which, by its nature, must have been directed toward an even greater number of people.

To these men who are out of the running as potential husbands for the modern Soviet woman must be added a considerable number of criminals who only partially overlap with the universe of alcoholics. Criminals in the USSR number several million (according to some estimates, about three million), and they are, in most cases, also exempt from the marriage market. Though infidelity may not be regarded as a great transgression, and though many women are involved in love affairs, often men are more sex-indulgent than women. Real philanderers are also not wanted as mates, and men's lasciviousness is another obstacle to marrying and contributes to the reduction of the available pool of potential mates.

A reviewer of modern Estonian literature (*Literaturnaia gazeta*, May 4, 1983) observed that in their works Estonian writers arouse alarm because Estonian women are short of decent husbands. The wife of the main character in Teet Kallas's *Eisen Street* says, "It sometimes seems that all the men have decided to drink themselves to death." In the same novel, four sisters discuss their husbands: "What's going on with them? They do stupid things, drink hard, play around with other men's wives, throw away money, and then come crying and asking for forgiveness . . . how few men we can respect."

Another Estonian writer, Eme Beekmen, describes life in a small town where all the unmarried men are satisfied spending all their free time in the local bar. Almost all of them are hard drinkers, and the heroine, Regina, who, after many affairs, wants to marry, is in a bind: whom to choose? At last she decides to marry a "tolerable alcoholic" and proposes to him herself.

A number of other Estonian writers, women and men, have lately published novels on, as the author of the piece in *Literaturnaia gazeta* put it, the shortage of "real men"—Linda Ruud (*Women of Leisure*), Ine Viiding (*Repeated Games*), Toomas Vint (*Family Games*).

Beyond the widespread problem of drunkenness and criminality among men, other factors account for the perception of women's moral superiority over men. In many other respects, Soviet women look better than men. It is accepted today in Soviet society that women are less likely than men to violate the dictates of established morality or to be tempted by greed into the abuses of privilege and position. They are also seen to be more commonly kind and fair toward others.

Soviet officials only rarely indulge in public discussion on such a subject so controversial in the Soviet context as the moral differences between groups within the population. Soviet ideology, with its emphasis on the determinant role of social milieu, avoids virtually any parallels or comparisons in this sphere. Because of this, the statements of the editor of a very popular Soviet magazine, *Rabotnitsa* (Woman Worker), look extremely impressive. She states that "sociological studies have shown that working women are more responsible in their work, better organized and disciplined. Thus, women fulfill work quotas better than men, waste less time than men, are more sensitive to deficiencies in their place of work, and more active in pursuing their elimination. At the same time, women react much more emotionally, more bravely to displays of rudeness or injustice, and attribute more importance to production conflicts" (Vavilina 1979, p. 166).

The recent Soviet film, *Without Witnesses*, by the leading Soviet director Nikita Mikhalkov, reflects exactly this view. The film is about "him" and "her," who discuss their relations and their lives. As the review of the movie in *Literaturnaia gazeta* states, "he" is presented as a "totally negative person" and "she" as "not simply positive, but an ideal heroine, spotless in her spiritual purity and integrity" (see *Literaturnaia gazeta*, November 23, 1983).

Of course, it would be erroneous to idealize Soviet women too much, even by Soviet standards. Emancipation, coupled with the specific Soviet conditions, has produced a more aggressive type of woman who is perceived as surpassing the most objectionable of Soviet men in self-centeredness and deceit. Antifeminist writers have in many recent works produced a highly critical portrait of such women. Yuri Trifonov was probably the first. In his famous novel, *Exchange*, he pinpointed such women, attributing to them the pejorative nickname of "women-bulldogs." Another prominent Soviet writer, Slutskis, in his novel, *The Trip to the Mountains and Back* (1983), traces the evolution of his heroine, a Lithuanian woman named Liongina, from a sensitive and bashful person to a conceited, consumption-oriented vamp.

It is not only male writers who are inclined to portray a negative image of this product of Soviet society; even female writers participate in the portrayal of an extremely repellent image of some members of their sex. Thus, Beliaieva, in her novel, *A Part that Was Not Played* (1982), also presents an image of an ordinary secretary in a local government office, Elizaveta, who all her adult life (in the novel, the dying heroine shares with a volunteer nurse the secrets of her life) has been absorbed in intrigues and schemes to attain her petty goals.

Even if Soviet sociology were as free as sociology in the United States, it is hardly possible that it could provide exact data on the distribution of "moral" and "immoral" Soviet men and women. But Soviet literature's various impressionistic data suggest that the last bastion of established morality in Soviet society is defended mostly by women.

THE HIGH DEATH RATE OF SOVIET MEN

As in any other country entering a period of intensive industrialization, over many decades in Russia and then in the Soviet Union, the female death rate decreased faster than the male. By 1958–59, the life expectancy of women was 71.7 years, of men 64.4 years—a difference of 7.3 years. In 1862, this difference had been 1.6 years; in 1926–27, 4.2 years (Urlanis 1978, p. 121).

In the 1960s, after the decrease of mortality over many decades, a new trend had emerged: the death rate of both sexes began to increase. This process has been continuing over the last two decades. In 1981, the death rate was 10.2, against 7.1 in 1960 (*Narodnoie Khosiastvo SSSR 1922–1982*, 1982, p. 27).

The most remarkable feature of this trend has been that male mortality has been rising much faster than female. Moreover, in the mid-1970s, the increase in female mortality rates practically stopped, whereas male mortality rates continued to grow. As a consequence, the difference between the life expectancy of women and of men has been growing and had, by 1971–72, reached 10 years, an extremely large difference. No other developed country in the world has a difference so great. (In the U.S. the gap is 7.8 years; in France, 7.6 years.) Since then, the USSR has stopped publishing data on life expectancy, but expert extrapolations (see Feshbach 1982, pp. 34–35) suggest that the difference between women's and men's life expectancy in 1980 was nearly 12 years.

According to various sources, the current mortality rate among men is three times that of women in all age groups over twenty. The table below illustrates the increase over the ten-year period between 1963–64 and 1973–74:

TABLE 10.1: Ratio of Male to Female Mortality Rate, 1963–64 and 1973–74, By Age Group

Age	1963–64	1973–74
20–24	2.2	3.1
25–29	2.3	3.4
30–34	2.5	3.1
35–39	2.4	3.0
40–44	2.2	2.9

Source: *Narodnoie Khosiastvo SSSR v 1964*, pp. 36–37; *Vestnik Statistiki* 1975, No. 12, p. 74.

The fact that the general death rate continued to grow during the second half of the 1970s suggests that by the beginning of the 1980s the "extramortality of men" (a term used by Boris Urlanis) was much higher than when the last direct data were published on male and female mortality. Many Soviet authors have underscored the ominousness of this trend (Perevedenstev 1982a; Biurukov 1979; Kaliniuk and Veselkova 1982; Suslov and Lebedev 1982).

All researchers, Soviet as well as foreign, have been inclined to attribute the unprecedented growth of male mortality to the increase in alcoholism and to related phenomena such as fatal accidents and occupational injuries. Discussing the rise of male mortality rates, one Soviet author writes,"the male organism is to a much greater extent than the female, exposed to pathological developments as a result of smoking, the use of alcohol, unbalanced diet, and so on" (Riabushkin 1981, p. 31).

According to official Soviet data, accidents, poisoning, and occupational injuries constitute the main causes of death for men aged 16 to 50 and for women 16 to 40. Eighty percent of all deaths of males 20 to 24 are attributed to this set of causes (Riabushkin 1981, p. 32).

In Kaluga in 1978, accidents, poisoning, and occupational injuries caused death to men four times as often as to women. In Murmansk, one-third of all the male deaths were by these causes. In the city, 30 to 40 percent of men who died were aged 30 to 44— few from natural causes (Suslov and Lebedev 1982, pp. 45–46).

Alcoholism affects length of life, however, not so much through accidents and poisoning as mostly through various diseases, with heart disease in first place. In the opinion of Soviet medical experts, such as Lisitsyn, every third death from heart disease is related to alcohol (see Litvinova 1981, p. 114). According to official Soviet data, heart disease was the cause in 52.4 percent of all the deaths in the country in 1981 (13.8 percent were to cancer) (*Vestnik Statistiki* 1982,11, pp. 65–66). Soviet experts argue that in general, alcohol abuse shortens life by about twenty years (Litvinova 1981, p.114).

According to the data of German Milner and Pavel Shul'gin, only 25 percent of all alcoholics reach the age of 50. They also contend that by comparing groups divided on the basis of low or high consumption of alcohol, significant differences can be observed. For example, occupational injuries are 1.7 times more frequent in the high consumption group than in the low consumption group. Children born to parents in the first group are 1.6 times more likely to have physical or mental handicaps than children born to parents in the second group (Nedelia 1984, 15).

Moreover, Timon Riabushkin and Galina Galetskaia point out that the mortality rate among men in the Slavic and Baltic republics is especially high; that is, in the very areas where Zaigraiev's data indicate the highest levels of alcohol consumption (Riabushkin and Galetskaia 1983, p. 147).

Another indication that alcoholism is the main cause of the growing male death rate is the fact that the death rate has been increasing especially fast in the countryside, where alcoholism is even more rampant than in the cities. According to the calculations of the Soviet demographer, Bednyi, the life expectancy of men living in villages is two years lower than that of male city dwellers (1980). Occupational injuries are now much more frequent in the country than in the cities. Of all retired collective farmers, 45 percent are handicapped in some way. Among industrial workers in rural areas, the handicapped make up only 10 to 29 percent (Nesterov 1977, p. 168; see also Kopyt 1971, pp. 79–82). The demographic situation in the countryside aggravates the problem of rural women wishing to find husbands (Kalinuk and Vasil'kova 1982, p. 13; Nauduzhas 1982, p. 70).

The higher death rate of men for about the last 15 years now explains why, despite the preponderance of male births over female births, in 1970 there were about 170 women of marriageable age for every 100 men of that age.* In the cities this ratio is even worse: there are twice as many single women as single men, and in Moscow even more (see Khorev and Kisilieva 1982, p. 60; Volkov 1981, p. 39). Illustratively, among ten thousand letters that came to *Literaturnaia gazeta* in response to only two lonely-hearts (one supposedly of a woman, the other of a man), only twenty percent were from men.

As in other countries, the U.S. included (see Hacker 1982, p. 38), age differences between spouses are not insignificant even in first marriages (about 2 to 3 years, see *Vestnik Statistiki* 1982,11, pp. 66–67), and they increase for second and later marriages. In other words, the older the man, the greater the difference between his age and his wife's.†

Because of the growing mortality rate of men above 30, the new generations of women who expect husbands from even older age groups find themselves in a more difficult situation than did

---

*The growth of the death rate of men especially aggravated the plight of women over 30 because of the differences in the ages of brides and grooms.

†In the U.S., if divorce comes when both are in their forties, the huband will generally choose a new mate nine to ten years his junior (Hacker 1982, p. 38).

previous cohorts.* The high wartime mortality rate of Soviet men, combined with their frequently disruptive behavior, accounts for why women perceive that a "good," or even tolerable, husband is as much a "scarce good" as the consumer products Soviet women search for incessantly.

The number of single women varies with ethnic origin, however, underscoring the decisive role of cultural factors in the lack of "normal" husbands. Thus, the proportion of unmarried women among Estonian females, age 30 to 39, was 23 percent in 1970, while it was 16 percent among Russians and 5 percent among Tadzhiks. In the age group between 50 to 59, unmarried women made up 55 percent of Estonian women, 47 percent among Russians, and 31 percent among Tadzhiks (Volkov 1983, p. 204).

LACK OF TIME—THE SOVIET WOMAN'S MAIN CONCERN

The tremendous progress of the Soviet women in occupational and career life was not accompanied by a commensurate improvement in living standards or liberation from many old household tasks. The chronic shortage of goods, the low level of public services, and the slow progress in the mechanization of housework, all have made the life of the Soviet woman in some ways more difficult and nerve-wracking than that of their grandmothers, who were only in charge of the four famous Ks—Küche, Kinder, Kleiden, and Kirche.

Soviet researchers have made an attempt to assess the amount of labor involved in housework. Though they came up with somewhat differing figures, they are almost unanimous that this input (perhaps 150 billion hours per year) differs only slightly—by no more than 18 percent—from labor expended in the Soviet public economy (Kharchev 1979, p. 283; Korchagin 1974, p. 32). Therefore, Soviet women, who mainly bear the burden of the "domestic economy," during their second shift do the same amount of work as the 115 million employed in industry, agriculture, construction, commerce, and all the other branches of the

---

*Since the birthrate is declining, Perevedentsev and some other demographers, expect that the position of women in the marriage market will improve. In the near future, the number of marriageable men will be greater than that of women. Because men are more likely to be older than the women they marry, they will have been born when the birthrate was higher than when their potential wives were born (Perevedentsev 1982a).

Soviet economy. This fact may be surprising in the same way as the data showing that Soviet peasants on their private plots (which take up 1 to 2 percent of all arable land) produce from one-quarter to one-third of all the agricultural output in the country. Having to play an active role in the public economy as well as the decisive role in the domestic economy puts tremendous pressure on the majority of Soviet women.

The chief complaint of Soviet women today is lack of time. They live under continual pressure of tasks at work and at home—tasks that they have to do but cannot do in time. The survey in Taganrog in the late 1960s, one of the best in the history of Soviet sociology, established that two-thirds of all the women of this typical industrial Russian city complained about their lack of time. Only one-quarter of the men made the same complaint (Gordon and Klopov 1972, p. 127).

Even Leonid Brezhnev, in his report to the 26th Congress of the Party, acknowledged that "it is not easy at times for the woman to combine a mother's duty with active production and public activity" (Brezhnev 1981, p. 55). The profound aversion of the late Soviet leader to confirming the existence of problems in Soviet society should be taken into account in assessing the significance of this "problem" that managed to force its way into the Kremlin where Brezhnev was making his last report to a Party congress.*

The continued pressure on Soviet women by society and by the family definitely affects their health. Although male mortality is higher, Soviet women fall sick much more often than Soviet men. A study by I. Velichkane, who explored the health of working men and women over one year, shows this. She found that after marriage, the number of days a woman was ill increased by fifty percent, whereas the number for men decreased. Moreover, the Lithuanian researcher discovered that the probability of a working woman's being ill increases with the number of children (see Boiko 1980, p. 165).

"Subjective" data about the health of working women are consonant with the "objective" data. In Boiko's survey, women complained about their health twice as often as men (Boiko 1980,

---

*The great burden that Soviet women have to carry at home and on the job is not a forbidden theme in Soviet literature. In many novels and stories, there are very vivid descriptions of the activity of the woman on two shifts. The best of these stories is Baranskaia's, "One Day in a Woman's Life," published in *Novyi Mir* at the height of its glory in the 1960s as a mouthpiece of the liberal intelligentsia (Baranskaia 1969).

pp. 164–65). A. Kotliar and S. Turchaninova asked working women how they felt at the beginning of the working day. Of women who did not have children, 69 percent said that they felt good when they started work. Among women with children, only 33 percent said they did (Kotliar and Turchaninova 1975, p. 123).

MEN AND WOMEN IN THE SOVIET KITCHEN

The Soviet man today plays a much more active role in domestic chores than did his father and, especially, his grandfather. Moreover, the younger the couple, the more active the husband in housework. A study in the Baltic republics found that 63 percent of husbands between 19 and 24 were very active in doing domestic chores, whereas only 40 percent between 30 and 39, and 36 percent 50 and over were as active at home (see Sysenko 1981, p. 51).

However, the Soviet man still does not do as much as the Soviet woman expects of him. He still does not want completely to forget the old division of labor between husband and wife. Not rarely he tries to ignore that this division does not work anymore and that his wife sometimes earns more than he. Roughly speaking, no more than one-third of Soviet husbands are active in the household.

The first studies of time budgeting in the USSR after Stalin found the contributions of men and women to domestic work are extremely uneven. The table below, based on data from the late 1960s, illustrates the time spent on domestic chores in families with both spouses working outside the home:

TABLE 10.2:   Hours per week spent on domestic chores in selected Soviet cities, by sex

	Women	Men
Krasnoiarsk	4.08	1.54
Sverdlovsk	3.87	1.73
Gorki	4.01	1.71
Ivanovo	3.45	1.55
Rostov–na–Donu	4.06	2.10
Pskov	3.20	1.10

Source: Compiled from data in Kolpakov, B., and V. Patrushev, 1971. *Budzhet Vremeni Gorodskogo Naseleniia*. Moscow: Statistika, pp. 117–18.

Thus, at this point, women spent about twice the time of men on household chores.

In the next decade, no significant changes took place. Zoia Iankova and Ira Rodzinskaia reviewed a series of recent studies on time budgeting and concluded that women still do about twice as much work at home as men (1982, p. 18; see also Rakitskii 1983).

Special studies in Taganrog, a typical industrial city of Russia, established that a man in a family without children spent 8 hours, 35 minutes a week on domestic chores, while his wife spent 25 hours, 50 minutes—three times as much. In families with children, the respective figures were 13 hours 25 minutes and 35 hours and 45 minutes (Gordon and Gruzdeva 1975, p. 37).

Even in Leningrad, where the level of education is much higher than in the country as a whole, and even in young families where the education of women is especially high, the differences between the involvement of wife and husband in domestic chores is very significant (see table 10.3).

The difficult life of the Soviet woman who, unlike her husband, has two shifts a day—one at the workplace, another at home—has been documented in numerous other investigations (see Kharchev and Golod 1971; Gordon and Klopov 1972; Gordon, Klopov and Onikov 1977; see also Sacks 1976, pp. 125–30).*

As can be judged from a rare Soviet longitudinal study, over the last two decades the domestic burden of Soviet women decreased very insignificantly, by less than 6 percent—from 35 hours a week in 1963 to 33 hours in 1980. It is remarkable that at the same time, men's efforts in the household declined by 10 percent, from 16.8 hours to 15.1 hours. These very representative data are for employees in industry in the Russian republic (Patrushev 1982, p. 29).

The unequal distribution of domestic chores between wife and husband is a major source of conflict inside the family and

---

*Involvement in the labor force has not released U.S. women from domestic chores either. Working wives in the U.S. continue to do the bulk of the housework. In families where both spouses work, 18 percent of women spend over 20 hours per week on housework, while only 4 percent of men spend equal amounts of time on domestic chores (Blumstein and Schwartz 1983, p. 270). However, if we take into account the great differences in living standards between the U.S. and the USSR (availability of food, mechanization of domestic work, and so on), the lives of U.S. women become incomparably easier than those of their Soviet counterparts.

TABLE 10.3: Percentage of wives and husbands who participate in selected domestic chores, Leningrad

	Wives	Husbands
Grocery shopping	83.6	39.6
Cooking	94.9	20.6
Housecleaning	83.3	39.9
Laundry	95.8	13.3

Source: Compiled from data in Ruzhzhe, V., et al. 1982. "KPD Semeinoi Gruppy." In Sovremenaia Sem'ia, edited by E. Vasil'ieva, Moscow: Finansy i Statistika, p. 79.

one of the most significant forces corroding the accord between spouses. A considerable proportion of Soviet women are dissatisfied with the domestic activity of their husbands.

Rodzinskaia, who analyzed Moscow families between 1976 and 1979, discovered that differences in the stability of marriages cannot be attributed to such material factors as income or housing conditions. She did not discover that happy families were wealthier or had better housing. Her data conspicuously indicate that the participation of the husband in housework makes an enormous difference. In happy families, only 18 percent of men did not take part in domestic chores, whereas in unhappy families, almost half (49 percent) did not take part. Two other figures accord well with these data: in unhappy families, only 14 percent of women are satisfied with the organization of domestic life; in happy families, almost 50 percent (Rodzinskaia 1981, p. 109).

It is even more characteristic that conflicts over domestic chores occur regularly in 78 percent of all the unhappy families (Rodzinskaia 1981, p. 109; Iankova and Rodzinskaia 1982, p. 23; see also Perevedenstev 1981, 1982a).

THE DECLINING ROLE OF THE GRANDMOTHER

The growing dissatisfaction of the Soviet woman with her domestic life should also, to a considerable degree, be ascribed to the declining role of the older generation in the household. The babushka, the famous Russian grandmother, helps her daughter raise the grandchildren less and less, though in many families the babushka continues to be an essential part of the family mechanism. A study in Leningrad (1979) shows that she helped in 41 percent of all young families with children, and even helped in 24 percent of those without children. What is more, grandmothers spent almost as much time on housework in the households of their daughters or daughters-in-law as did the young women themselves: in families with children, grandmothers worked 2.78 hours each day, young women 3.06; and in families without children, their contribution, though smaller, was proportionally larger than the young women's—1.80 hours as against 1.71 hours (Ruzhzhe *et al.* 1982, p. 76).* In the Ukraine, grandmothers help to bring up a new generation in one-sixth of all families in cities and in one-fifth of all families in the countryside (Ruzhzhe *et al.* 1983, p. 39).

New grandmothers and grandfathers are much more educated than their own grandparents, and even after retirement they have not wanted to devote all of their time to their children and grandchildren, as grandparents may have in the past.† The same process of the growth of aspiration that has brought so many changes to Soviet life has also been changing the relations between generations in the Soviet family. According to the data of Vladimir Shapiro, the best Soviet expert on the problems of the retired, only 16 percent of Moscow old people who were going to retire did so because they wished to participate in raising grandchildren (Shapiro 1980, p. 48). Outside Moscow the figure was even lower, at 12 percent (Kharchev 1982, p. 49).

Today, it is harder and harder for young people to ask their parents to help them bring up their children. Leningrad couples with children were asked about negative developments engendered in their lives by the birth of a child. The sociologists offered them 15 alternatives. "Dependence on grandmothers and grandfathers" ranked first—25 percent of the husbands and 20 percent of the wives checked this alternative. The respondents gave less consideration to such negative consequences of having a child as

---

*Strange as it may seem, U.S. data attest to the very active role of the older generations in child care in the United States. According to Hill's data (a study of 321 families in three-generation chains in the Twin Cities), 78 percent of all married couples had help with their children. In 16 percent of the cases, the couple's grandparents were among those who helped, and in 50 percent of the cases, the couple's parents helped (Hill 1970, p. 67).

†Since the age when a woman gives birth to her first child has decreased, the *babushka* has become younger than in the past. Because of this, the proportion of grandmothers continuing to work has also risen, a fact that also helps account for the diminishing role of grandmothers in raising grandchildren (see Chuiko and Nikitenko 1979, p. 59).

"material difficulties" (19 and 15 percent), "additional domestic chores" (23 and 15 percent), and so on (Boiko 1980, pp. 78–79).

The fact that the majority of couples now live in a nuclear family, without their parents, also accounts for the decreasing role of *babushka* in the lives of her children and grandchildren (Klupt 1982). Though dissatisfied with their parents' shirking their "duties" as grandparents, young Soviet couples are now oriented to living apart from them. According to Chuiko's Kiev data, 94 percent of newlyweds do not want to live with their parents (Chuiko and Nikitenko 1979, p. 59).* Here again is an example of a contradiction between values: young people wishing to have two opposing things—to live alone without the older generation and to enjoy their help around the house.

EQUAL BEFORE MARRIAGE, UNEQUAL AFTER

The constant shortage of time for Soviet women is related to another important manifestation of inequality between the sexes: occupational inequality. At the point of graduation from secondary or higher school (college), men and women with equivalent education fare about equally in the job market. Only in sectors where women currently predominate—for example, in health services and in the schools—are men hired ahead of women (a form of "affirmative action" generally approved of by public opinion).

But as soon as a woman marries, and especially after giving birth to a child, she begins to lag behind her husband. Promotion on the job requires considerable time for studying, attending evening classes, and participating in certain public activities. As has been shown, women have much less time for these activities.

An international study of time budgeting found that 26 percent of men in the typical Soviet city of Pskov were, in one way or another, engaged in life-long education. Among women, the proportion was 12.6 percent. In the U.S. city of Jackson, Michigan, by comparison, (which represented the U.S.A. in this study) a much

---

*One of the reasons for such an orientation is the role of conflicts with in-laws as a cause of divorce. An expert on this subject, L. Chuiko, supposes that the real number of families breaking up for this reason exceeds the figures that are to be found on the rolls of Soviet courts—5 percent when divorce is filed for by the man, and 3 percent when by the woman (see Chuiko and Nikitenko 1979, p. 60).

smaller proportion of the population was involved in continuing education, but the distribution of men and women was more equal—4.7 percent of men and 3.4 percent of women (Kolpakov and Patrushev 1971, p. 152).

In a more recent survey of 4000 urban dwellers, it was discovered that men spent 2.08 hours per week on education, while women spent only 1.10 hours (see Rakitskii 1983, p. 275; also Shishkan 1980).

Having to spend much more time than men on housework explains why after marriage, women lose what they have gained from their education and why, in middle life, they are behind men in occupational skills and social standing.

The very authoritative study carried out by A. Kotliar and S. Turchaninova in the early 1970s found that, in occupational standing, women are behind men with the same (or sometimes even less) education. The skill ratings of women in all branches of industry are significantly lower than men. In machine building, for example, the male skill rating was 3.5, the female was 2.1 (Kotliar and Turchaninova 1975, p. 81). While 38.9 percent of men in this industry were counted as highly skilled (skill rating 5 and 6), only 2.2 percent of the women were. Even in the textile industry, where women are in a majority, the respective percentages were 43.5 and 33.4 (p. 89).

Studies of factories in the late 1970s, found the same discrepancy between the high level of education of women and their low occupational standing. A study of a Novosibirsk instrument factory established that the highest category of qualification included 28 percent of all the men but only 1 percent of the women. And a 1978 study in the new Siberian city of Saianogorsk found that the average level of education of men employed in industry and construction was 9.7 years, and a bit higher for women at 10.0 years. However, 47 percent of men had a high skill rating (higher than 3), whereas only 8 percent of women had such a skill rating (Kuzev 1982, p. 163).

Given all this, it is only to be expected that women's incomes are significantly lower than those of men. In the Novosibirsk factory mentioned above, 45 percent of men had monthly salaries over 180 rubles, whereas only 25 percent of women were this well paid (Antosenkov and Kupriianova 1981, pp. 181–83). Data from a metallurgical factory in Karaganda support the same conclusion: eight percent of women, as against 63 percent of men, had the highest worker classification. Two percent of men and 16 percent of women were paid less than 120 rubles a month (Saprykin 1981, p. 208; see also Iankova 1979; Rotova 1982).*

Soviet publications rarely contain direct nationwide data on the average salaries of women and men. It is possible to flush out only indirect evidence on this subject. M. Sonin allows himself to say only that "the average salary in predominantly female domains is still lower than the average salary in the economy as a whole" (Sonin 1977, p. 25).

In the U.S., the average weekly salary for women in the late 1970s was about 61 percent of that of men (U.S. Bureau of the Census 1979). It is very likely, taking into account the difference in salary in male and female areas of the economy, that the difference in the USSR is of a similar magnitude. Comparing wages in transport, where the proportion of women is low (about 24 percent), we see that wages in trade (76 percent women) are only 68.9 percent as high; in health services (84 percent women), 62.9 percent as high; in education (73 percent women), 66.9 percent as high; in cultural institutions (73 percent women), 55.2 percent as high (*Narodnoie Khosiastvo SSSR*, 1922–1982, 1982, p. 406).

Women are consistently underrepresented in the highest echelons of prestige and authority—even in sectors where they are numerically predominant, such as health and education. In 1980–81, 71 percent of school teachers were women, but only 34 percent of secondary school principals were (*Zhenshchiny v SSSR*, 1982, p. 12). Among Soviet physicians, 69 percent are women, but the great majority of directors of hospitals are men. Women make up 44 percent of all engineers in the country, but of heads of various production units, only 24 percent are women; and of directors of enterprises, only 13 percent. And although women constitute the bulk of the labor force in agriculture, they make up less than 2 percent of all collective farm chairs, and only 17 percent of agricultural team leaders are women (see Lapidus 1982, p. 133).

---

*Women's salaries are lower than men's, usually even from the beginning of their work lives, largely because they are more concentrated in lighter and cleaner work and in sectors that are not as well paid. Women are more likely to be employed in schools, health services, commerce, and especially cultural institutions like libraries, museums, and so forth. In Chuiko's study of newly married couples in Kiev, men averaged a monthly salary of 116 rubles, while women only 86 rubles (1975, pp. 87–88; see also Shishkan 1980; Lapidus 1982). After this point, the gap increases.

Among scientific workers, women are also still underrepresented. Whereas 21 percent of all women scholars have a scientific degree, the figure for men is nearly twice as high—39 percent (*Narodnoie Khosiastvi SSSR, 1922–1982*, 1982, p. 125; *Zhenshchiny v SSSR*, 1982, p. 15; *Itogi Vsesouznoi Pereposi Naseleniia 1970 goda*, Vol. 6, pp. 165–67; Lapidus 1982, pp. 22–23).

Seemingly, few women hold a grudge against the men who almost everywhere—in factories, hospitals, schools, research institutes, collective farms—have positions superior to women's. With their greater emphasis on the family and on the emotional life, and with quite decent social status, they do not envy men—who have to spend much more time on the job than do their subordinates.* But there are some who do feel highly discriminated against—women who have to drudge in the most unattractive and arduous sectors of the economy, such as construction or agriculture, where they do the dirtiest and sometimes the hardest work. This fundamental fact of Soviet life arose unexpectedly during a visit by Andropov to a Moscow tool factory (January 1983): there a woman told him that she and her female coworkers had to wield machinery so heavy that it "shattered" those working with it and that men shunned the women's jobs because they were so dangerous (see Andropov 1983, pp. 227–28). There are also some particularly striking all-Union data on the proportion of people working in manual occupations among all workers en-

---

*Among those who argue against the advancement of women into various spheres of Soviet society, some of the most vocal target the proliferation of women in scientific research and scholarship. Two reasons are normally cited against the large proportion of women among scholars (40 percent in 1981; 28% of all Ph.D.s and 14% of higher doctoral degrees are held by women). First, the shortage of time in women's lives to commit themselves to scientific work, because of their "obligations" toward domestic chores (especially under Soviet conditions, with long lines in stores and poor facilities) lowers their suitability for this work. Second, women presumably possess weaker scientific capacities.

The last argument was recently advanced by two prominent male scholars— one the head of the Geological Section of the Academy of Science, the other a Senior Fellow in the Economic and Mathematical Institute at the Academy. They argue that "the increase in the number of women with scholarly degrees accounts for the decrease in the number of those who really develop science... the 'rebellious' spirit, the predisposition to search for new, nontraditional methods in science are more typical among men than women. This has been established by psychologists and experts in the science of science. Therefore, the broad feminization of science contributes to the slackening in the development of new branches of science, even if women make their contribution in the accumulation of facts" (Sokolov and Reimers 1983, p. 77).

gaged in earth work. For men, the figure was 18 percent, while for women it was 60 percent (*Ekonomika i Organizatsia Promyshlennogo Proizvodstva* 1978, p. 40).†

As we have seen, the drastic slowdown of educational and occupational progress of women after marriage accounts at least partially for their relatively low social mobility compared to men.

Studies of labor turnover conducted in Novosibirsk over a fifteen-year period (they are the best in Soviet sociology) established that women leave their jobs half as often because of dissatisfaction with the content of the work. And, with a smaller chance of enhancing their occupational status, they are also much less demanding about their salary. Among those who quit their jobs in 1970, the proportion of men who did so because of dissatisfaction with their salary was 19 percent, while only 5 percent of women abandoned jobs for this reason (Antosenkov and Kupriianova 1977, pp. 48–50, 72). The Novosibirsk data have been confirmed by other studies of labor turnover in the USSR. The authors of a survey of nineteen large and middle-sized Russian cities found that, among workers who rose to become engineers, only one-third were women. Since the total number of workers who change their social position is very small (no more than 2.3 percent of all workers), even more significant are data about mobility within the working class. The number of women who change their position within this class is half the number of men. Moreover, 59 percent of women who move from one workplace to another take a step down in their occupational status (Kotliar 1982, p. 100). Findings about Soviet construction workers are similar (S. Reznik 1982, p. 111).

Of special interest is the study of V. Lukina and S. Nekhoroshkov who explored in detail the differences between male and female mobility, using mid-1970s data relating to Leningrad and Bashkiria. They computed the number of couples aged 30 to 45 who moved after marriage to more skilled work. In childless

---

†Under pressure of public opinion, but largely for pronatalistic considerations, the Soviet government recently adopted a number of decisions that make many difficult manual occupations (about five hundred) inaccessible to women (see *Pravda*, November 21, 1983; see also Lapidus 1982, pp. 308–9). In a number of cases, however, women have protested furiously against these laws, demanding the permission to do whatever jobs they wish. Lena Solovieva published a long article in *Pravda* about the tribulations of a young woman who dreamed of becoming a truck driver but was not allowed to do so in spite of her high qualifications (*Pravda*, November 20, 1983).

families, the differences between wife and husband were not very significant. In Leningrad, women even progressed in their career a little faster than men. However, with each child they had, women lagged further behind. So, if in childless families 97 men were promoted for every 100 women, in three-child families, 122 men were. In Kazan, the figures rose from 108 men (in childless families) to 143 men (in three-child families) and to 270 (in four-child families) (Lukina and Nekhoroshkov 1982, p. 141).*

The unequal place of occupational and social career mobility of men and women after marriage leads to certain conflicts. Often moved by a desire to have a "prestigious" wife, men may leave their "backward" mate for a more successful partner (see Baranov 1981, p. 87). Soviet novels abound with stories about a man who finds, in his occupational surroundings, a woman with the same interests in science, art, or even in the over-fulfillment of the production plan—a woman who is much more capable than his wife of understanding all the worries and ambitions of a man in his middle or old age. Usually, it turns out, and it is the merest happenstance, that these sensitive and professionally active women are beautiful and young.†

THE CULTURAL SUPERIORITY OF SOVIET WOMEN

Falling behind her husband in a professional career, the Soviet woman, however, outruns him in the humanitarian and emotional spheres of life and they do this despite the fact that they have half the free time of men.‡

---

*That married women lag behind their husbands professionally is also, in part, accounted for by the fact that women change their place of residence less often than men (Baranov 1981, p. 73).

†To K. Ostrovitianov, the late vice-president of the Academy of Sciences of the USSR, Aron Katsenelinboigen ascribes the following contribution to the development of mathematical economics and sociology: an extremely simple but efficient formula for computing the age of the next wife of a member of the Academy— $y = 100 - x$, where y is the age of a new wife, x the age of an academician. This formula was inspired by the fact that each new wife seems to be younger than the previous one, while the husband gets older and older.

‡It is very peculiar that Soviet sociologists pay relatively little attention to sex as an independent variable in their analysis. As Tatiana Iaroshenko and Elena Petrenko established, sex was used by the authors of *Sotsiologicheskii Issledovaniia*, the Soviet sociological journal, in this capacity only in 3 percent of all articles, whereas occupation was so used in 40 percent, place of residence in 17 percent, age in 12 percent (see Petrenko and Iaroshenko 1979, p. 18). Sex as an independent variable has been almost completely ignored in many important

A study of free time in a number of large Russian cities in 1965–70 revealed that, even when women had less education than men, it was women who were more devoted to reading than men. This is especially clear when we control for marital status. Thus, unmarried women spent about 4.35 hours per week on reading, as against 3.25 hours for unmarried men. After marriage, women apparently had to curtail their reading time and, thus, read less than men—1.45 hours for women and 2.25 for men. However, if instead of time we use as an indicator the frequency of reading (i.e., the proportion of respondents who had read a book during the past month), it turns out that many more women take a book for reading than men, despite their domestic concerns. Among women with 8 to 10 years of education, 73 percent had read a book in the last month, whereas only 57 percent of similarly educated men had done so. For those with secondary and higher education, the figures were virtually identical, with 74 percent for women and 78 percent for men (Gordon and Gruzdeva 1975, pp. 51–53).*

An Estonian study revealed that among visitors to the theater, 70 percent were women and 30 percent were men (Kask 1977, p. 68). The same is largely true among visitors to exhibitions, where 64 percent were women (Laidmiae 1977, p. 102).†

Iadov's study of Leningrad engineers in the 1970s shows that women are considerably more oriented to aesthetic and emotional values than their male colleagues in factories and design bureaus. Offered a list of 18 terminal and 18 instrumental values, Leningrad female engineers attributed significantly more weight to

---

Soviet sociological publications (see Arutiunian 1980; Grushin and Onikov 1980; and others). Perusing my own Soviet publications, I also discovered, to my great amazement, how little attention I had paid to the variable, despite my perennial concern for the problems of women.

*According to data of Mikuletsky and Shanklin, U.S. women read an average of 14 minutes a day more than men and working women read a half hour more every day than their male counterparts (New York Times, September 8, 1983).

†In order to dispel any suspicions that such a divergence can be attributed to the difference between the number of old men and old women, the Estonian study cited figures on young people, which reveal the same results for young people. Of all visitors to the theater below the age of thirty, 75 percent were women, and among visitors to exhibitions of the same age, women represented 59 percent (Kask 1977, p. 68; Laidmiae 1977, p. 102).

Sergei Starodubtsev, an expert on the sociology of art, compared the composition of visitors to the famous Moscow-Paris exhibition in 1981. He found that the amount of interest in the exhibition was much more balanced between the sexes in Paris than in Moscow. While 34 percent of Soviet visitors were men, nearly half (47 percent) of French visitors were male (Starodubtsev 1983, p. 119).

human values such as beauty or cognition. Sixty-four percent of Leningrad women engineers said that aesthetic interests were for them the most important part of their leisure. Only 12.3 percent of men said the same (Iadov 1977, p. 196).

In another Leningrad study, the researchers, not without astonishment, found that women turned out to be more active than men in the family's cultural and spiritual life. In particular, women more often than their husbands, initiated conversations on books, plays, and movies (72 percent, against 62 percent). They also more frequently started discussions on the children (91 percent against 76 percent) and displayed more interest in the professional life of the other (71 percent against 58 percent), and so on (Suslov and Lebedev 1982, p. 149).

THE AGGRESSIVENESS OF SOVIET WOMEN

Almost all factors characterizing the lives of Soviet women today make them increasingly more aggressive toward their partners. The major cause of the bellicosity of Soviet females lies in the deep contradiction between their occupational and social status on the one hand, and the necessity for them to carry on their old roles in the family, on the other. Only recently has Soviet society sought to elaborate new norms and values that might significantly mitigate this conflict between roles.

Viktor Perevedentsev characterizes the psychological climate in the Soviet family: "The present transitional period implies that there is no consensus in couples on the nature of family life, about the roles of husband and wife, about their respective duties in housework, about the upbringing of children, and on many other questions. The modern, urban, educated woman is not inclined to be resigned to her low position in the family, since the Soviet woman legally is equal to the man in production and social life." (Perevedentsev 1982a, p. 30)

Iurii Riurikov, in the previously mentioned article from *Pravda*, elegantly and at the same time very bluntly wrote that "many families now have been turned into real fields of battle in direct and indirect ways" (Riurikov 1983, p. 5).*

Andrei Volkov, in his turn, underscores that "the family has become fragile and vulnerable" (see *Vestnik Statistiki* 3, 1983, p.

---

*Riurikov cleverly exploited the double meaning of the word *bran* in Russian–"swearing" and "battle."

68). The same view is supported by such usually cautious authors as Matskovskii and Kharchev who, in a summary chapter published in the very official edition, *Sociology in the USSR*, also assert that "the process of the involvement of women in professional and social activities (the creation of the conditions for the complex development of the woman, the increase in her freedom of choice of partners, and so on), has contributed to the exacerbation of conflicts between husbands and wives and to difficulties in their mutual understanding" (Matskovskii and Kharchev 1982, p. 161).

A recent study on family relations conducted in Leningrad is in accord with the opinion of these prominent Soviet sociologists. Generalizing the results of the study, N. Fedotova says that men and women have significantly different images of the "good husband" and the "good wife." Men adhere to the "traditional roles of husbands and wives," while women are more oriented to the "modern model of marriage" based on the equality of the sexes in all spheres of life (Fedotova 1982, p. 148).†

It is notable that, as this study found, women reckon men's contribution to domestic life as much lower than the men do themselves (see Suslov and Lebedev 1982, p. 148; Kharchev 1982, p. 77). In another Leningrad study (1973–74, 3220 respondents), 67 percent of husbands complained that women's working led to their becoming domineering in family life. Surprising as it may be, their wives say they are right about this, and in even greater proportion indicated that this trait of the modern woman is a direct consequence of her new social role (Boiko 1980, p. 208).

It is clear that men exhibit real reluctance to accept a more egalitarian relationship. The Moscow study conducted by Zoia Iankova, cited above, found evidence that the attempt of women to play the dominant role in the family brings marriage much more often to the verge of collapse. Women were dominant in 33.3 percent of all unstable marriages, and in only 7.4 percent of families who were the most stable (Iankova 1978, p. 238).

---

†According to this study, only about half (52 percent) of married people viewed their marriages as stable, and female respondents were more skeptical about their marriages than their spouses. Fifteen percent of all women in their first marriage evaluated their relationship "very negatively," or declined to answer the question on the stability of their marriage. Among men, this figure was 11 per cent. For respondents in their second marriage, the level of dissatisfaction was even higher, with 27 percent of women and 10 percent of men indicating very negative evaluations, or declining to answer (Boiko and Fedotova 1983, pp. 215–6).

A significant part of the younger generation, imitating older patterns of behavior in their family, still cling to old-fashioned images of the roles of men and women. The study conducted by Moscow sociologists in Moscow, Tbilisi, and Saransk among 600 families, found that 40 percent of the boys, and even 24 percent of the girls, still assumed that the contribution of both sexes to domestic chores cannot be equal (Kharchev 1982, p. 37).

As if their emerging liberation gave them extraordinary energy, many Soviet women look more and more active than their male partners. Analyzing data about divorces, E.-M. Tiit observes "the strength of character that is revealed in self-confidence, composure, the feeling of responsibility, and so forth, is a very important human trait. This is especially important of a man, and it is natural if a husband is superior to a wife in this respect. Unfortunately, this is not always the way things are. Our survey showed that in a considerable number of cases, divorce took place when a wife possessed a stronger character than a husband" (Tiit 1982, p. 32).

Dissatisfied with her husband, the Soviet woman not only demands that he increase his involvement in domestic affairs, but also maintains that she has to have the upper hand in many areas of family life, such as the budget or the upbringing of the children.

It should be said that Soviet women are on the way to attaining this goal. A survey of Moscow high school seniors found that young people recognize the mother as the main authority two to three times as often as they do the father. Sixty-four percent of them said their mother, and 23 percent said their father was the final authority in matters related to studies and social activity, and it was 45 and 17 when the question was of the authority in selecting friends and so on. Even in the domain of their choice of profession, the young people seemed to put their mother ahead of their father (60 percent and 37 percent) (Alekseieva 1976; see also Iankova and Pankratova 1979, pp. 21–22).

A special study of relations inside the family carried out by Sysenko in Moscow in 1976 provides us with an eloquent picture of women's attitudes toward their husbands. No less than one-third of women between 25 and 49 disapprove of the behavior of their husbands in some way. Concerning the organization of family leisure time, only 51 percent of the wives gave positive evaluations of the activity of their husbands. Almost half of all the respondents were dissatisfied with how the husbands use their time, how they spend money, and so on.

The wives are far from keeping their opinions of their husbands to themselves. About half of women draw the attention of their husband to the behavior of other men who could be regarded as models. Nineteen percent of the respondents used this device for teaching their husbands "very often." Forty percent praise their husbands either "never" or "seldom." Only 9 percent praise them regularly. Moreover, 67 percent of the women criticize their husbands in the presence of a third person. Thirteen percent do it, as they admit, "often" and "very often."

The same study discovered that once a conflict starts, there is little chance of settling it quickly. Only 15 percent of women said that in order not to exacerbate relations, they were ready to concede a point. Fifty-two percent acknowledged that they did it "very rarely." And, according to the women, their husbands are little more tolerant (Elistratkina 1979, pp. 85–91; Sysenko 1981, p. 61; see also Suslov and Lebedev 1982, p. 149).

A similar study in Leningrad (1974–75) produced results that support the Moscow data on relations inside Soviet families. Asked about other members of the family, 45 percent of married men gave positive judgments of them. However, even fewer (35 percent) of the married women did the same. The negative feelings of women are even more pronounced when we compare the figures for the divorced: 52 percent of the men and 38 percent of the women said only good things about their relatives. [It is curious that the situation changes radically if we compare the attitudes of the unmarried. Without the experience of marriage, women tend to be more lenient toward their folk than are men: 39 percent of them spoke of their relatives only positively, whereas only 32 percent of men did (Vasil'eva 1981, p. 93).] In evaluating these data, it must be taken into consideration that 27 percent of respondents avoided answering the question about relations inside their family. It is hardly to be doubted that if these respondents had been more forthcoming, the proportion of negative estimates would be larger. Besides, it is very likely that not all the respondents who did answer the question were wholly sincere and were not hiding, at least partially, their negative attitudes toward members of their family—their spouses above all.

Among more educated segments of society, there is some disagreement about the fair distribution of household duties. In a sample of Moscow residents (in which two-thirds had at least some higher education, and only 6 percent had not completed secondary education), women were more likely to discount differences between the kinds of jobs each of the spouses does at work when considering the appropriate distribution of housework. In other words, regardless of the arduousness (or prestige) of work carried out on the job, 20 percent of the women felt both partners should carry equal loads at home, while 12 percent of men agreed. Among the women, 35 percent expressed dissatisfaction with their husbands' contribution to domestic chores, and about one-fifth of the men complained that their wives did not understand the character of the work they did outside the home.

The authors of this study, summarizing data on conflicts in the family, observed that "in unstable families, women much more often insist that domestic chores should be divided between wife and husband whatever the circumstances, whereas in stable families, women recognize the necessity of taking into account the amount of work in the office, the specific character of each spouse" (Iankova and Rodzinskaia 1982, p. 23).

Under the unprecedented pressure of two types of roles, one in the workplace and another at home, the Soviet woman is often hard on her husband, often making him the scapegoat for the troubles she incurs when she decides to marry and continue in her career.

There is no question that Soviet men could greatly increase their contributions to domestic work to lessen the problems of the "double shift" for women. But, at the same time—indeed as a consequence of gender inequality—men tend to face additional burdens in their careers. Men generally have to expend more psychic energy and time on a professional career than women.* The husbands of Soviet women must waste more time than they on various political activities sponsored by the authorities—a fact women may not always take into consideration. Men are forced to participate much more than women in various intrigues at the

---

*An interesting letter was published in *Pravda* (December 12, 1983). The author, O. Litvinenko, reflecting on the statistics on unsuccessful marriages, appeals to all spouses to "achieve peaceful co-existence among themselves, whatever are the deprivations, sufferings, concessions, and compromises." Litvinenko, a 35-year-old woman and former Party professional worker, challenges the idea that emancipation has released women from "duties imposed on women by nature." She states with pride that she had always recognized the supremacy of the husband in the family. Moreover, in her opinion, conflicts in many families occur because women always grumble and are regularly discontent with everything around them. She admonishes women to be "more self-critical" and not shift the guilt for breaking up families to husbands.

workplace and are more exposed to the dangers of being labeled an unloyal citizen or an unfit Party member. (Although nationwide, Party members make up only about 15 percent of the population, among professionals, the proportion is closer to one-half. Party membership plays a significant role in professional career advancement.

Much of this is traceable to the underrepresentation of women in the Party. Women make up only 27 percent of Party members (*Narodnoie Khosiaistvo SSSR* 1922–1982, 1982, p. 48). This figure is informative because behind it are the great differences in the time that women and men spend on countless meetings, the fulfillment of numerous voluntary and involuntary assignments, and so on. Men are expected to spend more time than women in all kinds of public activities, such as participation in local government, Party committees, and other activities that demand time, take their toll on the nerves, and usually bring little intrinsic satisfaction. But they are regarded as necessary to survival and career advancement.* The figures mentioned here correlate with data from a 1974–75 survey of Leningrad families with wives aged 30 to 45, which found that in these families the wives were engaged in regular public activities in 31 percent of all the cases; the husbands in 39 percent (Lukina and Nekhoroshkov 1982, p. 153).

According to data from the survey of 4000 urban residents carried out by the Institute of Labor in different regions of the country, men spend 1.08 hours per week on public activities, while women spend one-third of that time (.37 hours) per week (Rakitskii 1983, p. 275). The following 1973 data, cited by Patrushev, on collective farmers in Rostov, show that in the countryside, differences are even more pronounced. Whereas men spent 1.01 hours a week in public service, women spent only .007 hours (Patrushev 1978, p. 247). Among professionals, where Party membership is much more widespread, the time spent in such activities is substantially greater.

---

*When discussing the political activity of Soviet women, such authors as Bohdan Harasymiv and Janet Maher unfortunately disregard the compulsory nature of this activity, which in many cases has nothing in common with the genuine involvement of women in the decision-making process in the USSR (see Yedlin 1980, pp. 140–212). The increase of the number of women who have to take part in the work of various political organizations simply erodes their balance of time, even if sometimes the election to governmental bodies opens access to some privileges and enhances women's prestige.

WOMEN AS INITIATORS OF DIVORCE

With the new image of the ideal, or even the simply tolerable husband, the Soviet woman more and more often emerges as the initiator of family conflict and, in the end, of divorce as well. This conclusion is substantiated by all Soviet studies that have touched this issue.

Of course, there are many causes of the mounting divorce rate. But it is well established that women's growing aspirations account for a considerable part of the present divorce rate (see Golod 1977, p. 56). In other words, in the past, many women would have bowed to their husbands and would not have decided to break up the family on the limited chance of finding a new partner. But today they often prefer to separate from their husbands in order to satisfy their needs better (Goldberg *et al.* 1982, p. 67). In fact, according to numerous data, it is more often women who file for divorce. Various sources witness that divorce proceedings were started by the woman in up to 70 percent of cases (see Chuiko 1975; Kharchev 1979; Chechot 1973; Iankova 1979).

It is remarkable that even in Central Asia, where in 1917 women did not even have the right to sue for divorce and where the average number of children is about four, 35 to 40 percent of all divorces now take place because the woman wanted it (Tashtemirov 1981, pp. 115–17).*

Since 1953, Soviet writers and film directors have presented women as heroes who throw out their husbands as nuisances and free themselves to pursue their professional and emotional life. In movies on this theme, such as *Strange Woman* (1976) or *Sun Wind* (1983), all the sympathies of the filmmakers are with a woman who is portrayed as superior to men in all respects (see *Pravda*, March 9, 1983). In the novel, *Sweet Woman*, a typical story in this respect, the author, I. Velembovskaia, derides an

---

*A special manifestation of the new aspirations of the Moslem woman is her unwillingness any longer to tolerate the interference of her husband's parents in the life of her own family. This circumstance is the first among motives named by men who initiated divorce proceedings (29 percent) and is second among motives that pushed women to break up the family (13 percent) (Tashtemirov 1981, p. 116). According to data obtained by Yuri Arutiunian, even in the late 1970s, 88 percent of the urban and 92 percent of the rural population of Uzbekistan deemed that parents had to give consent to the marriage of their children. The figures, for Estonia, the most Westernized region in the country, were 22 and 25 percent; for the Russian republic—38 and 34 percent (Arutiunian 1980, p. 79).

"outmoded" woman for her desire to have a family and compares her to a more modern woman.*

Many Soviet women not only leave husbands whom they regard as bad partners, but they also decline the opportunity to marry if the man who proposes does not fit their demands. A review of the ten thousand letters sent to *Literaturnaia gazeta* in 1976 established that a considerable proportion of single women (no less than one-fifth), said that they had opportunities to marry in the past—opportunities that they did not choose to avail themselves of because the suitors did not meet their demands.

EMBATTLED DOMINANCE

Describing the Soviet family as an arena of female struggle against male dominance, I do not want to suggest that this struggle is already finished, with the total victory to women. Not at all.

Of course, the role of women in the family today is incomparable with that in the prerevolutionary period or even before the Second World War. Moreover, a relatively new type of family has arisen—a family with authoritarian rule by the wife. In a Moscow study conducted in the late 1970s, sociologists discovered that 13 percent of all families were of this type (Iankova 1979, p. 124). The author of this survey had to acknowledge that the number of such families had been growing. She consoled herself and readers that this tendency could not be dominant because "any kind of authoritarianism is opposed to genuine equality."

However, even Zoia Iankova, with her classification of families as "old" (male dominant) and "new" (egalitarian), has to acknowledge that even in Moscow, officially declared a model socialist city in all respects, 35 percent of all families cannot be called "families with the new structure of activity, relations, and mentality" (Iankova 1974, p. 104). In other cities, the situation is even worse. Forty-seven percent of families in Penza and 50 percent of families in Yegoryevsk (a city near Moscow) also could not be treated as "egalitarian."

---

*Only recently, under the influence of antifeminist ideas that are spreading in the country, have some authors risked challenging this image of the independent and professional successful woman. Alexei Arbuzov, one of the oldest Soviet playwrights, in his latest play, *Lady Vanquisher*, describes the life of a brilliant scholar who, in pursuit of her career, found herself alone in mid-life, without family or close friends.

A large quantity of data indicates that in the majority of Soviet families the male, although subject every day to attacks by his aggressive wife, continues to be the real head of the family, even if not to the same extent as in the past.*

During our study of *Pravda* readers in 1976, we discovered that, in most cases, it is the man who represents the family in the outside world, not the woman. Visiting families randomly selected for the sample, the interviewer asked the members of each family to single out an individual for the interview. In cases when both spouses were home, almost always (83 percent of the time) it was the man who volunteered to answer the sociologist's questions (Petrenko and Iaroshenko 1979, p. 126).

SUMMARY

The last two decades witnessed the exacerbation of conflicts between Soviet women and men. The ultimate cause of this conflict was the growing educational and cultural progress of Soviet women. Today, Soviet women even surpass men in their level of education and in the intensity of their general cultural aspirations.

Although the Soviet authorities altered their previous position on women's participation in the economy and are ready to allow women to stay home, most Soviet women do not conceive of their lives now without some work that can bring them self-esteem, independence, and a social life.

Soviet women are in acerbic conflict with Soviet men in two areas: in the marriage market and at home. With their new aspirations, Soviet women cannot find decent husbands. Growing alcoholism is one of the main causes of the continuing demoralization of the Soviet male population. The same alcoholism, to some degree, also accounts for the high mortality rate of Soviet men as compared to women.

The principal cause of domestic conflicts is the permanent lack of time for women. Despite the important change in male attitudes toward domestic chores, women spend twice the time on

---

*Of course there are jokes that cast doubt on the efficiency of male leadership. According to one of them, which at the same time hints at the character of the Soviet political system, the husband in the Soviet family makes the most important decisions related to foreign affairs and the direction of the Soviet economy while his wife is engaged in decision-making about such minor issues as the family budget, the education of the children, the vacation, and so on.

household duties that men do, and women are not willing to acquiesce in this matter as before. This circumstance, and even more that of male alcoholism, explains why Soviet women are more likely to propose ending a marriage and to prefer the life of a divorcee to that of a wife.

11

Friendship in the Soviet Context: ─────────
An Institution Against the State

The attitude of Marxist ideology toward friendship, the infor-mal, intimate, and close relations between two individuals, has always been very ambivalent.* Claiming to be heir to all human-istic traditions, this ideology projects a rather positive stance toward friendship at an abstract level. Unlike marriage, friendship has never been attacked as an institution, nor was it ever declared a product of bourgeois or feudal society. Moreover, in the classical Marxist writings, especially the interpersonal correspondence between noted thinkers, it is possible to discover quite favorable remarks about friendship. And the friendship between Marx and Engels has been cited profusely by Soviet authors as a model for close relations between two persons united in the struggle for the liberation of humankind (see, for example, Zatsepin 1981, pp. 103–4).

SOVIET IDEOLOGY: HIDDEN ANIMOSITY

I will here discuss adult friendship, concentrating mostly on the place of friendship in the context of Soviet political and social structure. I will not address the numerous psychological problems of friendship, nor will I touch on friendships between children.†

---

*Friendship in the Soviet Union and in the United States, and the resistance of friendship to political repression, has been a subject of many discussions with Professor Stan Kaplowitz of Michigan State University.

†It is noticeable that the political implications of friendship have virtually never been addressed in Western publications on this subject (see, for instance,

The available definitions of friendship are often vague and inconsistent. All authors agree that it is very difficult to separate "true friendship" from other types of informal interactions between two people. For instance, John Reisman, in addition to "reciprocal friendship," which is viewed as "intimate" and "close," the "ideal," "true friendly relationship," identifies "associated friendship" (a superficial and casual friendship) and "receptive friendship" (in which one of the members is principally a giver to the other) (Reisman 1981a, p. 207). Robert Bell, author of a recent book on friendship, defines it as "a voluntary, close, and enduring social relationship" (Bell 1981, p. 402). Robert Paine (1969, p. 514), in his description of friendship in Western culture, employs three principal characteristics: autonomy (as opposed to ascription), unpredictability (in contrast to routinization), and terminality (rather than open–endedness). Throughout this chapter, I will adhere to the definition of friendship that mirrors Reisman's description of "reciprocal friendship."

The paucity of empirical data on friendship in the Soviet Union does not allow me in all cases to make a distinction between "friendship" and less intimate relations among the Soviet people, such as comradeship or friendly relations between colleagues. This circumstance is regrettable, for it does not permit a more refined analysis. But clear advances in understanding can be made nonetheless.

While never having engaged in vituperations against friendship, Soviet ideology has, however, never bestowed upon friendship the title of a significant social value. This may seem strange, given the role of collectivism as a fundamental of Soviet ideology. Indeed, friendship, as well as less intensive relations such as comradeship, can be treated as manifestations of collectivism (or at least as its initial forms). Some authors, such as Sokolov (1981) and Zatsepin (1981), are actually inclined to approach the issue in this way.* However, official ideology and the most sophisticated writers, such as Andreieva (1980), repudiate (usually implicitly) such identification of friendship with collectivism, simply because the latter involves the interactions of many people. Friendship, in

---

Bell 1981a, 1981b; Reisman 1981). Only recently have some authors, those dealing with the period of McCarthyism, touched on this aspect of friendship (for example, Navasky 1980).

*At the same time, it is obvious that many Soviet respondents, being unsophisticated in the subtleties of Soviet ideology, straightforwardly identify "friendship," "comradeship," and "collectivism" as synonomous concepts. It is important to keep this in mind when dealing with Soviet sociological data.

contrast, is normally dyadic and a personal, even private, type of relationship, closer to the individual than to the collective. Moreover, in the Soviet context, the collective presupposes the existence of external control, and it is just this characteristic that endears it so to the mentality of a Soviet *apparatchik*. However, the essence of friendship as such is the rejection of the idea of the intervention or control by any third party.

Thus, it is not possible to locate, in official Soviet documents, any hint of the importance of close relationships between individuals. Soviet mass media do use the term "friendship" profusely; however, this is almost always at a "macro level," as in "friendship among the people" or "friendship between the working class and peasants." Even if we examine the entire period of Soviet history, it is hardly possible to find in *Pravda* a single editorial devoted to personal friendships between Soviet individuals, though editorials are frequently addressed to issues of much lower social significance. The few articles in which personal friendship is touched upon generally praise "military" or "labor" friendships as beneficial to the society or the state, but almost never as relations that may be valuable for individuals *per se*.

If *Pravda's* lack of interest in friendship can be somewhat explainable in Soviet ideological terms, the absence of even a word of friendship in such a wordy Party document as "Main Directions in Reforming General and Professional Education" (it took almost the first two pages of *Pravda*, January 4, 1984) can hardly be accounted for other than by enmity to friendship. Devoting a special paragraph to the "moral and legal education" of students, the Central Committee, official author of the document, requires that "collectivism and mutual exactingness" be inured from early childhood and does not mention friendship, mutual support, or understanding of two or more people, though party officials could not ignore that friendship was one of the most important life problems for children and youth.

Such a hidden animosity toward friendship, as an institution purported to satisfy individual needs, is hardly amazing in a society that demands the submission of the individual to societal goals and only reluctantly tolerates human relations that are of no direct value to the state. Of course, a moderately repressive socialist society is much more tolerant to human needs than a highly repressive one of the Stalinist type. Yet, even such a society cannot overcome its endemic hostility to those spheres of human life where it suspects (and not without grounds) that some feelings antagonistic to the existing political order may emerge.

In comparison with friendship, the Soviet system displays much more tolerance, even benevolence, toward the institution of the family. As was indicated previously, the Soviet political elite realizes clearly that the family is an institution that helps people to confront the state, and that without it, people would have resisted the pressure of authorities much less successfully. Yet the family is vitally necessary for the state as a means of procreation and, further, as a means of socialization and social control of new generations. Moreover, the responsibility for a family forces people to yield to the demands of the system which they might otherwise repudiate. So, after having attempted to destroy the family and do without it in the first years after the Revolution, the Soviet system, as we have seen, had had to acquiesce to uncontrollable aspects of family life and has decided to consider the family as its principal official value. Friendship, in contrast, does not perform such positive functions for the state, and Soviet politicians and ideologues have never found grounds for the revision of their disguised enmity toward it.

Practically all other universal values with an individualistic hue share the same fate in Soviet ideology. Only rarely can an assiduous reader of official Soviet texts find even moderate commendation of such values as honesty and kindness, and almost never, broad–mindedness, independence, fairness, altruism, or compassion.

As is well known, when the Bolsheviks seized power in 1917, they declared an open war on all universal "abstract humanistic values" and proclaimed the class approach as the only one tolerated by the regime.* Since the mid–1950s, however, the ardor

---

*As an example of the evolution of official ideology, we can look at a value such as respect for, and care of, parents. The official ideology actively attacked, directly and indirectly, this value after the Revolution. Understandably, in the atmosphere of civil war, collectivization, and purges of various sorts, the authorities wanted their underlings to be ruthless to any enemy, even if this was their parents.

The case of the pioneer Pavlik Morosov is really symbolic here. In the early 1930s, this thirteen–year–old boy reported to the authorities that his father, together with some other peasants, had developed a plot against a collective farm. This report would have led unavoidably to the arrest and execution of the father and his friends. Learning of Pavlik's deed, his relatives killed the boy with an axe.

This case was put to use by the Soviet propaganda machine as an example of model behavior. There was no child or adult in the country who did not come to know this incident. Hundreds, perhaps thousands, of streets throughout the nation, and as many pioneer camps and detachments, were named in honor of poor Pavlik Morosov. His exploit was worked into all history textbooks. In treating this period of collectivization and the history of the communist youth movement,

of the denunciation of universal values of a humanistic nature, supported by Soviet intellectuals and writers, has cooled remarkably. In some fields of cultural life, it has practically been extinguished (Shlapentokh 1982a).* Simultaneously, the elite has ceased glorifying such values as mercilessness, the physical elimination of enemies, and such. However, Soviet ideology has not agreed to the complete, even formal, rehabilitation of humanistic values, and such values continue to be step–children. Accusations of "abstract humanism" have not all been dropped by Soviet ideologues, and occasionally some writers or philosphers are criticized for lauding "abstract humanistic values" and for undervaluing the class approach to moral issues (see, for example, the review of the Slavophile Davydov's *The Ethics of Love and the Metaphysics of Willfulness*, in *Communist* No. 5, 1983).

The Soviet system has serious grounds to be, if not hostile to, at least suspicious of close relationships between people, and especially to close, intimate friendships. In this respect, it does not differ from any other society with a nearly omnipotent state. The leadership of such societies will prefer to have the individual completely isolated from other people and, thus, more directly at the mercy of the authorities. Zamiatin and Orwell skillfuly grasped this important feature of the totalitarian society: friendship is an obstacle to the absolute dominance of the state over the individual.

Moreover, friendship frequently constitutes the basis for the creation of underground organizations and of antigovernmental activities of any sort. Russian Decembrists, the first revolutionaries in Russia, were linked by preexisting friendship networks. The same was true of Russian populists. The network of people based on friendships can easily develop into an organization

---

or the history of the class struggle, no one could omit the name of Pavlik Morosov. The ideological pressure proved to be rather effective. The majority of the population, especially youngsters, sincerely believed in the high moral character of this boy's act. The Morosov case was used by many experts to destroy positive attitudes toward humanistic values.

What is the fate of Pavlik Morosov in Soviet ideology today? He has been held in low profile. The 50th anniversary of the exploit was only lukewarmly commented on in the Soviet press. The present attitude of the elite to the story is yet another indicator of the changes in the system of values that have taken place in the country since the mid–1950s.

*It is certainly curious that, with all the boundless, idolatrous devotion to Lenin, the Soviet censors have not, since the mid–1950s, permitted the quotation of any work of Lenin in which he praised terror, the killing of enemies, and so forth.

comprising thousands of people. The same network can then serve as a basis for the creation of autonomous systems of information (e.g., the Soviet *Samizdat*) or education (such as the Polish "flying universities" of the 1970s and 1980s). Friends can develop into a primary "cell" of oppositional action, principally because it is so difficult, and in most cases, impossible for political police to penetrate a group consisting of friends. Indeed, it is for this reason that the illusion of friendship is often created by *agents provacateurs*, in order to gain information about suspicious activities (although this is rarely successful).

Of course, the state and the political leaders do not regard all friendships in the same way. They are virtually indifferent to close interpersonal relationships among persons who do not hold significant positions in society, in particular among workers or peasants. However, as a person's social status increases, personal relationships become a focus of greater and greater attention on the part of authorities, especially of the political police.

In this respect, the Stalin era can be regarded as an experimental phase in Soviet development, for at this time conformist political pressures on the people reached their peak. Stalin did not tolerate any kind of personal relationships among high Soviet officials and considered even weak forms of friendship to constitute possible conspiracies against him. (See Khrushchev's memoirs (1970) for illustrative observations on this matter. See also Orlov (1953) on friendships among high officials in the Soviet political police.)

THE CULT OF FRIENDS

As suggested previously, the hostile attitude of the state in socialist society toward friendship is quite understandable. To a considerable degree, the institution of friendship functions to protect the individual, as far as possible, from the arbitrariness of state authorities.

In general, friendship has always served as a refuge for the individual from external threats. All other things equal, the lower the sense of security among people and the weaker their confidence in the future, the more intense and vital are interpersonal relationships. This can be demonstrated by the closeness of relations among those belonging to an oppressed minority as compared to those of a dominant majority.

The role of friendship in Soviet life can be understood only in the social, economic, and especially the political context of the society. There is little doubt that friendship, as a social institution, was vigorous in prerevolutionary Russia. Russian classical literature of the nineteenth century, for example, praised camaraderie among the people, probably more strenuously than Western literature of the same period. Friendship is one of the leading themes in Pushkin's poetry, as well as in the novels of Turgenev, Tolstoy, and Goncharov. The recent Soviet film of Goncharov's novel *Oblomov* portrays well the intensity of friendship between the two heroes.

The virtual cult of friendship in tsarist Russia strongly supports the notion that a lack of political freedom can greatly contribute to the development and preservation of close human relationships. The glorification of friendship in the poetry of Pushkin is linked directly to political opposition against tsarist despotism and the yearning for freedom (Kon 1980, p. 82). The same character is revealed in the famous friendship between two great Russian figures of politics and literature—Gerzen and Ogarev. The Soviet system, which has increased the political pressures on its citizens, has only enhanced the significance of friendship in Russia.

Certainly it would be erroneous to reduce the role of friendship in Soviet society to purely political factors and underestimate the other stimuli that drive individuals to close relations with each other. To be sure, friendship plays a central role in the lives of people in democratic countries, such as the United States or France. Similarly, for many in the Soviet Union, a friend means, above all, someone to whom you can pour out your soul, who recognizes your virtues and is tolerant of your weaknesses, who is your advisor in intimate spheres of life, and with whom it is pleasant to spend your leisure time.

Indeed, the available data suggest that Soviet people attribute to friendship a much more prominent place in their system of values than do Americans. In a survey by Rokeach, conducted at the beginning of the 1970s, Americans put "friendship" in tenth place on a list of terminal values. (Those with some college education ranked friendship twelfth, while those with a completed college education placed friendship a bit higher on the scale, in seventh place.) A study by Iadov of Leningrad engineers, conducted at about the same time, found friendship ranked sixth on a list with the same number of values (Rokeach 1973, p. 64; Iadov 1979, p. 90).

Similarly, in a study of married people in Leningrad, when asked about the most important basis for a happy family life, 15 percent indicated friends, while only 12 percent cited "interesting leisure in the family," "good standing on the job," or "desirable education." It is interesting that the number of respondents who indicated as a precondition for a happy life, "confidence in the marriage," was only slightly higher (17 percent) than those indicating "friends." Only "children" (42 percent), "having own apartment" (47 percent), "mutual understanding between spouses" (50 percent), and "material well-being" (50 percent) significantly surpassed the role of friends in the perception of what is needed for a happy family life (Boiko 1980, p. 105).

As in other societies, the valuation of friendship is particularly strong among young people. A survey of Estonian students, conducted in the late 1970s, revealed a first place ranking for "communication with friends" from a list of nine life values, with a score of 3.29 on a five–point scale. "Communication with a loved person" received only 3.01, while "studies in school" scored 3.10. Perhaps most surprisingly, responses to "reading, theaters, concerts, exhibitions" scored only 3.13 on the scale (Titma 1981, p. 77). An earlier study, conducted on young Leningraders in the late 1960s, showed that 88 percent of all respondents pointed to "finding reliable friends" as their most important goal in life. Only the goal of "finding interesting work" surpassed the importance of friends among the respondents (Ikonnikova and Lisovskii 1969, p. 91).*

Some interesting facts may also be culled from the studies of very ideological sociologists. One study of Moscow students sought to determine the degree to which students had internalized the "Moral Code of Communist Builders." Of all the principles of this code, itself a mixture of Soviet slogans and universal values,

---

*Kvasov, an official in the Party's Central Committee, known for his ideological aggressiveness, published the results of a survey which is rather curious by Soviet ideological standards. The survey was carried out in a Moldavian cloth factory between 1974 and 1979. Asked about attitudes toward certain values, the majority of respondents (mostly women) clearly demonstrated that they assessed human relations much higher than official values. Asked what they value most in people, 77 indicated a dedication to hard work, 74 percent mentioned kindness, and 67 percent said modesty. At the same time, only 49 percent cited "devotion to the cause," and 45 percent "principles"—two officially supported values. Moreover, when asked about their life's priorities, love ranked in first place (73 percent), respect of other people (67 percent) was mentioned second most often, followed by "being useful to other people" and friendship (both mentioned by 64 percent) (Kvasov 1982, p. 189).

students revealed the greatest understanding of "friendship and collectivism," while other principles had been digested less well. "Patriotism" was best comprehended by 22 percent of respondents, while "honesty" (8 percent) and "internationalism" (5 percent) were even less adequately internalized (Goriachev *et al.* 1978, p. 59). (In evaluating these data, it is important to take into account not only the different emphases on these values in Soviet propaganda, but also the fact that respondents must adapt themselves to quite loaded questions with explicit ideological objectives.)*

Indeed, the role of friendship occupies so central a role in the Soviet mentality that, in a study of students at Tartu University in Estonia, 25 percent ranked as one of the most important characteristics of an occupation "its capacity to gain esteem among friends." Twenty–nine percent attributed similar importance to "broadening their knowledge about the world" and 25 percent to occupations "useful to the people." All other qualities of occupations, such as the "creative character of work," "good income," "social status," received much lower rankings (Solotareva 1973, p. 244).

It is curious that in order to persuade single women to have a child, Soviet sociologist Bestuzhev–Lada resorted to the role of friends in the life of Soviet people. He exclaims, "How simple, as it turns out, to implement the cherished dream of everybody about friends? How simple to get rid of solitude!" (*Literaturnaia gazeta*, September 14, 1983, p. 13).†

---

*Another, also ideologically oriented survey of 12,000 employees in various regions of the country in 1978–79 (sponsored by such institutions as the Academy of Social Science at the Central Committee, the Higher School of Young Communists, and the Institute of Sociological Research) also produced some interesting data (quite inadvertently, given the project's directors). The respondents were asked about which human traits they found widespread among their contemporaries. It turned out that 88 percent of the respondents supposed that "comradeship" was very widespread among Soviet people. However, only 72 percent thought the same about "ideological convictions" and the same proportion thought that a widespread characteristic was that "people's deeds and words did not differ from each other" (Sokolov 1981, p. 67).

†The warm and sincere article of Vladimir Voina, "Close Friend or an Ordinary Friend," in the Soviet weekly *Nedelia* (1984), stands out as an extremely rare example of a Soviet periodical's daring to praise friendship, as such, without linking it to social duties. "Friendship," writes Voina, "is a sacred thing.... Friendship is an invaluable gift, one of the highest existential values." Looking for the most convincing proofs of his thesis, the author cannot help citing examples from his personal life demonstrating that the friend's help when one is in confrontation with the state is the most serious test of friendship (Voina 1984).

THE RELATIVE IMPORTANCE OF FRIENDS AND FAMILY

Of special significance is the question of the relative significance of friends and family in the lives of Soviet individuals, and
the role of autonomy and ascription in the choice of persons with
whom to establish close relations. Historically, in many cases, the
best friend has also been a relative. However, some evidence
suggests that the friend–relative is more likely now to be replaced
by a friend who is not a member of the kin network. This is likely
the result of the expansion of education in the country, as people
become more selective in choosing their friends and are more
likely to choose from a larger pool of potential friends than simply
relatives.

Moreover, common occupational and professional interests
tend to play an increasing role in the establishment of close ties
among individuals, which will also diminish the probability that a
best friend will also be a brother or cousin (on this matter, see
Inkeles 1980, p. 51). A study of young workers in Moscow,
conducted in 1971, 1973, and 1975, asked respondents to rank
the importance of thirteen different leisure-time activities. In all
three surveys, meeting with friends was regarded as more important than meeting with relatives. Indeed, meeting with relatives
was ranked eleventh in all surveys, whereas meeting with friends
ranked seventh in the 1971 and 1975 surveys, and third in 1973
(Ermolaiev 1977, p. 87).* Studies by Zvorykin and Geluta of
engineers in Moscow, Kiev, and Kharkov in the late 1960s, and by
Resh of employees in Tumen' and Surgut, reveal similar results
(see Kon 1980, p. 106). Kon illustrates additionally how, in Soviet
life, friends may compete with family as objects of love and
devotion. Quoting from such authors as Lucian, Montaigne, or
Bacon, he uncovers frequent statements to the effect that friends
are more important figures in human life than wives or even
children (Kon 1980, p. 23, 64–65).

Other Soviet data support the thesis that the importance of
relatives in friendship tends to decline as education increases.

---

*Not only friends, but even colleagues on the whole are gaining on relatives in
frequency of communication. Data describing the network of human communication show that colleagues more and more supplant relatives and
neighbors as people with whom the individual is in regular contact. Unlike private
political or religious contacts, professional communication does not arouse the
anger of the authorities, and human relations based on common professional
interests are extraordinarily intense, much more so than here.

Sociologists in Sverdlovsk categorized respondents into groups depending on their preferences of those with whom they enjoy their leisure time. The largest group (53 percent) consisted mostly of workers and engineers and preferred to spend their free time with family, while those opting to spend time with friends (24 percent of the respondents) was made up of students and workers. The third group (12 percent of the total), consisting of students and professionals outside industry (teachers, scholars, physicians), chose to spend their leisure time with colleagues, who were also, of course, their friends (Kogan 1981, p. 97).

The potential competition between friends and family is revealed further in a study of the attitudes of Soviet young people by sociologist Vladimir Sokolov. Sokolov examined attitudes toward duties to society and the perceived obligations of norms in relation to family, friends, and colleagues. Interestingly, respondents condemned most strongly the violation of norms in interpersonal relations (55 percent felt there was not justification for such behavior). The shirking of responsibility in family was disapproved with the same intensity by only 36 percent of all respondents. Concerning violations of obligations toward society (for instance, avoidance of public service, unwillingness to participate in "voluntary Saturdays," *Subbotniks*) was perceived as a serious fault by only 30 percent of respondents (Sokolov 1981, p. 215).

Foreign visitors to the Soviet Union frequently emphasize that friends play a much more prominent role in the lives of Soviet people than in the West. Very few such visitors discuss this impassionately; most, like Hedrick Smith (1976, p. 146), cannot help praising the warmth of human relations in the USSR and note the contrast to the reserve of Soviet people toward those not considered friends.

THE FRIEND AS CONFESSOR

The emotional attachment between individuals, separate from any sexual modes of attraction, constitutes the core of friendship. Friends are important for us in the first place simply because we like them. In the first detailed Soviet treatment of friendship in decades, Igor Kon underscores that "friendship is a relation valuable in itself; friends help each other without egotistical interest" (1980, p. 9). Commonly, however, close friendship relations emerge because individuals, in the initial stages of interaction, discover some mutual utility to the relationship. Only after subsequent development are these relationships transformed from purely instrumental to emotional, affective ones. Yet, friends may also develop immediately as helpers in facing the various difficulties met in life.

As compared to Western countries, friendship in Soviet society more commonly embodies this expressive, less utilitarian function. One of the principal factors accounting for this is the absence of religious and church life among the majority of the Soviet people.

When allowed freer reign, religion absorbs a considerable amount of human emotion and establishes links between the individual and God. Regular prayers and dialogues with God allow religious people to express themselves emotionally and to find a being who is ready to listen to their complaints and doubts. The institution of confession only increases the possibility of the person's finding an outlet for his emotional tension.

Soviet people, however, are generally deprived of these opportunities. The proportion of the religious, even if we employ the most liberal measures, represents less than one–third of the population, and in cities an even smaller proportion. Yet, Soviet leaders have always been aware of this human need for confession and emotional discharge. In the past, they have attempted to assign to Party functionaries the task of playing the role of priests. In the first decades after the Revolution, a considerable proportion of the population in the cities, principally the young and members of the Party, actually were inclined to see their Party cell as a place where they could find answers to their questions and moral support at difficult times. The memoirs of such authors as Lev Kopelev (1975 and 1978), Evgenia Ginzburg (1979), and Piotr Grigorenko (1982) allow us to reconstruct this unique atmosphere, when young people were so committed to the Party and its cause that they regarded their Party bosses as benefactors and confessors.

These times are now long past, and today there are few mavericks whose attitudes toward the Party are so reverent as that of the earlier period. Now, for nearly everyone in the country, the Party represents a force with which it is necessary to maintain the best relations using any available means, most commonly hypocrisy and cheating. Even in the novels of hack writers, it is impossible to find characters who run to the Party secretary to confess doubts concerning official policy, or about abuses of official privilege. Such confession would be likely to yield results far different from absolution or forgiveness.

Today, Soviets do not have the possibility of finding comfort for their woes either in church or in any political organization. Lacking chances to find such consolation and support, they can only hope to find this inside the family or with friends.*

The family, however, is not always capable of satisfying the Soviet individual in this respect. This is due chiefly to the deep conflicts, discussed above, that are rampant in Soviet families. These conflicts are manifested in many families by spouses regularly lying to each other. As we have seen, lying to family members is only a part of a general pattern of lying in Soviet life, as the individual is compelled to do this many times, to varying degrees, each day in communications with superiors at work, with local officials, colleagues, and so on.† Thus, it is to friends that the Soviet people are more likely to turn to fulfill the expressive need in their lives.

This most important element of friendship, the expressive function, also constitutes the foundation for the more instrumental component of these relationships. The mutual assistance of friends is a natural outgrowth of mutual sympathy and liking. People render to their friends countless services, both trivial and significant. If, however, we wish to generalize the character of mutual aid that friends ask and render, this involves collusion against the external world. Of course, many actions that people undertake to help their friends do not fall into this category. Whereas in open societies this is especially the case, in Soviet society the most valuable actions of friends are those that help the individual to skirt the obstacles erected by various officials or institutions.

---

*When Soviet sociologists started the first surveys in the early 1960s, they were afraid that people, unaccustomed to being interviewed, would meet sociologists with hostility. In many cases, it turned out otherwise. Respondents often greeted interviewers with enthusiasm and used them for making confessions of various sorts. For interviewers, it was sometimes difficult to interrupt the conversation and leave the home (about this, see Shlapentokh 1970).

†In an extremely rare quota survey of 425 young workers in Moscow, Leningrad, and Minsk (1974–75), respondents were asked whether it was permissible to deceive their coworkers and superiors. Despite the loaded character of the question, especially in the Soviet context, 46 percent answered yes (Shalenko 1977, p. 71).

FRIENDS AS A THREAT TO THE FAMILY

It is useful to distinguish two levels of friends' collusion against the external world—a micro and a macro level. At the micro level, friendship, rooted in mutual trust, serves to aid the individual in opposition to members of the family (especially the spouse), as well as in relations with subordinates and coworkers.

For example, friends are completely informed about all love affairs the friend engages in, and they will not only withhold such information from their friend's spouse but even assist him in his philandering. Indeed, Soviet novels are replete with heroes and heroines who create for their friends of both sexes the most propitious conditions for adultery. The famous Trifonov novel, *Preliminary Summary*, well illustrates this practice.

The collusion of friends against the family, however, is probably most important in the domain of drinking. For many Soviets, especially among the noneducated, a drinking companion is almost equivalent to a friend. Considering the role of alcohol in Soviet life, it is a significant advantage to have somebody to drink with.

The importance of a steady drinking companion in the lives of many Soviet men, and not simply workers and peasants, is so great because drinking in Soviet society is not always simply for the consumption of alcohol. More important, drinking is a social event in which people can release themselves from various fears and troubles and pour out their souls. In fact, in many cases, drinking is an act with strong political overtones, for it involves the release of frustration generated by the strictures of Soviet life. Thus, to have a partner for drinking and warm conversation is very important for many Soviet people—including women, who are more and more realizing the social function of drinking.

However, and despite the increasing problem of female alcoholism, women regard the drinking of their husbands as the major difficulty in their family life. Thus, not only the authorities but also wives, understand the collusive character of friendship, and because of this, conflicts between newlyweds over their friends is very typical in Soviet society. Igor Kon, who briefly touched on this subject, attributes it simply to the desire of husbands and wives to monopolize the time of their partners and to compel them to spend all of their available time within the family (1980, p. 190). However, another cause of these conflicts is perhaps even more significant: husbands and wives do not feel secure if they know that their partners have confidants and aides who will assist them in activities that may be harmful to the family.

In this respect, a survey of engaged couples carried out by Gurko in Moscow in 1981 is of interest. The author of the survey very reasonably supposed that conflicts in the family, in many cases, are rooted in divergences between the spouses on various subjects. Asked what in their behavior aroused the anger of their partners, 22 percent of all men ascribed it to the fact that they spent too much time with their friends; 15 percent of all women explained the conflicts in the same way. It is also characteristic that 26 percent of men said that they wanted to able to spend their leisure time without their future wives (Gurko 1982, pp. 90–92).

In the realm of work, as well, when friends are also coworkers, it is expected that they must also be in permanent collusion against their superiors and, to a considerable degree, against other coworkers as well. In these circumstances, friends will exchange information, aid each other in lightening their work loads, and assist each other in securing raises or other benefits. It is widely, if not officially, admitted that the interests of friends on the job are more devotedly pursued than those of the organization that provides them with employment.

It is a prominent feature of Soviet life that people seek to develop friendships among their coworkers, their subordinates, and even their superiors. In the selection of cadre and the promotion of individuals to supportive positions, friendship plays a vital role. The strategic placement of friends helps to insulate the superior from those less trustworthy. Surrounded by friends, the Soviet man or woman can relax and diminish the intensity of work activity in order to devote more time to personal matters. Although the state has sought to eliminate this practice of appointment by friendship, it has been largely incapable of doing so. This is traceable to the fact that those most empowered to combat the practice are themselves most likely to be engaged in it.

As important as friends are as allies against other people in the microworld of the individual, friendship is much more important in the confrontation of Soviet people with their political and economic institutions, at both the central and regional level. Some Soviet data indirectly demonstrate that friendship in the USSR is especially dear to those who are at odds with the system, dearer than it is to those who have adjusted more comfortably to the system.

Kitvel, an Estonian sociologist, employed factor analysis to discover the relationship between participation in public work (an important indicator of conformism in Soviet society) and various other elements of social life. Using data from a 1973 survey of 2316 residents of the Estonian republic, he revealed that the role of friends is much more important in the lives of those who are dissatisfied with having to do public service than among those who find this work gratifying (Kitvel 1977, p. 124).

THE FRIEND AS A SUBSTITUTE FOR THE MASS MEDIA

Since the installation of the Soviet political system, Russian people have consistently felt a lack of important political information. The search for reliable information, especially about the intentions of the leadership and about the actual state of affairs in the economy and other spheres of social life, is an endemic feature of everyday Soviet life. Having drastically limited the flow of information to the public, the political elite has created an informational system that serves only the leadership and the party apparatus. *Apparatchiks* have their own magazines and bulletins inaccessible to the rank and file. Even such publications as *Illustrated America* and *England*, magazines that by agreement of the government with the U.S. and Great Britain are to be distributed freely to the population, are available normally only to Soviet bureaucrats (Kaplowitz and Shlapentokh 1982).

The Soviet people have responded to this informational policy of the leadership with the creation of their own networks of interpersonal communication, and these play an extremely important role in Soviet life. According to our studies, as well as those of other sociologists in the Soviet Union, no less than one-fourth of the population regards word–of–mouth information as a vital source of knowledge about the external world and, especially, about the internal life of the nation (Shlapentokh 1969 and 1970; see also Mickiewicz 1981).

Data obtained in other studies support this important role of informal interpersonal communication as a source of political information. A survey of Moscow students revealed that 23 percent of all respondents regularly seek out friends to gain information about events within the country, and another 41 percent do so occasionally (Goriachev *et al.* 1978, p. 39). According to a survey of workers in the Vladimir region, up to 50 percent of the respondents mentioned their friends and coworkers as sources of political information, whereas Party workers and agitators were mentioned by only 20 to 25 percent (Mansurov 1978, p. 17).

The exchange of sensitive political information in Soviet society presupposes that the participants in the exchange employ the same codes in their communication. Of course, as ethno-methodological studies have demonstrated, regular communication between people in any society requires the elaboration of symbols whose meanings are known only to members of a small group. Yet, in Soviet society, with the permanent fear of repression for tapping illicit sources of information or spreading this information, the development of codes in interpersonal communication plays a much more critical role than in freer societies.

A good example is the telephone conversation in the Soviet Union. Given the assumption that a conversation is being monitored, Soviet people, if they dare to discuss political information on the telephone at all, usually employ codes known only to friends or relatives with whom they have had regular contact. When Galina Andreieva, a prominent Soviet social psychologist, says in her book that people who communicate with each other "have to have a common language," she means business (Andreieva 1980, p. 101).

This exchange of information will only take place if people trust each other. For this reason, information flows most readily between friends. Only friends, for example, will swap news that they have learned from listening to foreign radio. And it is only with friends that it is possible to discuss, freely and without reservation, impressions of trips abroad or even of travels within the country.

Of course, in most cases, husbands and wives also completely trust each other, and the exchange of information inside the family is also intense. However, since quite often the spiritual closeness between friends is greater than that between husbands and wives, the role of friends in such interpersonal communication is probably greater. This is especially true among men.

Given that the reliability of information received may frequently be suspect, comparisons are often made with the information obtained by others to determine the likelihood of its accuracy. Here, friends also play a vital role. In the survey of Moscow students, mentioned above, nearly half (48.9 percent) of all respondents declared that in order to check the reliability of new information, they compared it to that of their friends. Less than one–fourth (23.5 percent) checked information with other students, and 20.9 percent with members of their families. Only 2.8 percent asked the opinions of their teachers, who are regarded as representatives of the administration (Goriachev *et al.* 1978, p. 40).

There is no doubt that in the more relaxed, post–Stalin era, people are more likely to trust each other than they were before 1953 and will quite often take the risk of expressing non-conformist political views with people not considered friends. On occasion, people will engage in political discussions even with casual acquaintances on trains or in rest houses. But the majority of Soviet people still tend to avoid expressions of their political views with persons who are not friends or family members.

WHEN A FRIEND FACES AN EMERGENCY

In all societies, the role of friend tends to carry the expectation that, in a state of emergency—when one's life, freedom, or survival is in jeopardy—a friend will offer assistance and comfort in full measure. In Soviet society, the expectation of friends' active assistance, even when they may be put at risk, is particularly high. Again, the arbitrariness of political power in this society is largely responsible for the extraordinary demands placed upon friends.

As in all societies, friends in the Soviet Union are expected to be of great help during times of personal emergency resulting from spontaneous, random tragedies (deaths in the family, grave illness, fire, and so on). But besides Soviet friends must also be available when emergencies stem from purposeful acts of re-pression by the state or its representatives. The addition of this realm of emergencies makes the ties of obligation between friends in the Soviet Union especially strong.

Since much earlier in its history, periods of political per-secution have been regarded in Russia as the strongest test of friendship. Those who did not desert their friends facing govern-mental harassment have been regarded as among the most noble of people. However strong and intimate friendship can be, the cost for aiding a target of official persecution can be high (including the loss of one's job, imprisonment, or even death), and, as a result, friendship has not always won out among other human values threatened by the state.

In the 1930s, with the Stalinist terror gradually enveloping the entire nation, only rarely could someone caught in the juggernaut machine of repression count on the support of friends.

The tragedy of human relations in this period was tellingly described in some books written by those who survived the 1930s. One of them belongs to Nadezhda Mandelstam, wife of the famous poet. Each day the mounting terror tested friendship and brought suffering to people who could not pass this test, cutting relations with friends in disgrace, refusing to help them or even reporting on them (Mandelstam 1970).*

The character of human relations in this period is also clearly portrayed in Vera Panova's memoirs, published in the Soviet Union (1975). In 1935–36, victims of persecution and members of their families could rely on the help of friends. However, one year later, when the terror became fully rampant, those who found themselves in Stalin's slaughterhouses could rarely expect the aid of their friends. In many cases during this period, friends were transformed by fear into assistants of the political police, providing to the torturers of their friends the necessary "evidence" of their fabricated crimes against Stalin, the Revolution, and "communism" (see also Ginzburg 1979; Kopelev 1975 and 1978; Grigorenko 1982; Solzhenitsyn 1975). Gradually, however, with the disappearance of mass terror, the Soviet people began to return to their previous attitudes toward friendship. As the Stalin era became more distant, more and more frequently people began to stand the test of friendship when their close comrades found themselves in conflict with the government.

The role of friends in the life of a dissident has been skillfully described by Amalrik (1982), whose work was cited above.

---

*One event in the development of the tragic fate of Osip Mandelstam is very notable. When Mandelstam was in exile in Voronezh in 1936 for his scathing poem about the Soviet supreme leader, Stalin suddenly called Boris Pasternak, another great poet, and started a conversation about the exiled Mandelstam. Stalin rebuked Pasternak for not addressing writers' organizations or "him" in order to bail out Mandelstam. And then Stalin added, "If I were a poet and my friend got in trouble, I would be beside myself to help him." Of course, it is one of many examples of Stalin's utter hypocrisy, so typical of this bloodthirsty man. One year later, he sent Mandelstam to the Gulag where he quickly died. However, this episode, which has been very hotly discussed in the Soviet intellectual community (Pasternak attempted to clarify his role in this conversation that disturbed many people), demonstrates the prestige of friendship in Russia even if Stalin decided to exploit it in his sadistic games with both poets (see Mandelstam 1970, pp. 153–54).

Although in permanent confrontation with the Soviet authorities for nearly two decades, Amalrik provides a generally quite positive assessment of the behavior of his friends toward him. Similar impressions can be drawn from the memoirs of General Grigorenko (1982). On the other hand, some of the friends of Andrei Sakharov did yield to the pressure of the authorities and ceased all relations with him (see *Sakharovoskii Sbornik* 1981).

I also have some interesting data, which I collected under some very special circumstances, and which serve to demonstrate the role of friendship in Soviet society.* As soon as I applied for an exit visa, in October of 1978, I began to carry a diary in which I collected observations on the attitudes of people around me. In some respects, this study bears the features of an experiment and a study in participant observation.†

---

*Vera Raskin was very helpful in the processing and analysis of the data of this study.

†A few words about the sample. It included about 300 people with whom I was in more or less regular contact before my declaration to go abroad. Most were scholars (79 percent) and other intellectuals—writers, literary critics, painters (8 percent). 57 percent were men and 43 percent women. Of all "observed" individuals, 22 percent were under 30 years of age, 48 percent were between 30 and 50 years old, and 30 percent were over 50. Thirty–seven percent of all the people in my environment were Party members. Of all the "units" in the sample, 44 percent were Russian, 40 percent Jews, and 10 percent half–Jews. Seventy–six percent were Muscovites.

My sample can be regarded as representing, in some ways, Moscow intellectuals with liberal views. Other segments of the intellectual community, particularly intellectuals with strong Slavophile tendencies, and official intellectuals, were not well represented in this study. Though the origin of this sample is very peculiar, the sociodemographic composition and the intercorrelations between various indicators suggest that it is similar to the population of the intellectual community, as described by official statistical sources or from licit surveys.

Thus, the proportion of members of the Party is close enough to the respective figures for the entire scientific community of the nation (which is somewhat higher at 40 to 50 percent). As should be expected, the proportion is higher for natural scientists than for social scientists. Among my fellow sociologists, 60 percent were Party members. It is also notable that in my sample, as elsewhere in the country, the proportion of Party members is lower among women (23 percent) than among men (48 percent).

As in the scientific community as a whole, Jews in my sample, as compared to Russians, are more likely than Russians to be engaged in research in the natural sciences than in the social sciences. Among Jews, the proportion of Party members (31 percent) is lower than among Russians (45 percent). And the proportion of Jews in the sample is not much higher than that of intellectuals in general. In 1972, when the last data were published, the percentage of Jews among those employed in science was about 20 percent. The percentage of Jews in the Writers' Union of Writers was even higher, about 30 to 40 percent.

After my decision to leave the Soviet Union, my status in society changed drastically. Previously, as a well-known Soviet sociologist and Senior Fellow in the prestigious Sociological Institute of the Academy of Science in Moscow, I enjoyed relatively high status in the scientific community, even if my status was higher among intellectuals than officials. After I applied for an exit visa, however, my status was radically altered.

Before examining the data I collected, we can look at a picture of the typical situation facing a scholar who has chosen to emigrate. Quickly the scholar will 1) be relieved of all teaching activities; 2) have his graduate students transferred to other supervisors; 3) be deprived of the possibility of publishing articles and books, and have all those in print destroyed; 4) have all his books removed from libraries; 5) have all invitations to participate in conferences and seminars cancelled; 6) be excluded from all councils and other bodies of which he is a member; 7) in some cases, also be deprived of scholarly titles and degrees; 8) in many cases, be fired without any prospect of finding another job; 9) have his children expelled from universities or colleges; 10) face special meetings in the institute, organized to make public denunciation of this antipatriotic act, with orchestrated speeches made by colleagues; and so on.

All these measures are dictated only partially by the desire of the authorities to punish those who challenge the official dogma that Soviet socialist society is superior to capitalist society. Rather, harassment of would-be emigrants is meant to convey to people in their surroundings the attitudes of the authorities toward individuals who betray the motherland and wish to join the ranks of its enemies. Each action taken against an applicant for an exit visa is an indicator of the utmost displeasure of the Soviet system with this act. Moreover, each act of harassment also signals to friends, colleagues, and acquaintances that the maintenance of good relations with the applicant for the visa would be regarded as unloyal behavior, with possible negative consequences for those who choose to ignore these warnings.

Under these circumstances, the maintenance of communication at the previous level with an applicant for an exit visa (the dependent variable in my study) should be viewed as an act of great courage. While on a scale of courage, the maintenance of good relations with an applicant is, at first glance, rather modest, especially compared to dissident activity, its seriousness within the Soviet context should not be underestimated.

It is possible to develop a measure of this "courage" in the behavior of people toward an emigrant. This measure encompasses forms of contact from the least to the most conspicuous, ranging from actions such as visits to an applicant's home, to meetings in public places (such as the library), inviting the applicant to parties (birthdays or celebration of other events), regular telephone calls (presumably taped by the KGB), participation in a farewell party (presumably watched by the KGB), up to the final parting at the airport. This last act is regarded as a feat equivalent to participation in a public demonstration: because departure to the West makes any future meetings very unlikely, not only close friends, but all good acquanitances are eager to come to the airport to say some last words to the emigrant. Only fear prevents many of them from coming to the terminal for a last chance to see their friend.

With all these circumstances taken into account, it was extremely interesting to register, during my six–month wait for a visa, the behavior of various sorts of acquaintances and to compare this behavior "after" with that "before" my application. The major conclusion of this study is that the majority of my acquaintances, despite the pressure of the authorities and the demoralizing impact of this pressure, behaved with a distinct lack of obedience to the regime. Fifty–six percent of all "units" in the sample increased or retained at the same level their interaction with me, while about one–third reduced their interaction (10 percent) or stopped having any contact at all (24 percent). It is noteworthy that 12 percent of all acquaintances actually increased their contacts with me. And of those who did sustain their relationships with me, 42 percent (or 30 percent of my sample) came to my farewell parties and 14 percent (10 percent of my sample) were at the airport.

In analyzing this data, I singled out the following categories of people with whom I had been in contact before the event of my application: close friends, friends, very good acquaintances, good acquaintances, and ordinary acquaintances. The categories are based on the frequency and character of our contacts in "normal" periods. For example, I considered "close friends" those whom I saw (if they lived in the same city) several times a week, or with whom I spoke on the telephone nearly every day (and with many, several times a day). "Close friends" I would meet at their homes or mine at least once a week. "Ordinary acquaintances" are those with whom I met only casually, in the library, at work, or in other public places. I never visited "ordinary acquaintances" in their homes and had never invited them to mine. All other categories of acquaintances are located on the scale of intensity of relationships between these two extremes.

The behavior of these friends after my application was affected by their attitudes toward official ideology and emigration, and toward such values as friendship and self–respect. Given the high place of friendship in Soviet society, it is expected that people will sustain friends who are feeling dejected and in low spirits. Since friendship is one of the few moral values truly respected by the majority of the population, those who desert their friends in times of trouble are despised, held in contempt, and lose their self–respect. Thus, even if some people did not feel an internal drive to support me, the strength of public expectations and their desire to preserve a good self–image compelled many to demonstrate their allegiance to our friendship.

It should be pointed out that positive behavior toward an applicant for an exit visa in the 1970s does not imply the severe reaction of the authorities that it would have under Stalin. However, it was believed that close contacts with a would–be emigrant could seriously endanger the careers of people, undermine their chances for promotion, or destroy their chances to go abroad on a mission, or to place their children in a good university.

Behavioral changes were not uniform, however, among my acquaintances. The analysis of my data demonstrates a very high inverse correlation between the official status of my friends and their determination to maintain the same relations with me after my visa application. Among all my acquaintances with high status (heads of various departments and units, prominent social scientists, writers, journalists, and others), 57 percent either reduced the intensity of our interaction or simply cut it out completely. Among those with moderate status (senior fellows in scientific institutes, editors), 37 percent behaved in this way, while among people with low status (graduate students, fellows in research institutes), only 21 percent did so. Given that those in higher positions are also most likely to be Party members, and in view of the higher exposure of Party members to political controls, it is not surprising that among my friends, those in higher rank were much more anxious to curtail or eliminate contact with me.

My universe of friends and acquaintances was not at all homogeneous with respect to attitudes toward Soviet ideology, particularly official patriotism. While many were more liberal, a number of them shared official views and some disapproved of my decision to emigrate for various political or personal reasons.

What my data reveal is that friendship turned out to be the strongest value and that people whom I regarded as close friends were ready to sacrifice other values for the sake of our relationship. The less close the friend, the more likely he was to alter his behavior toward me.

TABLE 11.1: Percentage of People Who Maintained Contacts at Previous Level, by Type of Relationship

Type of Relationship	Percentage of People Who Maintained Contacts at the Previous Level
Close Friends	93
Friends	82
Very Good Acquaintances	67
Good Acquaintances	53
Other Acquaintances	38

Source: Compiled by author.

Of special interest is the behavior of my colleagues, the sociologists in my institute and in other research units. My circumstances affected their behavior in the following ways:

TABLE 11.2: Percentage of People Who Curtailed or Ceased Contact, by Type of Relationship

Type of Relationship	Percentage Who Curtailed or Ceased Contact with Me
Colleagues in the Sociological Institute	73
Colleagues in Other Institutions	40
Graduate Students	38
Noncolleagues	19

Source: Compiled by author.

As these data reveal, friendship passed the test under the circumstances described above. Of course, if the political atmosphere in the country had been worse than it was in the late 1970s, and if I had not been a "legal" applicant for a visa but a dissident, all these figures would have been much different.

FRIENDSHIP IN EVERYDAY LIFE

However important the role of friends during periods of personal trouble, relationships themselves tend to be formed during "normal" circumstances. Unfortunately, this "normal" realm of life is not well documented by sociological data. But it is clear that friends are omnipresent concerns in the everyday lives of the Soviet people.

Given the Soviet conditions, the individual's life is nearly impossible without the regular assistance of friends. We can begin with a phenomenon that is probably not the most important but is still significant: the borrowing of money. The Soviet financial system does not provide such services as loans to individual citizens. Yet, Soviet people regularly need to borrow money in order to make ends meet or to obtain some valuable goods available only sporadically.* Without the frequent, mutual borrowing of money, Soviet people would find themselves in serious difficulties.

Much more important, however, than the borrowing of money is the assistance Soviet people provide each other in beating the system. Friends play an extremely vital role in the procurement of necessary goods, for they constantly buy each other food, clothing, shoes, or other things, should the chance to get them arise—that is, should they appear in stores. As Hedrick Smith aptly observed, Soviet people know by heart the sizes of all their friends and do not miss the opportunity to buy something that will fit someone they love. Even more important is the assistance of a friend who has access to closed stores or cafeterias. Friends have the moral right to ask to be brought some food or clothes regularly from places inaccessible to them.

Friends are extraordinarily active in providing assistance in all other important spheres of everyday life. They are the first of whom people inquire if it is necessary to find a job, place children in a good high school or college, or get into a hospital or health

---

*It is interesting that the frequent mutual borrowing of money is combined with relatively large savings among the Soviet people. According to Igor Birman's computations, the average savings of Soviet families reaches a relatively high figure: 2670 rubles. This is about one and one-half times the annual salary in the country (Birman 1983, p. 71). Partly because these savings are very unevenly distributed, even among people belonging to the same social group, and because people do not want to dip into their savings, they borrow very extensively from each other.

resort. The importance of friends is directly proportional to the unavailability of goods or services, and is inversely proportional to the importance of money in obtaining hard–to–find items.

With friends as the providers of all sorts of goods and services, the emergence of networks of "friends of friends" becomes unavoidable. Indeed, such a network can virtually extend across the entire country, and anyone can reach nearly anyone else through the mediation of one or, at most, two or three people. This neatly illustrates a phenomenon of the "small world," described by Milgram.

It is, thus, natural that the prominent role of friendship in the everyday lives of Soviet people is closely intertwined with the "second economy" and the relations based upon it. There are, however, two types of radically different relations involved here. On the one hand, people involved in the "second economy" maintain less intimate relations, based largely on bribes, extra payments, and covert exchanges of goods and services. Friends, on the other hand, render services to each other without material reward or compensation—aside from the emotional gratification of recognition as a friend. Yet, even with this, the rendering of services to friends also forces people to infringe upon rules or even laws. Because of this, friendship and family obligations in the Soviet context contribute significantly to the maintenance of the "second economy" and to corruption and the general moral decay of the society. The obligations of friendship, as well as those of the family, also tend to undermine the role of objective, universalistic criteria in social life. Professional performance, honesty, and fairness, which ideally should guide the distribution of rewards in a society striving for efficiency and justice, become subordinate to access based on whom one knows.

It is characteristic that Buieva, a Soviet social psychologist, and her coauthor, Alekseieva, in their article, "Communication as a Factor of the Development of Personality," underscore that "true collectivism" and "the defense of one's own people" (the authors preferred not to use the term "friendship") are incompatible with each other. They write, "The struggle against the relapses of Philistinism is, above all, the active denial of communication and knocking together of informal communities (and sometimes, even of whole offices), based on the principle "you–me, I–you" and also the denial of the submission of social activity to narrow egotistical interests" (Buieva and Alekseieva 1982, pp. 39–40). Having denounced friendship in Soviet society, as it really exists, as Philistinism, the authors reflect on a major problem in this society—the orientation of mutual relations between people against the state and official ideology.

It is curious, but understandable in this context, that social life in the Soviet Union, with all its claims to be the most advanced, resembles in many respects that in societies based on tribalism and patriarchy. For this reason, visitors from some African societies are better able to grasp the many phenomena of Soviet life than those from the West (which Weber took as the basis for his theory of formal authority and bureaucracy).

It is characteristic, too, that, of all the regions in the Soviet Union, Georgia and the other republics in the Caucasus and Central Asia, are the most "advanced" in this specific area of development, itself a throwback to times when personal relations played the dominant role. In these republics, the crucial role of personal relations in all spheres of social life is openly admitted (see, for example, Zemstov 1979; Simis 1982). The central leadership, even under Brezhnev, has undertaken a number of measures to mitigate the corruption in these regions, including replacing their leaders. In effect, the diminution of the role of friendship and family influence on decision–making was a central goal of this reshuffling. However, as might be expected, new leadership in the national republics could not significantly alter the style of life of the people or the importance of personal relations in social life. In fact, during the last two decades, with the general decline of labor morale and other social values, Russia and other parts of the Soviet Union have moved more toward the patterns of behavior flourishing in Georgia, Azerbaijan, and Central Asia. A kind of "Georgianization" of the entire country has been developing in the Soviet Union.

In this connection, it is interesting to note what was said by some Novosibirsk economists and sociologists in a paper presented recently at a seminar in Moscow (April, 1983), which became available to Western journalists. Advancing the notion that there are different types of workers, both productive and lazy, Soviet social scientists hinted that the distribution of people of these types corresponds to the cultural traditions of various ethnic groups. It is characteristic that the authors mentioned, besides Russians, only Estonians, Germans, and Georgians. Given that Estonians and Germans have always been regarded as model workers, it is clear that the Georgians were selected to represent the opposite pole (see *Deutsches Allgemeines Sonntagblatt*, August 21, 1983).

Indeed, in part because of their close personal relations

inherited from the recent past, Georgians and other Asian peoples have been able to resist the Soviet order much more successfully than Russians and other Soviet peoples. Friends and family relations emerge as a truly powerful weapon in this resistance, allowing the orientals to combat the bureaucratic, centralized planning in various ways. As suggested above, with the overwhelming presence of the cult of friends and family, Georgians have been exerting a visible influence on Soviet life in the last few decades. Their conspicuous success suggests to other Soviet people that friends and family are more important in this world than abstract concepts such as "the interests of society," "socialism," or "communism."

FRIENDS AND LEISURE TIME

Friends play a central role in the activities of Soviet people during their leisure time. Though the unmarried certainly spend more free time with their friends than the married, friends are still very important in the lives of Soviet people after marrying.

Studies by Sverdlovsk sociologists in the 1970s established that the frequency of communication with friends surpasses that of all other leisure activities, except watching television. According to their data on people in the Urals, 15.8 percent of all respondents meet with their friends every day. Ten percent meet with friends two to three times a week, while another 22.3 percent do so weekly. Nearly one–third (31.2 percent) meet with friends several times a month, another 12.3 percent do so three or more times a year, while only 8.4 percent meet with friends only once or twice a year. In other words, nearly half meet their friends each week, usually several times (Kogan 1981, p. 177).*

In a 1975 study of Estonian students, respondents were asked to evaluate, on a five–point scale, the importance of various leisure time activities. Parties with friends received a score of 4.55, while dating scored only 4.39, movies 4.34, and reading 4.20. Time with family received a score of 3.55, and public service only 2.54 (Erme 1977, p. 117).

---

*It is interesting to compare these data with some from the U.S. A survey in the 1970s by Michael Farrel and Stanley Rosenberg established that the average rate of contact with friends for young, unmarried people was 4.49 contacts per month, and between 3.08 and 3.55 for married men with children (1981, p. 196).

The prominent role of friends in the cultural activities of educated people must be attributed, to a great extent, to political factors. With the absence of a real political or religious life, the rare possibility for travel abroad, and the lack of regular information through the mass media, educated Soviets are much more involved in their national cultural life than their counterparts in the West. Soviet professionals read much more fiction than their Western colleagues, and more often display an interest in poetry and intellectual films.

Indeed, an extremely important part of Soviet life are regular and long discussions of films and novels. Since the diversity of cultural fare in Soviet society is much lower than in the West, Soviet people are annually offered only a few quality works of literature and art, and the majority of educated Soviet people see the same movies and read the same books. The consensus among Soviet people about what is good and bad is remarkably high. Some figures obtained by us from surveys of Soviet readers demonstrate this. Our survey of *Literaturnaia gazeta* readers (1968) established that 45 percent of them named Yevtushenko as their favorite poet. A considerable number of respondents chose as their favorite authors such writers as Simonov (14.1 percent), Bulgakov (13.8 percent), Solzhenitsyn (10.4 percent), and Ehrenburg (10.2 percent). A similar remarkable consensus among many educated people, who constitute the majority of the readership, was revealed in attitudes toward movies. Some films were chosen as favorites by as many as 32 percent of the respondents. This consensus on what is worth seeing or reading creates the preconditions for much more intensive cultural communication than in the West. Of course, however, such communication can yield satisfaction only if it is among people who trust each other.

Soviet figures in literature and the arts (besides those who have openly sold out to the political elite) perform two important social functions—civic and humanistic (I leave aside other functions such as escapism and entertainment). Being in open or hidden opposition to the existing system, Soviet intellectuals propagate democratic and humanistic values in their works. But since it is impossible openly to demonstrate allegiance to these values, the best Soviet writers and film directors (as well as their colleagues in the other domains of art), employ special languages of hints and allusions. This characteristic of Soviet literature and art stimulates heated debate as to the real meanings of these works and the intentions of their creators. Again, however, given the political overtones of such discussion, they can only be conducted among those who trust each other. A friend once more turns out to be indispensable to cultural communication.

TRUST: THE MOST IMPORTANT VIRTUE IN SOVIET FRIENDSHIP

A number of factors influence people's choices of friends. The scant Soviet data do not allow us to describe even briefly the mechanisms of attraction that make some people friends and repel others from this role.* But whatever factors of attraction are predominant in various social milieux, it is indisputable that confidence in a friend is of central importance.

The extraordinary role of mutual confidence in human relations in Soviet society is directly related to the existence of informers who, as agents of the KGB, either full or part time, voluntary or involuntary, collect information about the political views and behavior of their compatriots. Andrei Amalrik, in his brilliant and thoughtful book, *Notes of a Revolutionary*, vividly describes how informers, both real and imaginary, influence the lives of the Soviet people. This is true of people both in and out of prison, and not simply of dissidents or intellectuals, but of all strata of the population.

There are different estimates of the number of informants in the USSR. Whatever is the true figure, every person lives with the assumption that squealers are everywhere. People are always convinced that one of their colleagues at work regularly brings reports to the KGB agent responsible for their office or plant. It is also assumed that some of the guests at any large party are informers. No one can be absolutely sure that none of the people invited to their homes are informers, especially if there are people who have not been known for many years. For this reason, and despite all their hospitality, the Soviet people are very scared if their own acquaintances arrive at a party accompanied by a stranger. It is curious, as Western visitors have observed, that given the fear of contact with foreigners, when they are invited to the homes of Soviet people, their hosts are less fearful of the

---

*Galina Andreieva sadly states that "there are only a few studies of attraction in Soviet social psychology." She herself could only cite one (1980, p. 159).

foreigners themselves than of any unknown Soviets brought with them without permission.

Thus, the general level of suspiciousness in a society of the Soviet type is extremely high. In many cases, the people may suspect each other as informants, even though neither of them actually is. As Nadezhda Mandelstam aptly observed, two illnesses have developed in Soviet society, "one sort of people suspected everybody as squealers, another kind were afraid that they were regarded as squealers" (Mandelstam 1970, p. 93).

Of course, the KGB is pleased with such an atmosphere, for it helps to control the people much more easily than if such fear were not so widespread.

In a society with a strong state and with authorities lying in wait for citizens who make a wrong move, the role of mutual confidence in friendship is much greater than in open societies. It is not incidental that the famous Soviet sociologist, Igor Kon, writes that "ideal friendship . . . is the most profound sincerity, complete mutual trust, cautionless uncovering of the own intimate 'me'"(1980, p. 133).

In his book, *Friendship*, Kon cites the results of a study he conducted with Losenkov in Leningrad and in the countryside of three regions (Leningrad, Chita, and Cheliabinsk) in the early 1970s. Their respondents, senior pupils in high school, put closeness and mutual confidence as the most important feature of friendship (Kon 1980, p. 166).

In the survey of Moscow students (1971–1972 and 1980), Vladimir Sokolov obtained similar results. Asked about the most important merits of their friends, the majority of the respondents named loyalty and honesty. All other merits received many fewer votes (Sokolov 1981, p. 207). Residents of a worker's dormitory in Sverdlovsk (1968–74) also put mutual confidence in first place among qualities of their friends appreciated most (Pavlov 1975, p. 122). The same emphasis on sincerity and mutual trust was demonstrated by the workers and clerks interviewed by Gordon and Klopov (1972).*

---

*Western studies have also revealed that trust is regarded by many people as a very important trait in a friend. Thus Crawford writes that, in his study, two definitions of friendship were given most frequently: "a friend is someone I can talk to and trust," and "a friend is someone I can call on for help" (see Reisman 1981, p. 212). Robert Bell also contends that "when we asked people to describe what was important to friendship, their most common answer was 'trust'" (1981a, p. 16). However, when elaborating on this subject, Western authors link trust only to intimate aspects of personal life and with worries completely devoid of any political color.

Given the constant preoccupation with the question, "Can I trust this person?", Soviet people try as far as possible to have as friends those whom they have known for a long time. Of course, this tendency is universal; Americans and the French also prefer old friends to new ones. However, in Soviet society, this bent for people with whom "you have eaten a pud of salt" is much greater than in the West (a "pud" equals 16 kilograms). For this reason, and despite the radical changes occurring in peoples' lives that typically separate friends, Soviet people tend to retain as their best friends those whom they have known since childhood.

For example, in a study of Taganrog engineers, 40 percent of the respondents acquired their friends in high school or other school, whereas only 30 percent did so at work (Gordon and Klopov 1972, p. 152). It is notable as well that even young people, who are inclined to change friends rather often, attempt, given the effort required to check their reliability, not to look for new ones. According to the survey of Moscow students, cited above, 43 percent of senior students, age 21 to 24, and 38 percent over 24, continued the friendships they had made while they were sophomores (Goriachev et al. 1978, p. 46).

Friendship is an important social institution in Soviet society. It helps people cope with the system and solve various individual problems, from political problems to those related to the acquisition of goods and services. In all its major aspects, friendship is at odds with Soviet political and economic systems. It constitutes an important factor in the gradual change of the Soviet system, from the Stalinist model to the post–Stalinist one. With its political structure imposed by sheer force, and with the absence of an alternative, the result is the dominance of short–term, hedonistic values as the goals of human behavior.

SUMMARY

Unlike marriage, friendship has never been recognized by Soviet authorities and the official ideology as a positive social institution. Such hostility is understandable because friendship in Soviet society, even more than the modern family, is directed against the state.

At the same time, friendship is considered by the Soviet people as one of the leading personal values. In many cases, friends play a much more important role than relatives, and sometimes even than members of the family, in the lives of Soviet people.

Though friendship is based, in the first place, on mutual

emotional sympathy, friends assist each other in various ways in Soviet life, especially in cases of emergency. The most important quality of a friend in Soviet society is the trust and confidence that the friend is not an informer. For this reason, people regard as friends only those whom they have known since childhood and youth, or at least for a long time.

12

Conclusion: The Soviet People ────────── in a Moral Vacuum

With the analysis of the trends in the relations between men and women behind us, I will try to reconstruct the general picture of the moral atmosphere in Soviet society, building on the issues raised at the outset of the book.

Many of the trends in the private lives of the Soviet people described in this book can be seen to be relatively universal. Readers in the United States have undoubtedly found many opportunities to compare Soviet and U.S. society and have found many similarities between the two. For example, marriage is found to be in a similar situation in both societies: at once highly valued as an institution and as a life experience, yet undergoing multiple transformations amidst fearful claims that marriage is withering away. And premarital sex is extensively practiced in the two countries—young Americans and Soviets would not be likely to argue on this issue, as both appear quite permissive.

Similarly, among the educated, Soviet and U.S. women would find a great deal in common, especially in the struggle to get more assistance in domestic chores from their husbands. And many of these women in both countries will be materially and psychologically prepared should divorce become necessary.

Nonetheless, there remain radical differences in the developments of private life in Soviet and U.S. societies. The principal divergences can be traced to the different roles played by the state and official ideology in the two societies.

Compared to the Soviet Union, the state in U.S. society engages in much less direct intervention into the private lives of individuals, especially in the domain of marital and friendship relations. Moreover, social values in the United States are interpreted so differently by various social groups that, again, compared to Soviet society, it is often more difficult to determine what lifestyles and behavior are "deviant" in the United States. While the Soviet state is much less intrusive into the private lives of the citizenry than in the past, it continues to be an important force, defining the laws and principles by which interpersonal relations are expected to be conducted. Because the range of expected behavior is narrower in the Soviet Union, the actions of Soviet people—even when essentially identical to those of their U.S. counterparts—are likely to be labeled and treated as deviant.

This is because the norms and moral prescriptions in Soviet society are not only more numerous (according to the old dictum, in the USSR you can only do what is allowed, whereas in Western societies you can do anything that is not prohibited), but also because Soviet behavioral guidelines are more demanding. Indeed, it is commonly the more restrictive norms which are violated rather than the milder proscriptions, and the Soviet people appear rather more uninhibited in their behavior than Westerners if judged by some absolute standard. And despite the radically divergent perceptions of life in the United States, the majority of Soviet émigrés agree that, in comparison with Russians, people in the United States appear remarkably law–abiding and honest.

Of course, deviation from officially prescribed behavior in marital and sexual relations is not the most important difficulty facing Soviet society. As actual threats to the survival of the Soviet system, it is the behavior of individuals in the economic and political realm that is of paramount significance. It is enough here simply to mention the widely recognized difficulties the Soviet Union faces in labor morale, reflected in the nearly universal violation of norms and procedures and in absenteeism, corruption, and theft of state property. The problem of "labor ethics" in agriculture, industry, and commerce has been recognized many times by Soviet leaders, compelling the late Yuri Andropov to institute his nationwide campaign against corruption.

Nonetheless, Soviet society does not appear as completely anarchic. Despite the enormity of violations of norms, the majority of Soviet people do routinely observe most of the norms imposed from above. Yet these norms are generally not internalized, but are perceived merely as external roles, the observance of which depends largely on the efficiency of the mechanisms of external social control. The role of values as internalized processes of self–

restraint has been reduced to a minimum. Consistent with Durkheim's formulations on "deviant" behavior, the overwhelming presence of anomie in Soviet society is revealed in the distance between external rules and internalized values.

This cleavage between rule and values enters the awareness of the Soviet individual early in life. Most Soviets develop this awareness as they find themselves compelled to lie to each other and especially to their superiors—teachers, bosses, Party officials—nearly every day of their lives. While the majority despair at the anomic developments of their society, a substantial minority adapt simply by exploiting the situation to advance their interests at the expense of others.*

The anomie of Soviet society is illustrated as well by the deep cynicism characteristic of large numbers of the population who are convinced that everyone is driven by only the most selfish of motives. For many, it is considered almost unthinkable that people could perform a socially positive act motivated purely by altruism, or even patriotism. Some ulterior motive is always suspected. In fact, this image of the moral atmosphere of Soviet life held by large numbers of people greatly exaggerates the scale of demoralization; but as a classic "self-fulfilling prophecy," this image functions only to hasten the process.†

---

*An indicator of the anomie of Soviet society is the total dissatisfaction of each social group with the morals of other: city dwellers and villagers, the intelligentsia and the workers, old and young people, Russians and non–Russians—all accuse each other in demoralization.

†*Komsomolskaia Pravda*, the organ of the Young Communist League, recently published some excerpts from readers' letters that illustrate the perceptions of young people. One letter states, "I have asked many of my acquaintances about their attitudes toward their contemporaries. I became afraid of their answers because they all, as if competing with each other, answered, 'Everyone thinks only about himself.' " "I replied, 'But there are kind people.' 'We have not met them.' Then I understood. They were talking about themselves. How has this attitude emerged of thinking only about yourself? What is the origin of this corrosion? Maybe our well-being? Has the easy life expelled the soul? Let us look attentively at ourselves" (*Komsomolskaia Pravda*, December 12, 1983).

It is an indicator of the great concern among most of the population that articles on ethical issues arouse the interest of newspaper readers more than other topics. Nonetheless, readers are highly dissatisfied with the quality of such articles—many fewer than half of all readers evaluate these articles positively. A survey of the readers of *Trud* (the Soviet trade union organ) revealed that only 15 percent were satisfied with the treatment of relations between superiors and subordinates at work. When asked for recommendations on how to improve newspapers in general, readers suggested above all more objective and more

The general erosion of the acceptance of official ideology and the lack of internalization (more accurately, perhaps, the externalization) of social values have led to a variety of fundamental changes in the lives of the Soviet people. In this book, I have sought to detail the nature of these changes as they relate to the realm of interpersonal relations, especially between men and women. I will briefly summarize the most important of these:

The Psychological Differentiation of Soviet Society—As was indicated in the first chapter, the decline of ideology has been followed by the loss of any integrative force in Soviet society. Despite the leveling impact of centralized educational and mass media systems, the Soviet people are divided into numerous groups according to their attitudes toward significant social issues.

I have sought to demonstrate that there is no consensus among the Soviet population about the character of the "ideal" marriage. Rather, a variety of marital patterns are supported by various groups. Such widely divergent patterns as the romantic marriage, marriage based only on psychological compatability, permissive marriage, serial marriage, cohabitation, single motherhood, sexually oriented single life—each has its own constituency of substantial proportions. Though often linked to specific socio-demographic groups, idiosyncratic personality characteristics also play a role in defining the type of relationship one will prefer. No less divergence can be observed in connection with attitudes toward children, the place of a career in a woman's life, sexual pleasure, and other issues in this domain of Soviet life.

The attitudinal dissensus, as would be expected, extends into all spheres of Soviet life. Behavior in the workplace is particularly notable in this regard. As the acceptance of official ideology has declined, along with fear of the authorities, the leadership has sought to substitute material incentives to enhance labor morale. These attempts, for a variety of reasons, appear to have failed, and instead of a rejuvenated morale, there has emerged simply further differentiation. The diversity of attitudes equals that in relation to marriage: the population falls into myriad groups ranging from workaholics to committed "shirkers" and "bunglers" (in the words of the official lexicon). Again, personality differences intermix with environmental and social structural factors in distributing

---

comprehensive treatment of ethical issues. The discontent of Soviet readers with the coverage of such images reveals the pessimism about this domain in the nation (see Shlapentokh 1969; Fomicheva 1978).

individuals along this continuum. Persons with similar objective characteristics and social locations display variant attitudes toward work obligations.

The psychological differentiation, stemming from the weakening of social norms, creates a rather unique climate in society, as the Soviet individual interacts constantly with people who differ from each other in nearly every conceivable way. If we were to compare, for example, professionals in both societies, the diversity of viewpoints would be greater among the Soviets than their U.S. counterparts.

The Growth of Hedonism in Soviet Society—Earlier we saw that one of the most significant trends in Soviet life is the increasing role of hedonistic values. We can now look at this in greater detail.

It can be argued that the rising concern among the Soviet population for immediate gratification of desires is directly traceable to a perception that the future promises rather little. The belief in the "radiant future," which surrounded the excitement of building the new society in the first decades after the Revolution, has vanished. And although the post-Stalin period, especially in the 1960s and early 1970s, witnessed a relatively rapid rise in living standards, such improvements have nearly ceased, and in some areas even show evidence of decline.* Under Soviet conditions, the individual accumulation of money does not promise much. Savings cannot be invested in a burgeoning enterprise, nor directed toward personal consumption, for the quality of available goods is low. While there is no unemployment in the Soviet economy, the rate of upward mobility has slowed drastically and opportunities for promotion are bleak for most of the population.

Under these circumstances, workers and peasants cannot even dream of improving their social position (although they can still hope their children will move up), while members of the intelligentsia and the *apparatchiks* can never be certain that they will not be demoted tomorrow, whatever their prior contributions to society. Even a member of the Politburo—not to mention ordinary bureaucrats or intellectuals—may be downgraded with little warning.

---

*Even in the early of the 1970s, when the objective indicators of the standard of living were on the rise, only 45 percent of Leningrad residents believed that their income would rise during the period of the next Five-Year Plan and only 35 percent expected improvement in their housing conditions (Alekseiev *et al.* 1979, pp. 23–32).

This climate of deep ingratitude on the part of the authorities toward the efforts and sacrifices made by the citizenry for the sake of society contributes greatly to the general despondency about the future in Soviet society. In this context, the growing fears of nuclear annihilation only exacerbate the refusal of the Soviet people to look hopefully toward the future. The result (not uncommon among certain segments of U.S. society) is a focus on immediate gratification and the disregard of moral constraint.* Indeed, the corruption that has seeped into virtually every sphere of Soviet society—and that directly or indirectly involves a majority of the population—is able to thrive in large measure because people see little grounds for self-restraint in this atmosphere.

The tendency to adopt hedonistic values strongly influences behavior in the relations between men and women and is largely responsible for the growing incidence of premarital and extra-marital sex, as well as being a factor in the rising divorce and diminishing birth rates.

The cathectic focus on values linked to immediate gratification has increased the importance of conspicuous consumption. As never before, the self-images of Soviet people depend on their success in the acquisition of fashionable clothing (mostly foreign) and new electric appliances, as well as access to special hospitals, vacation resorts, or trips abroad.

Moreover, for a considerable number of both men and women, the number of sexual partners they have had is taken as an indicator of success in life and constitutes an important element in their self-images. The importance of one's sexual history— besides its role as a source of pleasure—is linked to its role as an ingredient of self-respect and as an antidote to feelings of inferiority. The refusal to marry, in this context, is a manifestation of the unwillingness of many to curb their desires and give up a constant source of immediate gratification and self-affirmation.

---

*Partially because the Soviet leaders radically changed the content of their propaganda and, contrary to the past, started in 1983 to emphasize the military might of the U.S. and the West as a whole, the Soviet people have entered a new stage in their mental development: a period in which they have begun to be afraid of nuclear war as much as or even more than people in the West. Now many Soviet people believe in the nuclear holocaust as something that cannot be averted or escaped. An unusual survey of genuine attitudes of the Soviet people to the threat of war is in the article of Fedor Burlatskii, one of the most brilliant Soviet political scientists and publicists, "1984: what it is preparing for mankind" (*Literaturnaia gazeta*, January 4, 1984, p. 15).

The pursuit of pleasure of all kinds, as a growing preoccupation of many in the Soviet Union, helps them to endure the difficulties and vicissitudes of life. Unlike followers of the dreary Protestant Ethic, many Soviets enjoy their everyday lives, perhaps more so than many of their Western counterparts.

Conflict between Men and Women—The withering of official norms regulating relations between the sexes has led to the exacerbation of conflicts between Soviet men and women. The most important cause of these elevated conflicts is the radical change in the status of Soviet women and the consequent reluctance of men to accept this change. Soviet women, with high educational attainment and cultural aspirations, are less and less willing to subordinate their desires for the sake of men. The conflict of hedonistic desires between lovers and spouses has become a typical phenomenon of contemporary Soviet life. In the absence of commonly accepted norms, men and women align with each other only to the degree that this does not infringe on their individual concerns. The general anomic atmosphere, with its barely hidden contempt of moral constraint, exerts its influence not only on relations between adults, but also between parents and children, reproducing the atmosphere for the next generation.

Psychological Adaptation to Life without Common Values—The egotistical approach to life among a growing proportion of the Soviet people views immediate gratification as essentially the only worthwhile thing. However, while followers of this approach are growing in number, the majority of the population still feels the need for some emotional ties to society, or at least some part of society.

A large proportion of Soviet society continues to adhere to the values of socialism and collectivism as extolled in official ideology. The rest of those who have not become completely cynical about the world view themselves as adherents to some other abstract values, such as religion, nationalism, or democracy. Nonetheless, whatever their ideological or value inclinations, many still manage to avoid the impact of abstract values on their behavior. It is the adherence to the distinction between "values for me" and "values for others" that makes possible allegiance to some system of values, even while these values achieve no reflection in action. The consequences of this are of great importance, for despite the variety of ideologies and value systems opposing the official ideology, anomie is not significantly reduced in society, nor is any formidable base of opposition likely to consolidate. In some way, it may be said that the Soviet system has managed to create the "unity" so highly praised by official ideologues—yet this "unity" is rooted largely in the rejection of moral constraints in everyday life.

The Soviet people have managed to elaborate certain special kinds of "surrogate" ideologies, which are active at a verbal level in communication with friends and like-minded people. Yet these remain largely irrelevant to "material behavior." Only insofar as these take on political overtones do "surrogate" ideologies appear socially significant.*

However, even in the realm of material behavior, the Soviet people cannot do without some moral values to guide, and make predictable, their behavior. And this reduces, to some degree, the anomie of society. As indicated above, the most significant here are the private values, above all those related to love, family, and friendship. These values (sometimes combined with those of professional excellence, devotion to scientific knowledge, support of colleagues, and so on) constitute the core of the moral mentality of those Soviet people who have not abandoned all moral constraint. One of the key messages of liberal intellectuals, writers, and filmmakers to the masses is that these universal values make possible a defense against the moral decay of society.

At the same time, Soviet people are developing new forms of personal relationships and lifestyles that are more or less adequate to the increased hedonistic orientations. Permissive marriage, cohabitation, and single motherhood are examples of these lifestyles. All these and some other patterns have been more or less legitimized in the public mentality and even encroached into official politics. Moreover, public opinion has increasingly absorbed the value of privacy, something nearly alien to the prior Soviet mentality.

Of course, even private values that are conspicuously directed against the state (friendship, for instance) cannot avoid the influence of the general moral degradation. The Soviet satirist Zhvanetskii, who today is probably the best identifier of trends in Soviet everyday life, has pinpointed this in his recent brilliant sketch, "The Second Half of the 20th Century." Among other changes in human behavior he mockingly describes, he mentions

---

*In this way, personal "surrogate" ideologies are much like official ideology—that is, there is very little coordination between what is said and what is actually done. Indeed, the parallel is hardly accidental, for the separation of verbal and "material" behavior is learned early in Soviet society.

that "friendship has been modified to such a degree that it allows treachery, does not require meetings of friends, nor hot exchanges of views between them, and even supposes that the existence of only one friend is enough for friendship. From here friendship goes smoothly to communication, by which people understand and obliterated forms of friendship. A swinging feeling that includes some mercilessness, cruelty, and harshness is known now as kindness. Under a microscope, you can see distinct but rather weak, forms of mutual assistance and support...." However, with all these, family and friendship are still unique institutions that, with the devotion of some people to their work, withstand the complete demoralization of Soviet society.

Russian patriotism in this respect deserves special attention. There is little doubt that this value is of great importance for the majority of Soviets. However, with all this patriotism and despite the regular appeal to it by the authorities, it has little impact on the everyday life of the Soviet people, particularly in human relations, and in no way overcomes the alienation of the majority of the population from the state and the Party apparatus. The anomic behavior of the Soviet people in any sphere is in no way impeded by devotion to the motherland. Only in times of crisis, as during the last war, can this value become a powerful factor in material behavior, compelling people to make sacrifices for the sake of their country.

The moral vacuum surrounding the Soviet people is a phenomenon of great importance. Whatever developments may take place "above" in the political structure of Soviet society, whatever type of leaders may emerge there—conservatives or reformers, Stalinists or liberals, chauvinists or "internationalists"—they all have to take into account that they have to rule a society in which people are deeply indifferent to the life of "others" and who are absorbed only by their own egoistical interests. The cleavage between the state and society, as was observed by Hegel, Marx and other philosophers and sociologists at the time of the decay of absolute monarchies in West Europe, is as deep and great now as then.

Alexander Zinoviev (1976, 1978, 1980), one of the most original modern thinkers, is not inclined to consider the present state of Soviet society as deeply conflicted and threatened with great future perturbations. His vision of Soviet society is based on the old Hegelian/functionalist principle that "everything that exists is rational," and from this perspective he regards the Soviet society as, in its way, a very smoothly working mechanism that does not need ethical values for its normal functioning and that cannot be compared with Western societies. His picture of Soviet society supposes that the majority of Soviet people are well adjusted to this mechanism and do not feel discomfort because they have to lie and violate officially declared values many times each day.

I do not share this view. For me, the anomic state of Soviet society cannot be stable simply because it engenders problems that are beyond the control of the Soviet political elite and bureaucracy. The economic decline is one example. The social behavior of the majority of the population engenders consequences that will be completely manifest only in the future.

Certainly, there is still a minority in Soviet society who continue, despite the adverse influence of social milieu, to muster examples of highly moral behavior—in the sphere of production, science, culture, and human relations. The role of this minority is important, for they provide norms of positive social behavior for the new generations. However, the Soviet system acts constantly to quiet these voices or control them—despite the Party's praise of hard workers and those who sacrifice their interests for society.

The skidding of the Soviet population into a moral vacuum is a fact of great domestic and international importance, with many ramifications. This process can hardly be stopped by a resurgence of mass repression and attempts to resort to new ideological brainwashing of the population, especially of the young. What the ramifications of the actual anomic state of Soviet society will be is difficult to predict in specific terms. What is clear, however, is that this development will have a great impact on the future history of the Soviet Union and the whole world.

Bibliography

Aksenov, V. (ed.). 1982. *Metropol*. New York: Norton.

Alekseieva, V. 1976. "Gorodskaia Sem'ia i Vospitaniie Lichnosti." In *Problemy Sotsiologicheskogo Izucheniia Sem'i*, pp. 15–25. Moscow: Institut Sotsiologicheskikh Issledovanii.

Alekseiev, V., *et al*. 1979. "Izmeneniie Obshchestvennogo Mneniia: Opyt i Problemy." *Sotsiologicheskiie Issledovaniia* 4:23–32.

Alliluieva, S. 1969. *Tol'ko Odin God*. New York: Harper and Row.

———. 1967. *Dvadtsat' Pisem Drugu*. New York: Harper and Row.

Amalrik, A. 1982. *Notes of a Revolutionary*. New York: Knopf.

Andreieva, G. 1980. *Sotsial'naia Psychologiia*. Moscow: Izdatel'stvo Moskovskogo Universiteta.

Andreieva, G., and A. Donstov (eds.) 1981. *Mezhlichnostnoie Vospitaniie v Gruppe*. Moscow: Izdatel'stvo Moskovskogo Universiteta.

Andropov, Yu. 1983. *Izbrannyie Rechi i Stat'i*. Moscow: Politizdat.

Antonov, A. 1980. *Sotsiologiia Rozhdaemosti*. Moscow: Statistika.

———. 1977. "Izmeneniie Struktury i Zhiznedeiatel'nosti Sem'i." In *Molodaia Sem'ia*, edited by D. Valentei, pp. 15–33. Moscow: Statistika.

Antosenkov, E., and Z. Kuprianova. 1981. *Vnutrizavodskoie Dvizheniie i Tekuchest' Rabochikh Kadrov*. Novosibirsk: Nauka.

———. 1977. *Tendentsii v Tekuchesti Rabochikh Kadrov*. Novosibirsk: Nauka.

Arutiunian, Iu. 1980. "Natsional'no-regional'noie Mnogoobraziie Sovietskoi Derevni." *Sotsiologicheskiie Issledovaniia* 3:73–81.

———. 1972. "Sotsial'no-Kul'turnyie Aspekty Razvitiia i Sblizheniia Natsii." *Sovietskaia Etnografiia* 3:3–25.

———. (ed.). 1980. *Opyt Etnosotsiologicheskogo Issledovania Obraza Zhizni (po materialam Moldavskoi SSR)*. Moscow: Nauka.

———. (ed.). 1973. *Sotsial'noie i Natsional'noie: Opyt Etnosotsiologicheskikh Issledovanii*. Moscow: Nauka.

257

Arutiunian, Iu., and Iu. Kakh (eds.). 1979. *Sotsiologicheskiie Ocherki o Sovietskoi Estonii.* Tallin: Periodika.

Asseiev, V., L. Gorchakov, and N. Kogan. 1981. "Kakim Ty Pridesh v Rabochii Klass." In *Sovietskaia Molodezh,* edited by E. Vasil'ieva, pp. 52–65. Moscow: Finansy i Statistika.

Babenyshev, A. (ed.). 1981. *Sakharovski Sbornik.* New York: Khronika Press.

Baranov, A. 1981. *Sotsial'no-Demograficheskoie Razvitiie Krupnogo Goroda.* Moscow: Finansy i Statistika.

Baranskaia, N. 1969. "Nedelia kak Nedelia." *Novyi Mir* 11 (November): 23–55.

Barbash, N., and V. Glushkova. 1983. "Nekotoryie Cherty Demograficheskoi Situatsii i Vnutrigorodskogo Rasseleniia v Moskve." In *Rasseleniie i Demograficheskiie Prozessy,* edited by D. Valentei, pp. 46–62. Moscow: Finansy i Statistika.

Barshis, V. 1982. "O Reproduktivnykh Ustanovkakh Muzhei i Zhen." In *Sovremennaia Sem'ia,* edited by E. Vasil'ieva, pp. 50–56. Moscow: Finansy i Statistika.

Bednyi, M. 1980. "O Putiakh Sovershenstvovania Issledovanii Sostoianiia Zdorov'ia Naseleniia." *Zdravokhraneniie Rossiiskoi Federatsii* 3: 4–16.

Belai, A. 1983. "Linia." *Novyi Mir* 4, pp. 11–86.

Belen'kaia, I., *et al.* 1981. "Osobennosti Demograficheskogo Razvitia Sel'skikh Regionov SSR." In *Demograficheskiie Prozessy v Sotsialisticheskom Obshchestve,* edited by T. Riabushkin and L. Rybakovskii, pp. 102–34. Moscow: Finansy i Statistika.

Bell, Robert. 1981a. *Worlds of Friendship.* Beverly Hills: Sage.

———. 1981b. "Friendships of Men and Women." *Psychology of Women Quarterly* 5 (Spring):402–17.

Belova, V. 1975. *Chislo Detei v Sem'ie.* Moscow: Statistika.

Belova, V., and L. Darskii. 1972. *Statistika Mnenii v Izuchenii Rozhdaemosti.* Moscow: Statistika.

Berger, Brigite, and Peter Berger. 1982. *Capturing the Middle Ground.* New York: Anchor Press.

Bestuzhev-Lada, I. 1981. "Druzhba, Lubov, Sem'ia." In *Demgrafy Dumaiut, Sporiat, Sovetuiut,* edited by G. Kisilieva, pp. 124–32. Moscow: Finansy i Statistika.

Biurukov, V. 1979. "Serdechno-Sosudistyie Zabolevaniia i Prodolzhitel'nost' Zhizni." In *Prodolzhitel'nost' Zhizni: Analiz i Modelirovaniie,* edited by E. Andreiev and A. Vishnevskii, pp. 61–79. Moscow: Statistika.

Birman, I. 1983. *Ekonomika Nedostachi.* New York: Chalidze.

Blekhter, F. 1979. *The Soviet Woman in the Family and Society: A Sociological Study.* New York: John Wiley.

Blumfelt, A. 1971. "Nekotoryie Aspekty Semeinykh Otnoshenii v Studenchestve." In *Trudy po Nauchnomu Kommunismu,* pp. 98–108. Tartu: Vypusk 276.

Blumstein, P., and P. Schwartz. 1983. *American Couples: Money, Work, and Sex.* New York: William Morrow.

Boiko, V. 1980. *Molodezhnaia Sem'ia.* Moscow: Statistika.

Boiko, V., and N. Fedotova. 1983. "Otsenka Prochnosti Braka" In *Demograficheskoie i Ekonomicheskoie Razvitiie v Regione* edited by G. Romanenkova and V. Boiko, Moscow: Finansy i Statistika.

Bondarskaia, G. 1977. *Rozhdaemost' v SSSR: Etnodemografisheskii Aspect.* Moscow: Statistika.

Bondarskaia, G., and I. Il'ina. 1979. "Etnicheskaia Differentsiatsiia Brachnosti Zhenshchin v SSSR." In *Demograficheskoie Razvitiie Sem'i,* edited by A. Volkov. pp. 7–38. Moscow: Statistika.

Borisov, V. 1976. *Perespektivy Rozhdaiemosti.* Moscow: Statistika.

Borovik, S. 1980. "My Tol'ko Znakomy." *Nash Sovremennik* 12: 140–55.

Brezhnev, L. 1981. *Otchetnyi Doklad Zentral'nogo Komiteta KPSS XXYI S'ezdu Kommunisticheskoi Partii Sovietskogo Souza i Ocherednyie Zadachi Partii v Oblasti Vnutrennei i Vneshnei Politiki.* Moscow: Politizdat.

———. 1976. *Otchet Zentral'nogo Komiteta KPSS i Ocherednyie Zadachi Partii v Oblasti Vnutrennei i Vneshnei Politiki.* Moscow: Politizdat.

Buieva, L., and V. Alekseieva. 1982. "Obshcheniie kak Faktor Razvitiia." *Sotsiologicheskiie Issledovaniia* 2:31–42.

Burlatskii, F. 1984. "1984—Chto On Gotovit dlia Cheloveschstva." *Literaturnaia gazeta,* January 4.

Burova, S. 1979. *Sotsiologiia i Pravo Razvoda.* Minsk: Izdatel'stvo BGU.

Buslov, K., and A. Chigir' (eds.). 1983. *Trudovyie i Nravstvennyie Osnovy Sovietskoi Sem'i.* Minsk: Nauka i Tekhnika.

Campbell, A., P. Converse, and W. Rodgers. 1976. *The Quality of American Life: Perceptions, Evaluations, and Satisfactions.* New York: Russell Sage Foundation.

Carr, E. 1958. *Socialism in One Country.* Vol. 1. London: Harmondsworth.

Casler, Lawrence. 1974. *Is Marriage Necessary?* New York: Human Sciences Press.

Changli, I. 1973. *Trud.* Moscow: Nauka.

Chechot, D. 1976. *Molodezh i Brak.* Leningrad: Znaniie.

———. 1973. *Sotsiologiia Braka i Razvoda.* Leningrad: Znaniie.

Cherlin, Andrew. 1981. *Marriage, Divorce, Remarriage.* Cambridge: Harvard University Press.

Chorvat, Fr. 1983. *Luvov', Materinstvo, Budushcheie.* Moscow: Progress.

Chuiko, L. 1982. "Lubov' i Domashneie Khosiastvo." In *Sovremenaia Semia,* edited by E. Vasil'ieva, pp. 44–49. Moscow: Finansy i Statistika.

———. 1975. *Braki i Razvody.* Moscow: Statistika.

———. 1974. "Opyt Analyza Mezhnatsional'nykh Brakov v SSSR." In *Razvitiie Naselaniia,* edited by D. Valentei, pp. 47–54. Moscow: Statistika.

Chuiko, L., and V. Nikitenko. 1979. "Pokoleniia v Sem'ie." In *Sem'ia*

Segodnia, edited by D. Valentei, pp. 51–62. Moscow: Statistika.

Chumakova, T. 1974. *Sem'ia, Moral', Pravo*. Minsk: Izdatel'stvo BGU.

Darskii, L. 1979. "Rozhdaeimost' i Reproduktivnaia Funktsiia Sem'i." In *Demograficheskoie Razvitiie Sem'i*, edited by A. Volkov, pp. 85–125. Moscow: Statistika.

———. 1972. *Formirovaniie Sem'i*. Moscow: Statistika.

Darskii, L. (ed.). 1978. *Rozhdaemost'*. Moscow: Statistika.

Davis, C., and M. Feshbach. 1980. "Rising Infant Mortality in the USSR in the 1970s." International Population Reports Series P-95, No. 74. Washington, DC: U.S. Bureau of Census, Foreign Demographic Analysis Division.

Davydov, Iu. 1982. *Etika Lubvi i Metafisika Svoevoliia*. Moscow: Molodaia Gvardiia.

De Lamates J., and P. MacCorquodal. 1964. *Premarital Sexuality: Attitudes, Relationships, Behavior*. Madison: University of Wisconsin Press.

Djilas, M. 1970. *Razgovory so Stalinym*. Frankfurt: Posev'.

Dmitriiev, A. 1980. *Sotsial'nyie Problemy Ludei Pozhilogo Vozrasta*. Leningrad: Nauka.

Dsarasova, I. 1979. "Struktura Sem'i v SSSR." In *Sem'ia Segodnia*, edited by D. Valentei, pp. 40–50. Moscow: Statistika.

Dubinin, N. 1983. *Chto Takoie Chelovek*. Moscow: Mysl'.

Dubinin, N., I. Karpets, and V. Kudriavstsev. 1982. *Genetika, Povedeniie, Otvetstvennost'*. Moscow: Politizdat.

Durkheim, Emile. 1933. *The Division of Labor in Society*. New York: Macmillan.

———. 1951. *Suicide*. Glencoe: The Free Press.

Duvignaud, Jean. 1973. *L'Anomie, hérésie et subversion*. Paris: Editions Anthropos.

Elistratkina, S. 1979. "Semeinyie Problemy Glazami Zamuzhnikh Zhenshchin." In *Sem'ia Segodnia*, edited by D. Valentei, pp. 85–92. Moscow: Statistika.

Eremeiev, B. 1982. "Brachnyie Ob'iavlenia Vchera i Segodnia." In *Sovremenaia Sem'ia*, edited by E. Vasil'ieva, pp. 103–14. Moscow: Finansy i Statistika.

Erme, I. 1977. "Izucheniie Orientatsii Starsheklassinikov v Sfere Svobodnogo Vremeni." In *Sotsial'naia i Professional'naia Orientatsiia Molodezhi i Problemy Kommunisticheskogo Vospitaniia*, edited by M. Titma, pp. 115–27. Tallin: Akademiia Nauk Estonskoi SSR.

Fainburg, Z. 1981. "Emotsial'no-Kul'turnyie Faktory Funktsionirovaniia Sem'i." *Sotsiologicheskiie Issledovaniia* 1:144–47.

———. 1978. "Sotsial'nyie Funktsii Sem'i i Genesis Poniatiia Ieie Stabil'nosti." In *Stabil'nost' Sem'i kak Sotsial'naia Problema*, edited by Z. Iankova, pp. 7–18. Moscow: Institut Sotsiologicheskikh Issledovanii.

———. 1977. "Problema Emotsianal'nykh Faktorov Formirovaniia Sem'i."

In *Izmeneniie Polozheniia Zhenshchinyi i Sem'ia,* edited by A. Kharchev, pp. 133–38. Moscow: Nauka.

————. 1977. "K Voprosu ob Eticheskoi Motivatsii Braka." In *Problemy Braka, Sem'i i Demografii.* Moscow: Statistika.

————. 1969. 'Tsennostnyie Orientatsii Lichnosti v Nekotorykh Sotsial'nykh Gruppakh Sotsialisticheskogo Obshchestva." In *Lichnost' i Ieie Tsennostnyie Orientatsii.* Vol. 2, edited by V. Iadov and I. Kon. Moscow: Institut Konkretnykh Sotsial'nykh Issledovanii.

Faisulin, F. 1978. "Ossobennosti Sotsial'nykh Peremeshchennii v Gorode." In *Ludi v Gorodakh i na Sele,* edited by D. Valentei. Moscow: Statistika.

Farrell, M., and S. Rosenberg. 1981. *Men at Midlife.* Boston: Auburn House.

Fedorina, N. 1983. *Sotsial'naia Psykhologiia: Ukazatel' Literatury.* Moscow: Izdatel'stvo Moskovskogo Universiteta.

Fedotova, N. 1982. "Nekotoryie Voprosy Obraza Zhizni Gorodskoi Sem'i." In *Problemy Sotsial'nogo Razvitiia Krupnykh Gorodov,* edited by Iu. Suslov and P. Lebedev, pp. 142–52. Leningrad: Izdatel'stvo Leningradskogo Universiteta.

Feshbach, M. 1983. "Issues in Soviet Health Problems." In *Soviet Economy in the 1980s: Problems and Prospects.* U.S. Congress, Joint Economic Committee. Joint Committee Print, Second Session, pp. 203–27.

————. 1982. "The Soviet Union: Population Trends and Dilemmas." *Population Bulletin* 37 (August):3–45.

Filist, G. 1977. *Nekotoryie Osobennosti Ateisticheskogo Vospitaniia Gorodskogo Naseleniia.* Minsk: Izdatel'stvo BGU.

Fisher, Wesley. 1980. *The Soviet Marriage Market: Mate-Selection in Russia and the USSR.* New York: Praeger.

Fomicheva, I. (ed.). 1978. *Literaturnaia gazeta i Ieie Auditoriia.* Moscow: Izdatel'stvo MGU.

Frank, D. 1974. "Current Conceptions of Competency Motivation and Self-Validation." In *Social Psychology for Sociologists,* edited by D. Field, pp. 68–82. New York: Halsted.

Gerasimov, I. 1983. "Probel v Kalendarie." *Novyi Mir* 3:pp. 6–143.

Gerasimova, I. 1976. *Struktura Sem'i.* Moscow: Statistika.

Ginsberg, R. 1980. *Anomie and Aspiration: A Reinterpretation of Durkheim's Theory.* New York: Arno Press.

Ginzburg, E. 1979 [1967]. *Journey Into the Whirlwind.* Translated by Paul Stevenson and Max Hayward. New York: Harcourt Brace and World.

Glick, Paul, and Arthur Norton. 1977. "Marrying, Divorcing, and Living Together in the U.S. Today." *Population Bulletin* 32:3–39.

Goldberg, A., V. Kamenetskii, and L. Akinfieva. 1982. "Preodolet' Trudnosti Podsteregaiushchiie Sem'iu." In *Sovremenaia Semia,* edited by E. Vasil'ieva, pp. 63–70. Moscow: Finansy i Statistika.

Golod, S. 1982. "Udovletvorennost' Supruzhestvom kak Faktor Stabilizatsii Sem'i." In *Sovremenaia Semia*, edited by E. Vasil'ieva, pp. 57–62. Moscow: Finansy i Statistika.

_____. 1977. "Sotsial'no-Psichologicheskie i Nravstvennyie Tsennosti Sem'i." In *Molodaia Semia*, edited by D. Valentei, pp. 47–56. Moscow: Statistika.

_____. 1975. "Molodaia Sem'a." In *Molodezh i Sovremennost'*, edited by V. Lisovskii and V. Iadov. Leningrad: Znanie.

Goriachev, M., M Syroiezhkina, and V. Sdobnov. 1978. "Nekotoryie Voprosy Povysheniia Effektivnosti Ideino-Po Liticheskogo i Nravstvennogo Vospitaniia Uchashcheisia Molodezhi." In *Sotsiologicheskiie Problemy Kommunisticheskogo Vospitaniia*, edited by N. Mansurov. Moscow: Institut Sotsiologicheskikh Issledovanii.

Gordon, L., and E. Gruzdeva. 1975. "Rasprostranennost' i Intensivnost' Chteniia v Gorodskoi Rabochei Srede." In *Problemy Sotsiologii i Psychologii Chteniia*, edited by E. Khrastestskii, pp. 47–64. Moscow: Kniga.

Gordon, L., and E. Klopov. 1972. *Chelovek Posle Raboty*. Moscow: Nauka.

Gordon, L., E. Klopov, and L. Onikov. 1977. *Cherty Sotsialisticheskogo Obraza Zhizhi: Byt Gorodskikh Rabochikh Vchera, Segodnia, Zavtra*. Moscow: Politizdat.

Gouldner, Alvin W. 1970. *The Coming Crisis of Western Sociology*. New York: Basic Books.

Grechin, A. 1983. "Opyt Sotsiologicheskogo Izucheniia Pravosoznaniia." *Sotsiologicheskiie Issledovaniia* 2:121–28.

Grigorenko, P. 1982. *Memoirs*. New York: Norton.

Grushin, B., and L. Onikov. 1980. *Massovoaia Informatsiia v Sovietskom Promyshlennom Gorode*. Moscow: Politizdat.

Gurko, T. 1982. "Vliianiie Dobrachnogo Povedeniia na Stabil'nost' Molodoi Sem'i." *Sotsiologicheskiie Issledovaniia* 2:88–93.

Hacker, Andrew. 1982. "Farewell to the Family." *New York Review of Books*, March 18, pp. 37–44.

Hill, R., et al. 1970. *Family Development in Three Generations: A Longitudinal Study of Changing Family Patterns of Planning and Achievement*. Cambridge: Schenkman.

Horn, P., and J. Horn. 1982. *Sex in the Office*. New York: Addison-Wesley.

Houseknecht, S. 1982. "Voluntary Childlessness in the 1980s: A Significant Increase?" *Marriage and Family Review* 5:51–69.

Houseknecht, S., and G. Grenier. 1980. "Marital Disruption and Higher Education among Women in the United States." *Sociological Quarterly* 21:375–89.

Iadov, V., V. Rozhin, and Z. Zdravomyslov. 1970 [1967]. *Man and His Work*. White Plains: International Arts and Science Press.

Iadov, V. (ed.). 1979. *Samoregulatsia i Prognozirovaniie Sotsial'nogo Povedeniia Lichnosti*. Leningrad: Nauka.

_____. (ed.) 1977. *Sotsial'no-Psychologicheskii Portret Inzhenera*. Moscow: Mysl'.

Iankova, Z. 1979. *Gorodskaia Sem'ia*. Moscow: Nauka.

_____. 1978. "Gorodskaia Sem'ia: Razvitiie, Ieie Struktura i Funktsii." In *Sotsiologiia i Problemy Sotsial'nogo Razvitiia*, edited by T. Riabushkin, *et al*. Moscow: Nauka.

_____. 1975. "Razvitie Lichnosti Zhenshchiny v Sovietskom Obshchestve." *Sotsiologicheskiie Issledovaniia* 4:62–73.

_____. 1974. "Struktura Gorodskoi Sem'i v Sotsialisticheskom Obshchestve." *Sotsiologicheskiie Issledovaniia* 1:100–109.

Iankova, Z., and M. Pankratova. 1979. "Funkstsii Sovremennoi Sovietskoi Sem'i." In *Sem'ia Segodnia*, edited by D. Valentei. Moscow: Statistika.

Iankova, Z., and I. Rodzinskaia. 1982. *Problemy Bol'shogo Goroda*. Moscow: Finansy i Statistika.

Iarve, M. 1977. "O Tsennostnykh Orientatsiakh v Ispol'zovanii Svobodnogo Vremeni." In *Problemy Razvitiia Kul'tury v Usloviiakh Industrial'nogo Regiona*, edited by L. Kogan and E. Rannik. Tallin: Institut Istorii Akademii Estonskoi SSR Nauk.

Igoshev, K. 1971. *Psychologiia Prestupnykh Proiavlenii sredi Molodezhi*. Moscow: Mysl'.

Ikonnikova, S., and V. Lisovskii. 1969. *Molodezh o Sebe, Svoikh Sverstnikakh*. Leningrad: Lenizdat.

Inkeles, Alex. 1980. "Modernization and Family Patterns: A Test of Convergence Theory." In *Conspectus of History* 1, edited by D. Hoover and J. Koumouldies, pp. 31–63.

Inkeles, A., and R. Bauer. 1959. *The Soviet Citizen: Daily Life in a Totalitarian Society*. Cambridge: Harvard University Press.

Iurkevitch, N. 1970. *Sovietskaia Sem'ia*. Minsk: Izdatel'stvo BGU.

Iurkevitch, N. and G. Iakovleva. 1977. "K Voprosy o Vnebrachnoi Rozhdaemosti i Polozhenii Odinokoi Materi." In *Vzaimootnosheniie Pokolenii*, pp. 170–85. Moscow: Statistika.

Ivanov, B. 1972. "Vklad Sem'i v Sotsializatsiiu Individa." In *Dinamika Izmeneniia Polozheniia Zhenshchiny i Sem'ia*, pp. 62–68. Moscow: Institut Konkretnykh Sotsial'nykh Issledovanii.

Jencks, Christopher. 1983. "Discrimination and Thomas Sowell." *New York Review of Books*, March 3.

Kaliniuk, I., and I. Veselkova. 1982. "Demograficheskiie Prozessy v SSSR." In *Naseleniie SSSR Segodnia*, edited by D. Valentei, pp. 7–19. Moscow: Finansy i Statistika.

Kaplowitz, S., and V. Shlapentokh. 1982. "Possible Falsification of Survey Data: An Analysis of a Mail Survey in the Soviet Union." *Public Opinion Quarterly* (April):2–21.

Kamenetskii B., and A. Aleksandrova. 1983. "Ispoved' Zhenshchiny." *Kontinent* 38:209–220.

Kask, K. 1977. "Teatr i Publika." In *Problemy Razvitiia Kul'tury v Usloviiakh Indusrial'nogo Regiona*, edited by L. Kogan and E. Rannik. Tallin: Akademiia Nauk Estonskoi SSR.

Kataiev, V. 1982. " Iunosheskii Roman Moiego Starogo Druga Pchelkina Rasskazannyi Im Samim." *Novyi Mir* 10:9–106.

Katkova, I. 1978a. "Materinskii Ukhod za Novorozhdennym." In *Zhenshchiny na Rabote i Doma*, edited by D. Valentei, pp. 38–46. Moscow: Statistika.

———. 1978b. "Mediko-Sotsial'nyie Osobennosti Formirovaniia Sem'i." In *Sotsiologiia i Problemy Sotsial'nogo Razvitiia*, edited by T. Raibushkin, pp. 218–26. Moscow: Nauka.

Kharchev, A. 1979. *Brak i Sem'ia v SSSR*. Moscow: Mysl'.

———. 1978. "Nauchno-Technisheskaia Revolutsiia i Sem'ia." In *Sotsiologiia i Problemy Sotsial'nogo Razvitiia*, edited by T. Riabushkin, pp. 206–217. Moscow: Nauka.

Kharchev, A. (ed.). 1982. *Sem'ia i Obshchestvo*. Moscow: Nauka.

———. (ed.). 1977. *Izmeneniie Polozheniia Zhenshchiny i Sem'ia*. Moscow: Nauka.

Kharchev, A., and M. Matskovskii. 1978 *Sovremennaia Sem'ia i Ieie Problemy*. Moscow: Statistika.

Kharchev, A., and S. Golod. 1971. *Professional'naia Rabota Zhenshchin i Sem'ia*. Leningrad: Nauka.

———. 1969. "Molodezh i Brak." In *Chelovek i Obshchestvo: Sotsial'nyie Problemy Molodezhi*. Leningrad: Izdatel'stvo LGU.

Kholmogorov, A. 1970. *International'nyie Cherty Sovietskikh Natsii (na materialakh konkretno-sotsiologicheskikh issledovanii v Pribaltike)*. Moscow: Mysl'.

Khorev, B., and G. Kisilieva. 1982. *Urbanizatsia i Demograficheskiie Prozessy*. Moscow: Finansy i Statistika.

Khrushchev, Nikita. 1970. *Khrushchev Remembers*. Boston: Little Brown.

Kisilieva, G. 1979. *Nuzhno li Povyshat' Rozhdaemost'*. Moscow: Statistika.

Kisilieva, G., and I. Rodzinskaia. 1982. "Vliianiie Stabil'nosti Braka na Rozhdaemost' v Krupneishikh Gorodakh." In *Naseleniie SSSR Segodnia*, edited by D. Valentei, pp. 74–82. Moscow: Finansy i Statistika.

Kitvel', T. 1977 "Otnosheniie k Trudu i Svobodnoie Vremia." In *Problemy Razvitiia Kul'tury v Usloviiakh Industrial'nogo Regiona*, edited by L. Kogan and I. Rannik, Tallin: Akademia Nauk Estonskoi SSR.

Kluckhohn, Clyde. 1951. "Values and Value Orientatins in the Theory of Action." In *Toward a General Theory of Action*, edited by Talcott Parsons and Edward Shills. Cambridge: Harvard University Press.

Klupt, M. 1982. "Ot Pokoleniia-k Pokoleniiu." In *Sovremenaia Sem'ia*, edited by E. Vasil'ieva, pp. 3–12. Moscow: Finansy i Statistika.

Kogan, L. (ed.). 1981. *Kul'turnaia Deiatel'nost': Opyt Sotsiologicheskogo Issledovaniia*.Moscow: Nauka.

Kolokol'nikov, V. 1976. "Brachno-Semeinyie Otnosheniia v Srede Kolkhoznogo Krestianstva." *Sotsiologicheskiie Issledovaniia* 3: 78–87.

Kolpakov, B., and V. Patrushev. 1971. *Budzhet Vrement Gorodskogo*

Naseleniia. Moscow: Statistika.

Kon, Igor. 1982. "O Sotsiologichskoi Interpretatsii Seksual'nogo Povedeniia." *Sotsiologicheskiie Issledovaniia* 2:113–22.

———. 1981. "Psykhologiia Polovykh Razlichii" *Voprosy Psykhologii* 2:47–57.

———. 1980. *Druzhba.* Mosocw: Politizdat.

———. 1978. *Otkrytiie "Ia".* Moscow: Politizdat.

———. 1973a. *Psychologiia Iunosheskoi Druzhby.* Moscow: Znanie.

———. 1973b. "Druzhba: Istoriko-Psikhologicheskii Etiud." *Novyi Mir* 7:165–83.

———. 1970. "Seks, Obshchestvo, Kul'tura." *Inostrannaia Literatura* 1:243–55.

———. 1967. *Sotsiologiia Lichnosti.* Moscow: Politizdat.

Kon, Igor, and V. Losenkov. 1974. "Problemy Issledovaniia Iunosheskoi Druzhby." *Sovietskaia Pedagogika* 10:35–45.

Kopelev, L. 1978. *Sotvorim Sebe Kumira.* Ann Arbor, Mich.: Ardis.

———. 1975. *Khranit' Vechno.* Ann Arbor, Mich.: Ardis.

Kopyt, N. 1971. *Opyt Organizatsii Mediko-Sanitarnoi Pomoshchi Rabochim Sovkhoza.* Moscow: Medizdat.

Korchagin, V. 1974. *Trudovyie Resursy v Usloviiakh Nauchno-Technicheskoi Revolutsii.* Moscow: Ekonomika.

Korenevskaia, B. 1972. "Sem'ia i Nravstvennaia Orientatsiia Zhenshchin." In *Dinamika Izmeneniia Polozheniia Zhenshchiny i Sem'ia.* Moscow: Institut Konkretnykh Sotsial'nykh Issledovanii.

Kositskii, G. 1981. "Infarkt ot Odinochestva." In *Demografy Dumaiut, Sporiat, Sovetuiut,* edited by G. Kisilieva, pp. 108–113. Moscow: Finansy i Statistika.

Kotliar, A. (ed.) 1982. *Dvizheniie Rabochei Sily v Krupnom Gorode.* Moscow: Finansy i Statistika.

Kotliar, A., and S. Turchaninova. 1975. *Zaniatost' Zhenshchin na Proizvodstve.* Moscow: Statistika.

Kozlov, V. 1982. *Nazional'nosti SSSR.* Moscow: Finansy i Statistika.

Kronik, A. 1982. *Mezhlichnostnoie Otsenivaniie v Malykh Gruppakh.* Kiev: Naukova Dumka.

Kudriavtsev, V. 1983. "Issledovatel'skaia Problema—Sotsial'nyie Otkloneniia." *Sotsiologicheskiie Issledovaniia* 2:111–17.

Kuzev, G. 1982. *Novyie Goroda.* Moscow: Finansy i Statistika.

Kuznetsova, L. 1981. "Pravo na Razborchivost." In *Demografy Dumaiut, Sporiat, Sovetuiut,* edited by G. Kisilieva, pp. 181–89. Moscow: Finansy i Statistika.

———. 1980. *Zhenshchina na Rabote i Doma.* Moscow: Politizdat.

Kvasov, G. 1982. "Kollektivism kak Obraz Zhizni: Analiz Stanovleniia Moral'nykh Tsennostei." In *Sovietskaia Sotsiologiia,* Vol. 1, edited by T. Riabushkin, pp. 181–89. Moscow: Nauka.

Laas, K. 1982. "Osobennosti Demograficheskikh Prozessov v Estonskoi SSSR i Zadachi Demografichesekoi Politiki." In *Naseleniie SSSR*

Segodnia, edited by D. Valentei, pp. 67–73. Moscow: Finansy i Statistika.

Laidmiae, V.-I. 1977. "Izobrazitel'noiie Iskusstvo v Sfere Dosuga." In *Problemy Razvitiia Kul'tury v Usloviiakh Industrial'nogo Regiona*, edited by L. Kogan and E. Rannik, pp. 100–108. Tallin: Akademiia Estonskoi SSR.

Lapidus, G. 1978. *Women in Soviet Society*. Berkeley: University of California Press.

Lapidus, G. (ed.). 1982. *Women, Work, and Family in the Soviet Union*. Armonk, NY: Sharp.

Larmin. O. 1974. *Metodologicheskiie Problemy Izucheniia Narodonaseleniia* Moscow: Statistika.

Lazarev, F., and P. Iakimov. 1977. *Partkom i Sotsial'noie Planirovaniie: Opyt Proizvodstvennogo Ob'edineniia "Apatity"*. Murmansk: Knizhoie Izdatel'stvo.

Levin, B. 1971. "Svobodonoie Vremia i Razvitiie Bytovykh Obshchnostei." In *Sotsial'nyie Issledovaniia*, Vol. 7, edited by A. Kharchev and Z. Iankova, pp. 104–117. Mowcow: Nauka.

Lisovskii, Yu. 1969. *Eskiz k Portretu Molodezhi*. Moscow: Molodaia Gvardiia.

Litvinova. G. 1981. *Pravo i Demografichskiie Prozessy v. SSSR*. Moscow: Nauka.

Loiberg, M. 1982. *Stabilizatsia Proizvodstvennykh Kollektivov v Lesnoi i Derevoobrabatyvaushchei Promyshlennosti*. Moscow: Lesnaia Promyshlennost'.

Lukina, V., and S. Nekhoroshkov. 1982. *Dinamika Sotsial'noi Struktury Naseleniia SSSR*. Moscow: Finansy i Statistika.

Magun, V. 1983. *Potrebnosti i Psychologiia Sotsial'noi Deiatel'nosti Lichnosti*. Leningrad: Nauka.

Mandelstam, N. 1970. *Vospominaniia*. Paris: Imka.

Mansimov, Ch., and E. Foteieva. 1982. "Osobennosti Predstavlennii Molodezhi Azerbaidjanskoi SSR o Semeinoi Zhizni." *Sotsiologicheskiie Issledovaniia* 3:128–32.

Mansurov, N. 1978. "Komplexnyi Podkhod k Vospitaniiu." In *Sotsiologichiskiie Problemy Kommunisticheskogo Vospitaniia*, edited by N. Mansurov, pp. 7–30. Moscow: Institut Sotsiologicheskikh Issledovanii.

Marx, K. and F. Engels. 1961. *Sobraniie Sochinenii v. 21*. Moscow: Cospolitizdat.

Maslow, Abraham. 1972. *The Farther Reaches of Human Nature*. New York: Viking Press.

Masnik, George, and Mary Jo Bane, *et al.* 1982. *The Nation's Families, 1969–1982*. Boston: Auburn House.

Matskovskii, M. 1982. "Opty Razrabotki i Ispol'zovaniia Tematicheskogo Rubrikatora Sem'i." Sotsiologicheskiie Issledovaniia 4:70–77.

_____. 1981. "Zachem Cheloveku Brat." In *Demografy Dumaiut, Sporiat, Sovetuiut*, edited by G. Kisilieva, pp. 71–77. Moscow: Finansy i Statistika.

Matskovskii, M., and A. Kharchev. 1982. "Osnovnyie Tendentsii Izmeneniia Brachno-Semeinykh Otnoshenii v SSSR." In *Sovietskaia Sotsiologiia*, edited by T. Riabushkin and G. Osipov, pp. 152–63. Moscow: Nauka.

McClelland, D. 1961. *The Achieving Society*. Princeton: Van Nostrand.

Merton, R. 1957 *Social Theory and Social Structure*. New York: Free Press.

Mickievicz, E. 1981. *Media and the Russian Public*. New York: Praeger.

Morris, Desmond. 1967. *The Naked Ape*. London: Cape.

Moses, J. 1978. "The Politics of Female Labor in the Soviet Union." *Western Societies Program Occasional Papers*, no. 10 (September).

Muchnik, I., E. Petrenko, E. Sinitsyn, and T. Iaroshenko. 1980. *Territorial'naia Vyborka v Sotsiologicheskikh Issledovaniiakh*. Moscow: Nauka.

Muchnik, I., E. Petrenko, E. Sinitsyn, V. Shlapentokh, and T. Iaroshenko. 1978. "Problemy Postroeniia Vsesoiuznoi Territorial'noi Vyborki dlia Sotsiologicheskikh Issledovanii." *Sotsiologicheskiie Issledovaniia* 1:162–76.

Murphy, Cullen. 1983. "Watching the Russians." *Atlantic Monthly* (February):33–52.

Nabatnikova, T. 1983. "Doch." *Sibirskiie Ogni* 8.

Nafikov, Z. 1974. *Sotsialisticheskaia Sem'ia*. Ufa.

Nauduzhas, V. 1982. "Aktual'nyie Demograficheskiie Problemy v Litovskoi SSR." In *Naselenie SSSR Segodnia*, edited by D. Valentei, p. 57–66. Moscow: Finansy i Statistika.

Navasky, V. 1980. *Naming Names*. New York: Viking Press.

Nemirovskii, D. 1982. "Ob Otnoshenii Molodezhi k Dobrachnoi Polovoi Zhizni." *Sotsiologicheskiie Issledovaniia* 1:119–21.

Nesterov, V. 1977. *Statistika Invalidnosti*. Moscow: Medizdat.

Neubert, G. 1965. *Novaia Kniga of Supruzheskoi Zhizni*. Moscow: Progress.

Orlov, A. 1953. *The Secret History of Stalin's Crimes*. New York: Random House.

Osipov, G., and I. Szczepanski. (eds.). 1969. *Sotsial'nyie Problemy Truda i Proizvodstva: Sovietstko-Pol'skoie Issledovaniie*. Moscow: Mysl'.

Paine, R. 1969. "In Search of Friendship: An Exploratory Analysis in 'Middle Class' Culture." *Man* 14 (October):505–524.

Pankhurst, J. 1982. "Childless and One-Child Families in the Soviet Union." *Journal of Family Issues* 4 (December):493–515.

Pankhurst, J., and S. Houseknecht. 1983. "The Family, Politics, and Religion in the 1980s." *Journal of Family Issues* 1 (March):5–34.

Pankratova, M. 1972. "Izmeneniia v Semeinykh Otnosheniiakh Sel'skikh Zhitelei." In *Dinamika Izmeneniia Polozheniia Zhenshchiny i Sem'ia*. Moscow: Institut Konkretnykh Sotsial'nykh Issledovanii.

Panova, V. 1975. *O Moiei Zhizni, Knigakh i Chitateliakh*. Leningrad: Lenizdat.

Parygin, B. (ed.) 1982. *Sotsial'no-Psychologicheskiie Problemy Nauchno-Technicheskogo Progressa*. Leningrad: Nauka.

Patrushev, V. 1982. "Vozmozhnyiie Izmeneniia v Ispol'zovanii Budzhetov

Vremeni." *Sotsiologicheskiie Issledovaniia* 1:28–35.

_____. 1978. "Obraz Zhizni: Tendentsii Razvitiia Svobodnogo Vremeni." In *Sotsiologiia i Problemy Sotsial'nogo Razvitiia*, edited by T. Riabushkin, pp. 241–51. Moscow: Nauka.

Pavlov, B. 1975. "Razvitie Kollektivisma v Bytu Rabochei Molodezhi." In *Issledovaniie i Planirovaniie Dukhovnoi Kultury Trudiashchikhsia Urala*, edited by L. Kogan and A. Sharova, pp.104–124. Swerdlovsk: Ural'skii Nauchnyi Zentr AN SSSR.

Peach, Ceri. 1974. "Homogamy, Propinquity, and Segregation: A Reevaluation." *American Sociological Review* 39 (October):636–41.

Pelevin, S. 1972. *Voprosy Effektivnosti Pravovogo Regulirovaniia Razvodov*. Leningrad.

Perevedentsev, V. 1982a. *270 Millionov*. Moscow: Finansy i Statistika.

_____. 1982b. "Vosproizvodstvo Naseleniia i Sem'ia." *Sotsiologicheskiie Issledovaniia* 2:80–87.

_____. 1981. "Dvoie v Semeinoi Lodke." In *Demografy Dumaiut, Sporiat, Sovetuiut*, edited by G. Kisilieva. Moscow: Finansy i Statistika.

_____. 1975. *Metody Izucheniia Migratsii Naseleniia*. Moscow: Nauka.

Petrenko, E., and T. Iaroshenko. 1979. *Sotsial'no-Demograficheskiie Pokazateli v Sotsiologicheskikh Issledovaniiakh*. Moscow: Statistika.

Pogosian, G. 1983. "Forma Voprosa i Tselevaia Ustanovka Issledovatelia." *Sotsiologicheskiie Issledovaniia* 3:162–67.

Rakitskii, R. 1983. *Strategiia Blagosostoianiia*. Moscow: Molodaia.

Rapavy, S. and G. Baldwin. 1983. "Demographic Trends in the Soviet Union: 1950–2000." In *Soviet Economy in the 1980s: Problems and Prospects*. U.S. Congress, Joint Economic Committee. Joint Committee Print, 97th Congress, 2d. sess.

Rappoport, S. 1977. "O Sisteme Norm Semeinogo Povedeniia." In *Molodaia Sem'ia*, edited by D. Valentei, pp. 57–66. Moscow: Statistika.

Rasputin, V. 1980. *Povesti*. Moscow: Molodaia Gvardiia.

Reisman, J. 1981. "Adult Friendships." In *Personal Relationships*, Vol. 2, edited by S. Duck and R. Gilmour, pp. 205–230. London: Academic Press.

Reznik, S. 1982. *Trudovyie Resursy v Stroitel'stve*. Moscow: Stroiizdat.

Riabushkin, T. (ed.). 1981. *Regional'nyie Osobennosti Vosproizvodstva i Migratsii Naselenia v SSSR*. Moscow: Finansy i Statistika.

_____. (ed.). 1978. *Demograficheskiie Problemy Sem'i*. Moscow: Nauka.

Riabushkin, T., and R. Galetskaia. 1983. *Naseleniie i Sotsialisticheskoie Obshchestvo*, Moscow: Finansy i Statistika.

Riabushkin, T., and R. Galetskaia. 1981. "Struktura i Vosproizvodstvo Naseleniia Sovietskogo Souza." In *Demograficheskiie Prozessy in Sotsialisticheskom Obshchestve*, edited by T. Riabushkin and L. Rybakovskii, pp. 144–75. Moscow: Finansy i Statistika.

Riurikov, Iu. 1983. "Mestorozhdeniia Shchast'ia." *Pravda*, June 9.

_____. 1967. *Tri Vlecheniia*. Moscow: Iskusstvo.

Rodzinskaia, I. 1981. "Material'noie Blagosostoianiie i Stabil'nost' Sem'i." *Sotsiologicheskiie Issledovaniia* 1:106–13.

Rogovin, V. 1980. *Sotsial'naia Politika v Razvitom Sotsialisticheskom Obshchestve*. Moscow: Nauka.

Rokeach, M. 1973. *The Nature of Human Values*. New York: The Free Press.

Rosenberg, M. 1979. *Conceiving the Self*. New York: Basic Book.

Rotova, R. (ed.). 1982. *Osobennosti Demograficheskogo Razvitiia v SSSR*. Moscow: Nauka.

Rozhanovskaia, Z. 1981. "Sotsial'no-Psychologicheskiie Aspekty Regulirovaniia Suprezheskikh Otnoshenii." In *Nauchno-Technicheskaia Revolutsiia i Sotsial'naia Psychologia*, edited by B. Parygin, pp. 114–17. Moscow: Nauka.

Rubin, Z. 1973. *Liking and Loving: An Invitation to Social Psychology*. New York: Holt, Rinehart and Winston.

Ruzhzhe, V., I. Eliseieva, and T. Kadibur. 1983. *Struktura i Funktsii Semeinykh Grup*. Moscow: Finansy i Statistika.

———. 1982. "KPD Semeinoi Gruppy." In *Sovremenaia Sem'ia*, edited by E. Vasil'ieva, pp. 77–81. Moscow: Finansy i Statistika.

Ryvkina, R. 1979. *Obraz Zhizni Sel'skogo Naseleniia*. Novosibirsk: Nauka.

———. 1976. "Tradizionnyie i Urbanisticheskiie Tsennosti Sel'skovo Naseleniia." In *Sibirskaia Derevnia v Usloviiakh Urbanizatssii*, edited by T. Zaslavskaia and V. Kalmyk, pp. 116–34. Novosibirsk: Nauka.

Sacks, M. 1982. *Work and Equality in Soviet Society*. New York: Praeger.

———. 1976. *Women's Work in Soviet Russia*. New York: Praeger.

Sadvokasova, E. 1969. *Sotsial'no-Gigienicheskiie Aspekty Regulirovaniia Razmerov Sem'i*. Moscow: Medgiz.

Sankova, K. 1981. "Dinamika Sotsial'no-Geterogennykh Brakov Gorodskogo Naseleniia." *Sotsiologicheskie Issledovaniia* 4:119–23.

Saprykin, V. 1981. *Urbanizatsiia, Ateism, Religia*. Alma-Ata: Kazakhstan.

Savenkova, L. 1966. *Vozrast Krasoty*. Moscow.

Schuman, H., and M. Johnson. 1976. "Attitudes and Behavior." *Annual Review of Sociology*, Vol. 2.

Semenova, V. 1979. 1979. "Trudovoi Kollektiv kak Faktor Vliiaushchii na Nravstvennoiie Razvitiie Lichnosti." In *Trud kak Osnova Sotsialisticheskogo Obraza Zhizni*, edited by V. Staroverov, pp. 165–82. Moscow: Institut Sotsiologicheskikh Issledovanii.

Severina, A., and G. Zaikina. 1983. "Sluzhba Sem'i i Voprosy ieie Dal'neishego Sovershenstvovaniia." *Sotsiologicheskiie Issledovaniia* 2:85–91.

Shalenko, V. 1977. "Nravstvennoie Vospitaniie, Trudovoi Kollektiv i Lichnost'." In *Kompleksnyi Podkhod k Kommunisticheskomy Vospitaniiu*, edited by N. Mansurov, pp. 64–78. Moscow: Institut

Sotsiologicheskikh Issledovanii.

Shapiro, V. 1980. *Chelovek na Pensii.* Moscow: Mysl'.

Sheinin, Iu. 1980. "Usloviia Nauchnogo Truda." In *Nauka v Sotsial'nykh, Gnoseologicheskikh i Tsennostnykh Aspektakh,* edited by L. Bashenov and M. Akhundov. Moscow: Nauka.

Shenderezka, A. 1979. "Uchitel'skaia Sem'ia." In *Sem'ia Segodnia,* edited by D. Valentei, pp. 74–84. Moscow: Statistika.

Shilova, L. 1978. "Kharakter Provedeniia Semeinogo Dosuga i Udovletvorennost' Brakom." In *Stabil'nost' Sem'i kak Sotsial'naia Problema,* edited by Z. Iankova, pp. 129–35. Moscow: Institut Sotsiologicheskikh Issledovanii.

Shishkan, N. 1980. *Sotsial'no-Ekonomicheskie Problemy Zhenskogo Truda.* Moscow: Ekonomika.

Shlapentokh, V. 1982a. "The Study of Values as a Social Phenomenon: The Soviet Case." *Social Forces* 61 (Spring):403–17.

_____. 1982b. "Human Aspirations as a Cause of the Failure of Soviet Agriculture." *The Rural Sociologist* 2 (May):138–49.

_____. 1980. *Essays in Sociology. International Journal of Sociology* 10 (Spring) Special Issue.

_____. 1977a. "Etot Mnogolikii Prestizh." *Molodoi Kommunist* 1:82–88.

_____. 1977b. "Problemy Svoi i Chuzhiie." *Literaturnaia gazeta,* November 30.

_____. 1976. *Problemy Representativnosti Sotsiologicheskoi Informatsii.* Moscow: Statistika.

_____. 1973. *Problemy Dostovernosti Statisticheskoi Informatsii v Sotsiologicheskikh Issledovaniiakh.* Moscow: Statistika.

_____. 1971. "Znakomstvy i Svad'by." *Literaturnaia Gazeta,* June 6, p. 12.

_____. 1970. *Sotsiologiia dlia Veskh.* Moscow: Sovietskaia Rossiia.

Shlapentokh, V. (ed.). 1969. *Chitatel' i Gazeta,* Vols. 1 and 2. Moscow: Institut Konkretnykh Sotsial'nykh Issledovanii.

Shlapentokh, V., and V. Chernets. 1977. "Korrektirovka Vyborki". In *Proektirovaniie i Organisatsiia Vyborochnogo Sotsiologicheskogo Issledovaniia.* Edited by E. Petrenko. Moscow: Institut Sotsiologicheskikh Issledovanii.

Shubkin, V. 1970. *Sotsiologicheskiie Opyty.* Moscow: Mysl'.

Sifman, P. 1976. "Dinamika Rozhdaemosti i Tempy Formirovaniia Sem'i v SSSR." In *Demograficheskaia Situatsia v SSSR.* Moscow: Statistika.

Silka, L., and S. Kiesler. 1977. "Couples Who Choose to Remain Childless." *Family Planning Perspectives* 9 (Jan./Feb.):16–25.

Simis, K. 1982. *The Corrupt Society: The Secret World of Soviet Capitalism.* New York: Simon and Schuster.

Sinel'nikov, A. 1978. "Statistika Brachnosti i Sluzhba Zhakomstv." In *Stabil'nost' Sem'ia kak Sotsial'naia Problema,* edited by Z. Iankova, pp. 146–60. Moscow: Institut Sotsiologicheskikh Issledovanii.

Slesarev, G. 1978. *Demograficheskiie Prozessy i Sotsial'naia Struktura*

Sotsialisticheskogo Obshchestva. Moscow: Nauka.

Smirnov, G. 1971. *Sovietskii Chelovek.* Moscow: Politizdat.

Smith, Hedrick. 1976. *The Russians.* New York: Ballantine.

Sokolov, B., and I. Reimers. 1983. "Instensivno li Razvivautsia Glavnyie Dvigateli Intensifikatsii." *EKO* 9:72–80.

Sokolov, V. 1981. *Nravstvennyi Mir Sovietskogo Cheloveka.* Moscow: Politizdat.

Solotareva, O. 1973. "Prestizh i Privlekatel'nost' Professii u Postupauzhikh v Vuzy ESSR: Sravnitel'nyi Analiz." In *Sotsial'no-Professional'naia Orientsiia Molodezhi,* edited by M. Titma, pp. 250–62. Tartu: Tartusskii Universitet.

Solov'iev, N. 1981. *Sem'ia v Sotsialisticheskom Obshchestve.* Moscow: Politizdat.

_____. 1977. *Brak i Sem'ia Segodnia.* Vilnius: Mintis.

_____. 1962. *Sem'a v Sovietskom Obshchestve.* Moscow: Politizdat.

Solzhenitsyn, A. 1975. *The Gulag Archipelago, 1918–1956.* New York: Harper and Row.

Sonin, M. 1981. "Ne Khochu Zhenistsia." In *Demografy Dumaiut, Sporiat, Sovetuiut,* edited by G. Kisilieva, pp. 189–94. Moscow: Finansy i Statistika.

_____. 1977. "Sotsial'no-Ekonomicheskiie Problemy Zaniatsosti Zhenshchin." In *Izmenenie Polozheniia Zhenshchiny i Sem'ia,* edited by A. Kharchev, pp. 22–31. Moscow: Nauka.

Starodubtsev, S. 1983. "Sravnitel'noie Issledovaniie Posetitelei Vystavki Moskwa-Parizh," *Sotsiologicheskiie Issledovania,* 4:118–20.

Starr, S. Frederick. 1983. *Red and Hot: The Fate of Jazz in the Soviet Union, 1917–1980.* New York: Oxford University Press.

Stern, M. 1979. *La Vie sexuelle en URSS.* Paris: Albin Michel.

Stites, R. 1978. *The Women's Liberation Movement in Russia.* Princeton: Princeton University Press.

Suslov, Iu., and P. Lebedev (eds.). 1982. *Problemy Sotsial'nogo Razvitiia Krupnykh Gorodov.* Leningrad: Nauka.

Swayze, H. 1962. *Political Control of Literature in the USSR, 1946–1959.* Cambridge: Harvard University Press.

Sysenko, V. 1982. "Razvody: Dinamika, Motivy, Posledstviia." *Sotsiologicheskiie Issledovania* 2:99–104.

_____. 1981. *Ustoichivost' Braka: Problemy, Faktory, Uslovia.* Moscow: Finansy i Statistika.

_____. 1979. "Sluzhba Sem'i: Problemy, Poiski, Rescheniia." In *Sem'ia Segodnia,* edited by D. Valentei, pp. 93–99. Moscow: Statistika.

Tashtemirov, U. 1981. "Motivy Razvodov v Odnonatsional'nykh Uzbekskikh Sem'iakh." *Sotsiologicheskie Issledovaniia* 2:115–19.

Tatarinova, N. 1979. *Primeneniie Truda Zhenzhin v Narodnom Khosiastve SSSR.* Moscow: Ekonomika.

Ter-Sarkisiants, A. 1973. "O Natsional'nom Aspekte Brakov v Armianskoi SSSR (Po Materialam Zagsov)." *Sovietskaia Etnografiia* 4.

Tiit, E. 1982. "Problemy Vybora Budushchego Sputnika Zhizni u

Molodezhi." In *Sovremenaia Semia*, edited by E. Vasil'ieva, pp. 25–38. Moscow: Finansy i Statistika.

_____. 1978. "Faktory Vliiaiushchiie na Stabil'nost' Braka." In *Stabil'-nost' Sem'i kak Sotsial'naia Problema*, edited by Z. Iankova. Moscow: Institut Sotsiologicheskikh Issledovanii.

Titarenko, A. (ed.). 1980. *Marksistkaia Etika*. Moscow: Politizdat.

Titma, M. 1981. *Sotsial'no-Professional'naia Orientatsiia Student-chestva*. Vilnus: Institut Filosofii, Sotsiologii i Prava AN Litovskoi SSR.

Tolchinskii, L. 1979. "Otsenka Urovnia Razvodimosti v SSSR." In *Demo-graficheskoie Razvitiie Sem'i*, edited by A. Volkov, pp. 185–90. Moscow: Statistika.

Tolts, M. 1979. "Nekotoryie Obobshchaushchiie Kharakteristiki Brach-nosti, Prekrashcheniia i Dlitel'nosti Braka." In *Demografisheskoie Razvitiie Sem'i*, edited by A. Volkov, pp. 39–58. Moscow: Statistika.

_____. 1974. *Kharakteristika Nekotorykh Komponentov Rozhdaemosti v Bol'shom Gorode*. Moscow: Statistika.

Treml, V. 1982a. *Alcohol in the USSR: A Statistical Study*. Durham: Duke University Press.

_____. 1982b. "Deaths from Alcohol Poisoning in the USSR." *Soviet Studies* 34 (October):487–505.

Ts. S.U. 1983 *Narodnoie Khosiastvo SSSR v 1982 godu*, Moscow: Finansy i Statistika.

Ts. S.U. SSSR. 1982. *Narodnoie Khosiastvo SSR. 1929–1982*. Moscow: Finansy i Statistika.

_____. 1982. *Zhenshchiny v SSSR*. Moscow: Finansy i Statistika.

_____. 1980. *Narodnoie Khosiastvo SSSR v 1979 godu*. Moscow: Statistika.

_____. 1979. *Deti v SSSR*. Moscow: Statistika.

_____. 1975 *Itogi Vesouznoi Perepisi Naseleniia 1970 goda*, v. 6. Moscow: Statistika.

Ts. S.U. 1965. *Narodnoie Khosiastvo SSSR v. 1964 godu*. Moscow: Statistika.

Upp, M. 1983. "Zhenshchiny Rossii." *Novoye Russkoie Slovo*, November 10.

Urlanis, B. 1978. *Evolutsiia Prodolzhitel'nosti Zhizni*. Moscow: Sta-tistika.

_____. 1977. "Sem'ia i Problemy Demografii." In *Molodaia Sem'ia*, edited by D. Valentei. Moscow: Statistika.

Vasil'ieva, E. 1981. *Obraz Zhizni Gorodskoi Sem'i*. Moscow: Finansy i Statistika.

Vavilina, V. 1979. "Ob Ideale Sovremennoi Zhenshchiny." In *Rol' Sredstv Massovoi Informatsii i Propagandy v Nravstvennom Vospitannii*, edited by I. Kalin, R. Kosolapov, and I. Chkhikvishvili, pp. 162–71. Moscow: Mysl'.

Veevers, J. 1980. *Childless by Choice*. Toronto: Butterworth.

Vishnevskii, A. 1982. *Vosproizvodstvo Naseleniia i Obshchestvo*.

Moscow: Finansy i Statistika.

Vishnevskii, A., and A. Volkov (eds.). 1983. *Vosproizvodstvo Naseleniia SSSR*. Moscow: Finansy i Statistika.

Voina, V. 1984. "Drug ili Priiatel'." *Nedelia* 16, p. 14.

Volkov, A. 1983. "'Rozhdaemost'" i "Defizit Zhenikhov" In *Rozhdaemost': Izvestnoie i Neizvestnoie*, edited by E. Vasil'eva. Moscow: Financy i Statistika.

Volkov, A. 1981. "Sem'ia kak Faktor Izmeneniia Demograficheskoi Situatsii." *Sotsiologicheskiie Issledovaniia* 1:34–42.

———. 1979. "Ob Ozhidaiemoi Prodolzhitel'nosti Braka i Ieie Demograficheskikh Faktorakh." In *Demograficheskoi Razvitiie Sem'i*, edited by A. Volkov, pp. 59–84. Moscow: Statistika.

———. 1977. "Izmeneniie Polozheniia Zhenshchiny i Demograficheskoie Razvitiie Sem'i." In *Izmenenie Polozheniia Zhenshchiny i Sem'ia*, edited by A. Kharchev, pp. 43–52. Moscow: Nauka.

Volkov, B. 1982. *Motivy Prestuplenii*. Kazan: Izdatel'stvo Kazanskogo Universiteta.

Voslenski, M. 1980. *La Nomenclature: Les Privilèges en URSS*. Paris: Pierre Belfon.

Vospominaniia o V. I. Lenine. 1957. Moscow: Cospolitizdat.

Walster, E., and G.W. Walster. 1978. *A New Look at Love*. Reading: Addison-Wesley.

Yedlin, T. (ed.). 1980. *Women In Eastern Europe and the Soviet Union*. New York: Praeger.

Zaigraiev, G. 1983. "O Nekotorykh Osobennostiakh Profilaktiki P'ianstva," *Sotsiologicheskiie Issledovaniia*, 4, 1983.

Zaslavskaia, T., and V. Kalmyk (eds.). 1975. *Sovremennaia Sibirskaia Derevnia*. Novosibirsk: Nauka.

Zatsepin, V. 1981. *Shchast'ie kak Problema Sotsial'noi Psychologii*. L'vov: Vyshcha Shkola.

Zemtsov, I. 1976. *Patiia ili Mafiia./Razvororannaia Respublika*. Paris: Les Editeurs Reunis.

Zhirnova, G. 1980. *Brak i Svad'by Russkikh Gorozhan v Proshlom i Nastoiashchem*. Moscow: Nauka.

Zhukhovitskii, L. 1977. "Lubov' i Demografiia." *Literaturnaia gazeta*, May 4.

———. 1976. "Devushka Ishchet Dublenku." *Molodoi Kommunist* 10.

Zinoviev, A. 1980. *Zheltyi Dom*. Lausanne: L'age d'homme.

———. 1978. *Svetloie Budushcheie*. Lausanne: L'age d'homme.

———. 1976. *Ziianshchiie Vysoty*. Lansanne: L'age d'homme.

Zvidrinsh, P. 1981. "Studencheskeiia Sem'ia v Latvii." In *Sovietskaia Molodezh*, edited by E. Vasil'ieva, pp. 80–87. Moscow: Finansy i Statistika.

Zvidrinsh, P., and A. Lapin'sh. 1979. "Obsledovaniie Molodezhi v Latviiskoi SSR." In *Sem'ia Segodnia*, edited by D. Valentei. Moscow: Statistika.

Index ─────────────────────────────

romantic marriage, 80, 99, 101,
105, 120, 250; and Lenin, 105;
and Stalin, 79–80, 84

"Second economy," 6, 74, 90, 98,
238
serial marriage, 81, 121–29
sex, 49–55, 56–57, 85, 105,
109–10, 141, 252 (*see also*
extramarital sex; love;
premarital sex)
single men, 119, 132, 135, 188
(*see also* single people)
single mothers, 116, 118, 124,
138–39, 141, 151, 250, 254
(*see also* single women)
single people, 135, 163, 166, 167,
200, 205, 240 (*see also* single
men; single women)

single women, 10, 97, 113, 119,
132, 136, 150–55, 159, 167,
179, 188, 189, 221 (*see also*
single mothers)
Soviet marital codes, 20, 22, 27, 31
Soviet sociology, 13–18, 28, 30, 44,
46, 49, 50, 51–52, 61–62, 81,
140
Soviet surveys, 11–12, 45–46, 50,
79, 142, 143, 178, 209
Stalin, J., 1, 21, 24–30, 34, 40, 41,
49, 52, 58, 63–64, 79–80, 151,
156, 218, 231–32

United States, 13, 87, 103, 112,
137, 186, 197, 247–48;
friendship in, 219; sexual
behavior in, 116

About the Author

VLADIMIR E. SHLAPENTOKH is a Professor of Sociology at Michigan State University in East Lansing. Until 1979, the year of his emigration from the Soviet Union, he was a Senior Fellow in the Sociological Institute in Moscow and belonged to the group of most prominent Soviet sociologists.

He conducted the first nationwide survey of public opinion in the Soviet Union. He has published widely in the field of sociology. As author, co-author, or editor, he published thirteen books in the USSR. Since coming to the United States, he has published several articles in sociological journals and in newspapers, including *Social Forces, Public Opinion Quarterly,* and the *New York Times.* His "Essays in Sociology" appears as a special issue of the *International Journal of Sociology* in 1980.

He holds three scholarly degrees from the Soviet Union. He studied at Kiev University, the Moscow Statistical Institute, and the Institute of International Economics and Relations of the Academy of Science of the USSR, Moscow.